Leabhra ar iasacht ar feadh 21 lá ón dáta eisiúna.

Fineáil ar leabhra thar am. 10c ar gach seachtain nó cuid de sheachtain móide costas an phostas san aisghabála.

Books are on loan for 21 days from date of issue.

Fines for overdue books: 10c for each week or portion of a week plus cost of postage incurred in recovery.

LIFFEY GREEN
DANUBE BLUE

The Musical Life and Loves of László Gede

LIFFEY GREEN DANUBE BLUE

The Musical Life and Loves of László Gede

EIBHLÍN MAC MÁIGHISTIR GEDE
with Antoinette Walker

MERRION
PRESS

LIFFEY GREEN DANUBE BLUE
Published in 2016 by Merrion Press
8 Chapel Lane
Sallins
Co. Kildare

British Library Cataloguing in Publications Data
An entry can be found on request

978-1-78537-070-0 (Cloth)
978-1-78537-071-7 (PDF)
978-1-78537-072-4 (Epub)
978-1-78537-073-1 (Kindle)

Library of Congress Cataloguing in Publication Data
An entry can be found on request

Design and layout by Oldtown

10 9 8 7 6 5 4 3 2 1

M223.404
€24.95

For my husband László and his parents,
Papa István Gede and Mama Zsuzsánna Bara Gede

Contents

Foreword

This is the story of a human heart; the sensitivity of soul; the transporting power of music; the vulnerability of youth; the terror of poverty; the reality of human frailty; the loss of a child; the love of a nation; the horrors of war; the loneliness of exile; and the triumph of goodness over adversity.

In these pages I endeavour to tell the story of my husband László with as much accuracy and devoid of sentiment as I can muster. It has been a most challenging journey for me because of my deep love and devotion to him, and of the tremendous difficulty I had to go on living without him. Notwithstanding this, I am pleased to have undertaken the task and to share it with you. László was not alone in his sufferings and in his quiet hidden heroism. For this world of ours always was and will forever be filled with acts of heroism; we do not have to look too far from our own hall door to find them.

In the last passage of *Middlemarch*, George Eliot eloquently sums up the effect her heroine Dorothea had on those around her. Her words fill me with courage, knowing that we do not have to live superhuman or extraordinary lives to make an impact.

> We insignificant people with our daily words and acts are preparing the lives of many Dorotheas, some of which may present a far sadder sacrifice than that of the Dorothea whose story we know. For there is no creature whose inward being is so strong that it is not greatly determined by what lies outside it. Dorothea's finely-touched spirit had still its fine issues, though they were not widely visible. Her full nature, spent itself in channels which had no great name on the earth. But the effect of her being on those around her was incalculably diffusive: for the growing good of the world is partly dependent on unhistoric acts;

and that things are not so ill with you and me as they might have been, is half owing to the number who lived faithfully a hidden life, and rest in unvisited tombs.

Most of the human race are ordinary people of little consequence, but we can still in our own quiet and gentle ways give hope and courage to many. László was one such person.

PART I

EUROPE IN TURMOIL

1.

LAST REQUEST

Little Lamb who made thee?
Dost thou know who made thee?
Gave thee life & bid thee feed
By the stream and o'er the mead;
Gave thee clothing of delight,
Softest clothing, woolly, bright;
Gave thee such a tender voice,
Making all the vales rejoice!
Little Lamb who made thee?
Dost thou know who made thee?

From 'The Lamb' by William Blake

AT THE AGE OF NINETY, my Hungarian husband lay dying in our home in Drinklange, a hamlet high in the Ardennes in northern Luxembourg. Despite enjoying near rude good health all his life, his time had come. The slow decline in the last year of his life had heralded his end. His voice now struggled to whisper his final words to me.

'Find … find … find…'

Slowly, he reached out for my hand and with all the strength he could muster tried to squeeze it. At the same time he feebly repeated the words.

'Find … find … find…'

As I looked into his eyes, dullness had replaced their once brilliant blueness. Time was quickly running out, yet still he persisted.

'Find … find … find…'

Through my tears and a heart in smithereens, I struggled to understand.

'What is it, darling? What do you wish me to find?'

But at that very moment the slight pressure left my hand and dearest László was gone. It was early morning, around twenty to six, on Thursday, 13 October 2005. The light had gone out for the most remarkable man I had ever met. One of the noblest souls that had ever walked the earth. One whose talents and virtues knew no bounds. One who had lived through the most turbulent periods of the twentieth century and had survived. He was now finally at peace. In my mind, there was none his equal, except for my father.

With a mind deep in turmoil, I nonetheless carried out his previously expressed wish to have his remains cremated. It was completed within two days. And gathering myself together, the following Wednesday, I took his ashes and returned to Ireland, my homeland. There, in my apartment in Dublin, his urn resided for six long months. Heartbroken and bereft, I was at a loss what to do and could not bear to be parted from him. As long as his ashes were with me, his spirit was somehow alive, or so I thought. He was there with me in the drawing of a curtain, the washing of a cup, the lighting of a fire. Finally, my strength returned and I knew it was time to let him go.

Through the good graces of the Augustinian Fathers, a requiem mass was held for him in John's Lane Church on Thomas Street in Dublin. László's urn sat in a small casket in the splendid shrine of Our Lady of Good Counsel to the east of the high altar. The church held particular significance for me. On the first Saturday of each month during my childhood, my father, occasionally with my mother, would walk me and my two siblings to evening devotions in honour of Our Lady of Good Counsel. We invariably sat midway down the church and directly in front of her shrine. My grandfather John Joseph Masterson, who worked as a brass finisher and gas fitter at Guinness Brewery, had made several huge brass candelabras that adorned the high altar and many of the side altars.

These were brought out on special occasions, holy days and feast days, such as Our Lady of Good Counsel's.

The requiem on that sunny yet showery Wednesday coincided with her feast day on 26 April and so the church was filled to capacity. The solemnity of the requiem was enhanced all the more by the music of the choir and organ. It was perhaps more a comfort to me than to László, who had professed no belief in the afterlife. But as the light streamed through the magnificent Harry Clarke stained-glass windows, I felt his soul was bathed in a heavenly light.

It was a momentous day for me and brought the life we had spent together to a close. Afterwards László was interred in Dublin's Glasnevin Cemetery in the ground vaults of its Garden of Remembrance amid foliage and birdsong. For someone who in life was devoted to music and nature, it was indeed a fitting resting place. He could rest in peace among patriots and poets, artists and artisans, scholars and statesmen – lives like his that had burned bright and touched the hearts of many.

In the weeks and months after his death, I pondered on my husband's last words. What was it that he wanted me to find? Was it someone or something, an object of some description, something that had been lost? I was at a loss to understand what it all could mean. Could it have something to do with his work as a musician, a clarinettist, and a music professor? There had been several places in several countries that László had once called home. To which was it linked? Then ever so slowly it dawned on me that just three weeks before his death he had mentioned young people, especially the underprivileged, striving to have a roof over their heads. Homelessness, exile and the struggle for survival were things that had partly dogged his life. Nearing the end of his days had they been foremost in his mind? I came to the conclusion that he wished me to help music students. Embedded in my mind was also the thought that perhaps he wished me to locate his family. And so I went about fulfilling his wishes and putting his affairs in order. All the signs were very much pointing in the direction of Hungary.

In May, the following month, I found myself in Budapest with a friend Maurice; he and his wife Yvonne had been loyal friends of László, especially in the last years of his life. My reason for undertaking the journey was now firm and resolute. It was for the purpose of setting up a kind of endowment or scholarship for Hungarian music students and also to try and make contact with his relatives. Our first port of call was the Liszt Academy of Music. I imagined that László wanted to help music students in some way, especially regarding accommodation. Our home in Luxembourg had been well and truly sold by now and I had reserved the funds to buy three modest apartments being constructed in one of the many new residential blocks springing up around Budapest. The intention was to gift them to the academy. As I saw it, this would be in keeping with the spirit of László's wishes. I was helped in this endeavour by a Budapest firm of solicitors, HGBV-Szabó, in particular by solicitor Dr Viktor Benedek.

However, to my great disappointment, the Liszt Academy did not agree to the proposal. It was not in accordance with their policy or perhaps they thought it would be difficult to operate in reality. Either way, my morale took a hit. Fortunately, they did accept my donation of László's two clarinets, along with his extensive music collection, scores of old and rare pieces of music as well as a number of small items. These were handed over to Judit Szekér, secretary general of the academy, at the time.

That August, re-energised, Yvonne and I found ourselves in eastern Hungary on the trail of László's family. As we drove in a hired car, with an open map of the country resting upon my lap, I thought of this historical land and of its people. Tribes and empires had fought over it for centuries, as László had reminded me. It made me happy that the Celts had once roamed its lands, as it formed a connection with Ireland for me. For four centuries before the birth of Christ various Celtic tribes had conquered lands there, often settling near rivers, such as the Rába, Sava and Danube. After all, water held spiritual significance for them and they worshipped river deities – which appealed to me.

Later there were the Romans who conquered land west of the Danube, realising the abundance of thermal springs. Later again in the fifth century they were overthrown by Attila the Hun and his Hunnic Empire, extending from the Ural River to the Rhine River and from the Danube River to the Baltic Sea. Then nomadic Magyar tribes under the leadership of Árpád settled in the Carpathian Basin in the ninth century. His descendent Saint Stephen (István) became the first king of Hungary in the eleventh century, following conversion to Christianity. This dynasty ruled much of central Europe for several generations. And even when the dynasty was in decline, István V as a minor was married to Elizabeth, daughter of a Cuman chief, to strengthen the declining dynasty from marauding armies.

Every empire under the sun seemed to me to dominate Hungary in some shape or form. Even Genghis Khan, who ruled over the largest land empire in the history of humankind, from the Caspian Sea to the Sea of Japan, invaded Hungary in 1241 AD. Then there were long spells when the Ottoman Empire ruled the region, followed by the Hapsburg Empire, then the Dual Monarchy of Austria and Hungary in 1867, which finally came to an end after the First World War.

But history was not something confined to dusty tomes. It was very much alive and kicking in my husband's lifetime too; witnessing the end of the Dual Monarchy, then the Hungarian Republic with vast regions of land forfeited, the country allied with Nazi Germany during the Second World War and subsequently occupied, and in the postwar years dominated by communism and the Soviet Union. It was hard to believe so much history could take place in one nation. The roads Yvonne and I now travelled over must surely have seen much trampling upon by cavalry, artillery and infantry over the centuries, not to mention tanks that dominated wars in the twentieth century.

Putting thoughts of war aside, my focus was now on the eastern city of Debrecen, close to the Romanian and Ukrainian borders. This delightful city, the second largest in Hungary, was renowned as the 'Calvinist Rome', after the Reformation that took roots in the city in the sixteenth century. It was also the city of László's birth. I tried to imagine what life was like growing up in this flat, great plain region, with the great arc of the Carpathian Mountains in the distance and the Tisza River coursing through in all her majesty. Knowing László as I had, it was not hard to believe that Debrecen had been an important cultural and intellectual centre for centuries, flourishing under the various empires. It made it all the more exciting searching for his family home.

'His old house must be here somewhere,' Yvonne reckoned, pointing to the map.

'Yes, it must be. But will we ever find it?'

'Let's visit the civic office to check their records,' she suggested.

The civic offices were located in the centre of town, which became our first destination. Inquiring at the office, I explained that we were trying to find the house where my husband once lived as a child. Politely, we were told to wait and before long the receptionist returned, accompanied by a young office clerk. Between hand gestures and broken German, English and a little Hungarian, somehow we made ourselves understood. Directly, we were brought into a large, airy open office with tall windows radiating light upon staff busily absorbed in their work. The walls were painted in pale cream, and my first impression was one of spotlessness and diligent employees.

To our great relief, a clerk spoke English with relative ease. Again I repeated my request.

'Is it at all possible to find the house where my husband lived as a child? His name is László Gede.'

'Everything is possible,' I was politely told.

The kind-heartedness shown me was a trait I knew so well in my Debrecen-born husband. Although the Hungarians are noted as a reserved and rather formal people, I found them quite the opposite in their friendliness and helpfulness. After a long search of files, a house was located that belonged to the Gede grandparents. We were told to go to Szív Street. Thanking all the officials for their kindness, we left overjoyed with this news, realising that our quest had finally begun.

To take stock, we decided to adjourn for coffee in a quaint little café in the town square. There beside an elaborate modern fountain we relaxed and indulged ourselves. Oh, such tasteful delights, who could surpass these skilled Hungarian bakers? In its day, Hungarian café society rivalled that of Vienna and Paris. It was not hard to see why.

Drinking coffee and eating scrumptious Hungarian gateaux, we took in the enormous, pedestrianised Kossuth Square, a sight in itself and a far cry from its marketplace origins. The nearby Millennium Foundation was quite impressive – a large musical fountain depicting the arrival of the Magyars in the country as well as a phoenix, the symbol of the rebirth of the city. Across the square I observed the colossal Great Reformed Church with two stout bell towers, glowing in vivid yellow. This noble edifice dominated the horizon and was indeed a statement of power. Almost immediately I realised that this church would have been the place of worship for all the Gede family.

Yvonne, with tourist booklet in hand, informed me that the city was staging a Béla Bartók International Choir Competition. Over one thousand singers with twenty-one choirs from fifteen countries were participating. László would certainly have enjoyed that! Secretly, I hoped that in between my search for his roots time might be found to sample the local celebrations. Finishing our coffee, we continued our search.

The house we were referred to was not far from the city centre in the central district, according to the Debrecen city map, and a short walk from the railway station. We were getting a feel for the city and its mixture of building styles, modern and old. Debrecen had fallen victim to the vagaries of nature and war throughout the centuries. Half of the city was destroyed in a great fire in 1802 and rebuilt, only for half of the buildings to lay in ruins after the Second World War and nearly another quarter badly damaged. The Battle of Debrecen in October 1944 against the Red Army had been particularly savage. The Soviet-style buildings that replaced the ruins did little to grace the once-beautiful city. Finally, after some wrong turns here and there, we found Szív Street nestled in an avenue of trees lit by the sun's rays dancing upon its leaves. It was a peaceful, pleasant street with a mishmash of one, two and three-storey buildings; some were newly painted and looked quite striking, while others were rundown, shabby and neglected. Tall barnlike buildings behind high concrete walls could also be seen. The street was in existence since the nineteenth century, and I later learnt that *szív* meant 'heart' in Hungarian. As I continued to look more closely, it did feel we were getting to the heart of the matter.

9

With the car safely parked and after a short walk following the house numbers, we eventually came to a huge entrance with massive solid wooden gates. Together we both gave a sigh of relief.

'Ah, there it is,' said Yvonne.

I grew apprehensive and my hand trembled as I knocked on the heavy doors. Concerned at the lack of a response after repeated knocks, Yvonne discovered a concealed doorbell, yet still no answer came. As we were about to leave, the gates opened and a tall grey-haired man appeared, who smiled at us. Within lay a beautiful courtyard that revealed a tall, newly painted yellow house. Once again we told our story and understood from his answer that a widow named Gede had sold the property some years before and was now living with her daughter in Budapest. He also mentioned that someone in the Gede family had excelled at music and had become a member of the Hungarian State Opera House in Budapest. I informed him that this very person had been my husband László!

After such a promising start, we rewarded ourselves by attending the festival later that night. Listening to various choral recitals, we watched the whole city centre come alive with excitement and joy. The diverse choirs in vibrant dress seemed to delight the very heavens with song! Yvonne and I both shared in the appreciation of this music. Immersed in the atmosphere, I reflected upon the man whom I had married and on his deep and abiding love of music.

* * *

The following day, I was anxious to find the grave of Papa and Mama Gede with the limited information I had. László's two brothers, István and Zoltán, also filled my mind and the details of what had once been relayed to me. István had died many years previously, but I had no knowledge of the younger brother Zoltán. Was he still alive? Returning to the civic offices once more, further enquiries followed, but this task proved far more difficult. After fruitless forays in various locations, I had detected a reluctance, or rather a little hesitancy, to provide us with the information we sought. I now understand more fully that this, perhaps, was due to the upheaval that ravaged Hungary during the Second World War and the oppressive rule of communism that followed. Similar to other European countries, the Hungarians suffered unimaginable cruelty and brutality at the hands of those regimes.

After numerous visits to the civic offices, an office clerk eventually informed us that my husband's parents were buried at a cemetery located in the northeast of the city. He also confirmed that Zoltán, the youngest brother, was dead. It was sad news to hear but at least we were making progress. Ravenous after all our trekking about, we decided to dine out later that evening. It would be another chance for me to taste Hungarian food on Hungarian soil. The meal started with asparagus soup served with dumplings (*galuska*), leading to the main course of Wiener schnitzel served with green beans, mashed potatoes and a fresh salad, followed by walnut pudding wrapped in pancakes. Although the meal was indeed scrumptious, the Wiener schnitzel would have failed to reach the exacting high standards of my husband's cooking. I had been the apprentice and he the chef in our kitchen! He had been very particular about his food and in today's terms would be labelled a 'faddy eater'.

In the mild late evening the city centre and surrounding streets were still a riot of colour. The festival was in full swing with performers dressed in their various national folk costumes of bright and brilliant reds, blues, yellows, whites, greens and purples. To our delight, suddenly some singers gathered in front of the nearby concert hall and we were treated to an exuberant choral street performance! The crowds went wild with excitement and enthusiasm as they listened to the folk music of the various nations participating. Truly, an unforgettable experience.

* * *

The next morning in warm bright sunshine, on our last day in Debrecen, I was anxious to find the cemetery. Thus, with Yvonne once again at the wheel and me directing, we eventually came upon it near the forested fringe of the city. The public cemetery known as Debreceni Köztemető was relatively new, built in 1932, but many bodies had been re-interred there after the city authorities closed down some older and smaller cemeteries in the city. Now it could boast splendid manicured gardens, mortuaries and a crematorium. The records office was located just inside the main gates. Once inside, we were greeted by a young blonde woman, tall and fair of face, who proved quite helpful.

In answer to our enquiry, she disappeared through swinging doors leaving us to wait. My eyes wandered about the office, which was rather small and sparse, yet pleasingly spotless. On her return she carried a large, old and worn leather-bound book, similar to the school roll books of my youth. My curiosity mounted. Delicately she opened the book, turned the pages and with her index finger searched each line before finally striking gold.

On a map provided, she indicated the grave site where my parents-in-law were buried, and pointed us in the right direction. With a sense of excitement, if not trepidation, we walked into the brightness of sunshine and the silence of headstones. Much thought and planning had gone into the design of the cemetery with its monuments, flowerbeds, fountains and avenues of trees. Taking centre stage was a magnificent brick-red Memorial Service Building in Art Nouveau style. The beautifully decorated frescos, stained-glass windows, arcades and various works of art were held in great esteem by the city dwellers. As we navigated down numbered pathways of graves, Yvonne took my hand.

'We've found them, Eibhlín,' she said, quietly beckoning. 'Look, they're here.'

Following a week of perfect cloudless skies, now for a few brief seconds, raindrops fell. It was an extraordinary moment and a sign that said *welcome and thank you for coming such a long way*. And there, partly hidden, surrounded by a carpet of green foliage I spotted an old weather-beaten sign marked with the names of István Gede and Zsuzsánna Bara. My eyes gently lingered over the grave, their souls at rest in a woodland cemetery filled with birdsong and fragranced by beautiful pine trees.

2.

Early Years

My Son, if thou be humbled, poor,
Hopeless of honour and of gain,
Oh! do not dread thy mother's door;
Think not of me with grief and pain:
I now can see with better eyes;
And worldly grandeur I despise,
And fortune with her gifts and lies.

From 'The Afflictions of Margaret' by William Wordsworth

My husband László Gede was born on 21 June 1915 in the city of Debrecen, Hajdú-Bihar County, in eastern Hungary. At that time it was part of the Austro-Hungarian Empire, which dissolved after the catastrophic carnage of the Great War. László's Debrecen-born father, István Gede, had married Zsuzsánna Bara of Monostorpályi, a small town some twenty-three kilometres southeast of Debrecen. Not a typical Hungarian surname, Gede is possibly of Saxon origin coming from Hamburg in Germany. László's relatives believed that the family first settled in south-eastern Hungary at a date unknown. Bara, on the other hand, is most likely French and originated from Provence or Galician Spain. Both Gede and Bara families were of the Calvinist faith, and Monostorpályi like Debrecen was staunchly Calvinist. Consequently, hard work and discipline in all aspects of life were stressed. This indeed proved to be the guiding principle for my husband throughout his life. The Gede ancestors included the Balog and Kálmán families, also committed Calvinists. Some months after my visit to Debrecen, I learned that a devastating fire had destroyed the Great Reformed Church in Debrecen in 1802 and that the above families had generously contributed to the restoration of the church. For their beneficence, a monument was erected in their honour, which today is found in the public cemetery in Debrecen.

When László was born in 1915, his father István was on military service. In fact, he was absent for the entire duration of the First World War. I have no knowledge of his regiment or which battles he fought in, but more than likely he was in the Royal Hungarian Honvéd, or territorial army. At that time, there were cavalry and Hussar regiments attached to Debrecen as well as an infantry division, that is, the 3rd Debrecen Honved Infantry Regiment. By all accounts, Hungarian soldiers fought fearlessly and distinguished themselves on every front contested by Austria-Hungary during the war. They saw combat especially on the Eastern Front and at the Battles of the Isonzo on the Italian Front. The 11th Debrecen Cavalry, commanded by Lieutenant-General Josef Roth, memorably took part in the Battle of Limanowa, southeast of Krakow in December 1914, and along with the other military divisions successfully held back the Russian Third Army. However, the Siege of Przemysl resulted in a defeat for the Hungarian forces against the Russian Third and Eleventh Armies in March 1915. At the Eastern Front, the Brusilov Offensive in 1916 proved a costly victory for Austria-Hungary with over half a million casualties and a significant retreat. How László's father managed to survive the war for so long was a miracle, given that over a million Austro-Hungarian soldiers lost their lives.

At a political level, it was the aggressive foreign policies pursued by Austria-Hungary that had precipitated the war, but at a human level their soldiers and citizens had paid the ultimate price. It is believed that Hungarian soldiers were far more trustworthy and disciplined than soldiers from other ethnic groups in the empire, and easier to mobilise. If István Gede was anything like his son, then I imagine he would have fought with great pride and patriotism.

In those absent years it fell to Zsuzsánna Gede to rear her son. The family home was then on Hajnal Street, a main thoroughfare in the east of the city, and where László was born. As a child László was blessed with good looks and developed into a most handsome boy. Though he never reached the two metres he aspired to, his average height never impaired his drive to succeed. As a youngster he had blond hair and brilliant pale-blue eyes, and like many children his hair darkened with age, though his perceptive eyes always kept their same sparkling brilliance. His mother adored her firstborn son and he equally adored her; she called him Laci, the diminutive of László. She would on occasions bring him to Monostorpályi to visit her father, Adrás Bara, owner of a substantial farm and vineyards. According to László, Grandfather Bara was much respected in the locality; in cases where a dispute arose, he would be called upon to act as mediator between the quarrelling parties.

Young László delighted in observing the working of his grandfather's farm. There was much to feast his eyes on: horse-drawn carriages, droves of cattle grazing in fields or cows being herded into milking parlours; wee piglets squealing and running amuck in the piggery; and horses freely galloping across green paddocks. As in most farms, there were geese, hens, dogs and cats wandering about and vying for his attention. He also felt the thrill of adventure as he ran through vast avenues of vineyards. Here, in this setting, László's heart opened up and his devotion and love of nature grew.

Although he respected his grandfather, László could not bear for the man to touch him. The young boy had developed an aversion to facial hair and tobacco smoke; a pipe was forever lodged in his grandfather's mouth and he wore an enormous moustache, or so it seemed to the young child! Hence, a closer friendship evaded grandfather and grandson.

This was not the case, however, with his paternal grandmother, Julianna Kálmán Gede. Visits to this grandmother, who lived some distance away in a house on Szív Street dating from around 1900, were particularly special. The affection László held for her was deep and enduring. In later life, he would often speak kindly of her and held her in high esteem.

Born to János Kálmán and his wife Julianna Balog in January 1863, little Julianna was however orphaned at six years of age. I have no knowledge of how both her parents died, then aged in their thirties.

Luckily for Julianna, she was adopted by a kind local farmer and his wife. These good people made their home a haven of love and security for her. In time she learnt the rudiments of farming, in particular the raising of geese, and impressed the farmer with her bright and quick mind. Upon marriage in December 1886, it was a fine, hardworking, stoic woman who set up home with László's grandfather, István Gede. She was just twenty-three years of age and he a year younger. With her characteristic inner strength and resilience, she lived well into old age. To László, however, she was simply Goose Grandmother. The geese on the farm were highly valued in particular and it was said that goose liver from the family's geese ended up on the tables of Queen Victoria in England. Goose liver was indeed a symbol of Hungarian cuisine, reserved for special family occasions and festivities. From this grandmother, László's love of nature was enhanced all the more. Though I never met the woman, I have such warm feelings towards her that I give her a big mental hug every time I think of her.

László was three years of age by the time he clapped eyes on his father, István Gede, for the first time. Small and short in stature, István returned from the war a changed man. Indeed much had changed in the meantime. Austria-Hungary was no longer one of the great powers of Europe, boasting fifty-two million subjects, with its ethnic groups now calling for independence. By 1920, after the Treaty of Trianon, Hungary itself would lose two-thirds of all its territory and more than half its population. Eight million Hungarians would be left in Hungary, while more than three million ethnic Hungarians would be cut off outside the newly established borders. In time this would sow seeds of great discontent and result in more bloodshed. Certainly the horrors that István Gede had encountered during the war influenced his life's philosophy. According to László, his father had a deep abhorrence of war and instructed his children, over and over again, to stay clear of aggression and to avoid politics.

Speaking of children, the end of the war and István Gede's employment as a locksmith in the engineering department with the Hungarian State

Railways was an opportunity for the family to expand. László was soon joined by two brothers, István Jnr and Zoltán. Zoltán, the youngest, in time came to adore his older brother László.

On returning home from war, István had observed a sensitive and placid boy in László and quickly resolved to toughen him up! László recalled working side by side with his father at the family home at weekends and after school. István was a skilled craftsman, capable of working with iron and other metals and also with wood. By all accounts, István had a wonderful brain and wonderful hands and could shape any object into whatever he wished to create. There was a story that László relayed about his father designing some essential piece of equipment for the State Railways so that the new rails and wheels fitted perfectly.

Under his father's tutelage, László acquired basic carving and metalwork skills, which would later stand him in good stead. No project seemed too big or two small for the intrepid pair – gates and doors, pots and bins, and even repairing roofs. Together they made enormous wooden gates for the entrance to the family home. When László turned eight, István undertook the making of a large cooking stove. During the construction of this range, the young boy at one point was placed within the structure, given a hammer and told which parts to hit. Even as an adult, László would smile as he recalled the thundering sound – notes of music within the iron drum!

Across the road close to the Gede family home stood Bocskai Barracks with its extensive parade grounds and splendid neoclassical pavilion. For all Austro-Hungarian soldiers, the military band held a special place with its own insignias and ranks. In the playing of national anthems and patriotic songs, they boosted morale, especially with troops leaving for the Front. As a baby, so I was told, László would clap his little hands together at the sound of the military band, whether playing ceremonial or marching music, no doubt fostering his earliest love of music. Zsuzsánna, being an attentive mother, later discreetly sent the young boy to study music, without her husband's knowledge. He was taught violin, piano and, in his teenage years, the clarinet. Of the three, it was the clarinet that became his lifelong companion.

Later when his father discovered what was happening, he was absolutely furious.

'No, no, no,' he said. 'There will be no music.'

He relented somewhat when his wife explained that music was just a hobby.

Even in those early years László possessed a quick, bright mind and at school would sometimes allow some of his fellow pupils to copy his homework, usually algebra and geometry. It was done out of sheer goodness and sometimes for the reward of a sweet or such like. Of course, whenever the teachers found out László was severely punished. Yet, despite this, it did not deter him from helping the pupils again. This characteristic goodness stayed with him all his life.

* * *

Around 1919 the family moved further down the street to a house István Gede had built. The low building was situated off the street and opened onto a small courtyard, typical of many Hungarian dwellings. Sadly that August, at the age of sixteen, László lost the one person he loved the most. Zsuzsánna Gede died suddenly aged thirty-seven, leaving a distraught husband to raise three children. So great was István's grief that he spent an enormous amount of money on her funeral and ordered a lead-lined coffin. In addition to coping with the tragedy, László had another mighty struggle to contend with – his father's absolute refusal to allow him to enter the Debrecen School of Music, his one burning desire and ambition. It was made all the more painful knowing his mother would have wished it with all her heart. The Debrecen School of Music was a prestigious institution on Vár Street in the city centre. Ironically, it was founded in 1861 by a Ferenc Farkas, chair of the Society for the School of Music, who not only was an amateur musician but also an ironmonger!

István, quite adamant, had made up his mind that his son should study engineering and accomplish more than he had working as a locksmith. In István's eyes, László's sharp intellect and excellence at mathematics made him ideally suited to engineering. He naturally wished his son to achieve in life, but that did not extend to a musical career. To István, earning a living in a regular job and providing for his family should be László's focus. However, his son had his own dreams to follow. His devotion and love of music convinced him that he should leave home and travel westwards to Budapest. The tension between father and son grew, making further discussion nigh on impossible. László had made his decision.

Taking matters into his own hands, László immediately visited an uncle on his mother's side of the family. Uncle Bara, as he was called, listened intently as László explained his predicament: his father's refusal to allow him enter the Debrecen School of Music and his plans to fulfil his ambitions in Budapest. László had given the matter great thought and now expressed his hopes and desires earnestly. More than anything he wished to attend the Liszt Academy of Music; to compose his own music; to conduct his own orchestra; to be a member of the Hungarian State Opera House. All his dreams came tumbling out and were laid at the feet of his uncle.

In László, Uncle Bara observed a sixteen-year-old with the same stubborn, obstinate, strong-willed character as the father he was running from. No amount of persuading would change the mind of this bright intelligent youth. Of that, Bara was certain. However, László did need to see things from his father's perspective. Uncle Bara began by telling his nephew that money was very scarce and reminding him of the deprivation that surrounded him. The Great Depression had not escaped Hungary. After the Wall Street Crash of 1929 world grain prices plummeted, leading to a catastrophic decline in Hungary's grain exports and collapse of its economy. To stay afloat, it had to seek financial relief from the League of Nations whose austerity measures unhappily led to greater unemployment.

'Look about you, László,' he said. 'What do you see only poverty and hunger everywhere.'

László remained silent as his uncle spoke.

'You have a wonderful father who provides well for you and your brothers.'

László nodded, knowing too well that life had been grindingly hard for most people since the war. By now Bara was convinced that László was earnest in his hopes for the future, and would do his utmost to achieve his dreams. And so with great foresight, he gave the youth a gold watch and some money to assist him on his way. It was the nearest thing to a family blessing and they parted with a firm handshake. Despite his father's wishes, László quietly left the family home early one morning shortly afterwards as the household slept.

Even at such a tender age, László knew he would have to fend for himself. Military service was also a fact of life in Hungary. And so, on 18 August 1931, he enlisted in the Royal Hungarian Army. Conveniently, the barracks were located some distance from his home, north of the city, in the old hussar barracks on Kassai Street with its distinctive ornate fountain. In years to come during communism those barracks would be occupied by Russians before being splendidly renovated and converted to a university campus in the twenty-first century. Back in 1931, perhaps László's strongest reason for enlisting was that he stood an excellent chance of getting a good musical education within the army structure. After all, band music had been ringing in his ears since his cradle days.

Before long, having come through the catering and canteen sections, László found himself selected for the military band, playing the clarinet. While playing in the band, he also applied to study at the Debrecen School of Music. However, not much is known about how he fared there. I can only imagine how satisfied he must have been in the band, although with his aptitude and interest in cooking, I'm sure his stint with the canteen services was no great chore.

When his remarkable powers of concentration and keen engineering skills manifested themselves, however, László was earmarked as a marksman in the army. He may have been somewhat reluctant to perform this duty, though he had to abide by army discipline and had little or no say in the matter. The platoon rifle competitions, an important part of all army training, undoubtedly gave him great personal satisfaction and recognition within the ranks. Throughout his life he maintained that he never once fired a gun in anger.

During this period his father married again. Like Zsuzsánna, his stepmother Borbála Molnár came from farming stock; she was small, dark-haired and quietly spoken. In later years László spoke much of her kindness and good qualities, adroitly taking over the running of the household and paying special attention to his younger siblings and grandmother. That Borbála was continuing the care that Zsuzsánna had lavished on the ailing Goose Grandmother, now nearing the age of seventy, came as a relief. Indeed the knowledge that his entire family was in good hands was a great consolation to László. Borbála's brother Antal was equally kind-hearted and favourably disposed to the Gede family. In time, Antal would be a great support and ally to István and his sons.

Soon afterwards, in 1932, László was transferred to Budapest. The length of military service at the time was three years and so he remained in the army until around 1934. By that time he had attained the rank of sergeant. Turmoil at the borders flared up from time to time during this period. Since the Treaty of Trianon in 1920, Hungary was essentially a kingdom without a king. Instead, a prince regent named Admiral Miklós Horthy ruled and pursued foreign policies aimed at recovering lost Hungarian territories and bringing ethnic Hungarians back into the fold. So much territory had been lost, it greatly saddened and angered Hungarians: Romania acquired Transylvania; Yugoslavia gained Croatia, Slavonia and Vojvodina; Slovakia became a part of Czechoslovakia; and Austria also acquired a small piece of prewar Hungarian territory. There was also unrest in the country as standards of living were very low or just subsistent and unemployment high. László's family, like many others, could barely survive. To boost its economy, Hungary out of necessity became major trading partners with Nazi Germany and Fascist Italy, then led by Benito Mussolini. But for László and his fellow Hungarians it was an alliance they would regret in years to come.

* * *

Once in Budapest László did not reside in the army barracks. He had no intention of relinquishing his newfound freedom and independence. However, his meagre army wages were not sufficient to live on. Thus, the gold watch given to him by Uncle Bara kept him alive during those first months living in Budapest, pawned when money was scarce and retrieved when means allowed! In fact, the pawn shops of Budapest were something of an institution. The Empress Maria Theresa herself had approved the licensing of pawnbrokers in 1773 to prevent exploitation by moneylenders. They flourished in Budapest and became part of the fabric of life, especially in László's time. It was said that money was so tight in those decades that people would pawn their summer clothes in winter and winter clothes in summer. In January 1933, the Associated Press reported that the winter had been so severe that the city authorities were forced to redeem 40,000 overcoats from the public pawn shops and return them to their insolvent owners, but that 400,000 overcoats still remained in hock! It certainly gives a flavour of the hardship that László and his fellow city dwellers must have endured.

In that vast city he spent much time finding suitable lodgings and accommodation, not an easy task for a youth intent on following a musical career. Having very little money he wound up more often than not lodging in rather poor rundown areas, such as backstreets off main thoroughfares. In some boarding houses all that he was offered was a bed at night-time that he had to vacate early each morning to allow the person on shift work to occupy it during the day. It gives new meanings to the words sleep-share, bed-share or hot-bedding! Dissatisfied, he realised that this was the price to be paid for success, while economic depression gripped Europe. Soon afterwards László changed lodgings once more and rented a room at the back of a baker's shop. This brought an unforeseen bonus. In wintertime he was warm and cosy, thanks to the ovens giving out great heat!

* * *

Eventually László's luck began to turn. He found employment in a large music shop owned by a kind, elderly Jewish gentleman, in the Jewish Quarter. The Jewish Quarter was located in the district of Erzebetvaros in the city, with the Hungarian State Opera and Liszt Academy of Music at its outer fringes. Shrewd as ever, László seized upon an opportunity that presented itself one morning. On entering the shop, intending to purchase some reeds for his clarinet, he observed that a sales assistant was required. As he tried out various instruments he noticed that some were out of tune. Then on requesting music sheets he perceived a filing system in need of some upgrading. Immediately he struck up a conversation with the owner, Mr Weisz, and mentioned his observations. The discussion ended with the owner asking the teenager if he would care to work in the establishment and help put things in order. It goes without saying that the impecunious youngster jumped at the chance. As a result, a sincere and warm friendship began between the elderly Jew and the penniless Calvinist youth. The extra little money he earned now offered security and guaranteed him the basics of life. From the beginning, Mr Weisz looked after him through all those early difficult years in the capital. It was always with deep gratitude and affection that László remembered this man. If struggling artists need a benefactor on occasion, then Mr Weisz was truly his.

In Hungary, with its centuries of high culture and patronage, music held a special place. It was not seen as the preserve of the elite and sophisticated but of interest to the general masses as well. If ever there was a musical gene, then the Hungarian nation seemed to have inherited it in abundance. Mindful of this, the postwar government wished to give all workers every opportunity to avail of a musical training and the experience of being part of a band or orchestra in the workplace. It was a most opportune time for László. Through his army connections he became a member of the Ganz factory orchestra while an army sergeant based at the factory. He also helped to teach some of the members.

The Ganz Works, founded in 1844, was a vast engineering plant located near the Keleti railway station east of the city in the Józsefváros district. Throughout its long history Ganz was best known for manufacturing heavy machinery such as tramcars, trains, ships, planes, bridges, generators, and among one of the first European firms to pioneer the transition from steam to electric railways. It numbered thousands among its employees and had no shortage of takers for its orchestra. The development also reflected some progressive thinking throughout Europe. In Britain and elsewhere, workers' brass bands and orchestras had been in existence since the nineteenth century, especially at collieries. They brought nothing but positives. They kept workers out of trouble, were a source of civic pride for local communities, increased worker morale and nipped any signs of political activity in the bud.

The orchestral work was also another small income for László, constantly struggling to make a living. He could immerse himself in music once again, rehearsing and performing at festivals and special events, and sometimes major concerts. There was no shortage of music composed for brass bands either. Liszt was a firm favourite and a national treasure. He had composed quite an amount for brass, such as the Hungarian Battle March; Les Preludes, Symphonic Poem No. 3; and Hungarian Rhapsody No. 2. The experience also perhaps brought László back to his youth when the military bands in Debrecen gave such intense joy to the local people. It is no surprise today that Debrecen regularly hosts the International Festival of Military Bands.

During this early period, László also applied to the National Music School on Nagymező Street. This school was located near Andrássy Avenue and not far from the State Opera House. The school had the distinction of being the first Hungarian music school that catered for students at high school or secondary school level. Fortunate to obtain a scholarship – a sure indication of his talent – László studied extremely hard, mastering the intricacies and technicalities of playing his clarinet and absorbing every detail in the theory of music. Not only that but he had to familiarise himself with the history of music and learn all about the various composers and their compositions. This he did with great diligence and achieved the grades desired. Sadly, records of his time at the school were lost given the later upheavals in his country as well as its eventual amalgamation with the Liszt Academy of Music.

How wonderful it was for László, bringing to life the music of composers who had written specific parts for clarinet. Beginning with Bach, in the early days of the instrument, to Mozart and down to Weber and Brahms, the experience must have been deeply gratifying for him. It was said that Mozart in his later years considered the clarinet his favourite instrument and created the most famous of all clarinet concertos for his friend Anton Stadler: the delightful Clarinet Concerto in A major. What pride too László felt immersed in the rich musical heritage of his land listening to Liszt, Dohnányi, Bartók and Kodály. In his midst was also another esteemed Hungarian composer, Dr László Lajtha, under whose tutelage László benefited greatly. At the school, Dr Lajtha taught composition, chamber music, music theory, methodology, and music history, despite a hectic schedule of composing, touring, teaching and researching. Like Bartók and Kodály, Lajtha was dedicated to Hungarian folk music research, which also influenced his compositions along with French impressionism.

It was an exciting period for László in this hothouse of creativity. It spawned him to do something similarly creative and modern as he grew into maturity. In the mid-1930s he felt confident enough to form a little band with his young fellow musicians, calling themselves Goldwin Gede. Popular music had become the modern craze and was cutting edge for some musicians. The Jazz Age of 1920s America had left its mark throughout European capitals, notably Paris and Budapest, where it also fell under the spell of gipsy music. The Swing Era was about to take off, and virtuoso bandleaders were suddenly in vogue. László was aware that the clarinet was a perfect instrument for jazz and swing jazz, with no shortage of sheet music. Leading American clarinettist and bandleader Benny Goodman popularised many songs during the 1930s that became standards internationally, such as 'Darn that Dream', 'How Deep is the Ocean', and 'Stompin' at the Savoy' – all of which László was acquainted with. The American King of Swing, whose parents had hailed from Eastern Europe, was just as popular in Hungary. In fact, Goodman's first classical recording took place in 1938 when he recorded Mozart's Clarinet Quintet in A major with the Budapest Quartet.

However, it was American composer George Gershwin, who was writing thrilling parts for clarinet in compositions such as *Rhapsody in Blue* and 'Summertime' from *Porgy and Bess*, that caught László's attention. He was hooked and perhaps the choice of Goldwin for his band was a play on the name Gershwin as well as a tribute. Slowly and painstakingly, line by line, László transcribed the music and songs for their repertoire and divided them into two songbooks. Swing nestled among the rumbas, foxtrots, tangoes, and slow waltzes. The songs inscribed were in English, German and Hungarian: 'Alexander's Ragtime Band', 'The Big Apple', 'The Umbrella Man', 'Tea for Two', 'Rock Around the Clock', 'September in the Rain', 'Bei der blonden Kathrein', 'Lili Marlen', 'Juliett-nek Nincsegy

Szdknnyája' and 'En Mulatok Minden Ejszakát', to name but a few. During this period László also turned his attention to composing and improvisation; he adapted and arranged many a Hungarian folk song to the new modern music.

There was no shortage of venues for the band to play in. There were hotels, clubs, private functions, and, of course, cafés such as the Budavár Coffee House on Széna Square. The elegant coffee houses of Budapest were legendary, numbering over five hundred at one time, and part of the cultural life of the city. They were also home to artists, writers and poets. Café Gerbeaud and the New York Café, in particular, were among the most sumptuous and opulent. It was in this milieu that László could play his beloved clarinet and on occasion another instrument close to his heart: the saxophone. Now if his music professors knew about that, they would not have been amused; certainly, in those days, the saxophone was rather frowned upon in the higher echelons of the musical establishment!

The band provided extra welcome funds for László and his fellow students to finance their studies and lifestyles. That said, László spent very little money being frugal and thrifty by nature. On one occasion, in those early years at the National Music School, he became quite ill and suddenly collapsed. Exhaustion and poor nutrition were to blame. His schedule was phenomenally busy: studying at the music school, playing with the Ganz orchestra and military band, and long evenings playing at various venues with Goldwin Gede. It is easy for me to understand the reason for his ill-health and what motivated him in this regard, for he had a most dreadful fear of poverty. Perhaps irrational at times, this fear remained with him throughout life, and even during our marriage I had to ensure that I kept a well-stocked fridge and that nothing was ever wasted.

His failing health did not go unnoticed and became a cause of concern. Soon the professors at the music school began to worry about him, in particular Dr Lajtha. This most kindly man, despite his own busy schedule and esteemed position, would sometimes bring László to his family home on Váci Street, a couple of streets away. There, Dr Lajtha made sure that the young student had good nourishing food and plenty of it. A close bond was forged between the two men and László looked upon Dr Lajtha as a mentor and friend. In the coming years that bond would be furthered deepened as they sought to protect their city from wartime oppressors. When their paths diverged years later they would still keep in contact, but sadly their correspondence was lost over time.

3.

WAR AND RESISTANCE

The glory of Hungary, is it
a falling star which sparkled,
fell
and was swallowed forever?

From 'About Our Country' by Sándor Petőfi

AROUND 1935 László finally finished his studies at the National Music School on Nagymező Street. At last, he could rejoice that he had received a proper musical education at the hands of some of the country's finest teachers. His future seemed brighter than ever before. He continued to perfect his musicianship, seeing that it was his life's great passion, and frequently met with like-minded people. They formed his close circle of friends and helped broaden his understanding of music both at home and abroad. The Goldwin Gede Band was also much in demand and over the next decade he continued to play at various venues in the city and beyond.

Occasionally Sunday mornings saw László play clarinet at Saint Stephen's Basilica in the city and also at other church venues. It was a great honour for him to play in such auspicious surroundings as the basilica. The magnificent neoclassical building was constructed in 1905 and dedicated to Saint Stephen, the first King of Hungary from the tenth century. Interestingly, his incorrupt right hand is today housed in a highly ornate reliquary there. Music had been an integral part of the basilica since its consecration and featured many eminent musicians as organists and soloists over the years. Despite his Calvinist upbringing, László could appreciate the fine musical traditions of the Catholic Church and relished the opportunity of playing at the basilica.

In his spare time, not that much existed, László dabbled in various DIY projects. His engineering skills were rarely neglected and his resourceful nature came in handy at a time when many Hungarians were struggling to make ends meet. Building up a makeshift workshop and acquiring tools became another preoccupation over the years. He once built himself a motorbike from old discarded ones left for scrap. It was such a success he could travel around the city as he pleased and sometimes further afield to Lake Balaton, a short run from Budapest. The achievement filled him with pride and delight, all the more so when his music professors viewed his work and congratulated him on his talent and dexterity. Soon he progressed to a clapped-out motor car. Hours were spent tinkering with engine and bodywork and restoring them to their former life.

* * *

The outbreak of war in Europe in 1939 unleashed a turbulent period in the history of the Hungarian nation. László and his family could scarcely imagine what would soon befall their beloved country. The war and its aftermath would take its toll on every Hungarian, destroying lives, livelihoods, property and practically the nation itself. Years later, recalling the period, László would sigh time and again.

'Ah, poor Hungary, poor, poor Hungary.'

For many decades both German and Hungarian defence forces had worked together and looked upon each another as allies. The Trianon Treaty of 1920 had been severely punitive and a humiliating blow to national pride. Many Hungarians, indeed many of them László's friends and relatives, were under the impression that the country would soon regain territories lost under the treaty. In the late 1930s, however, Miklós Horthy began to walk a tightrope act as regent. The country soon benefited from its unholy alliance with Nazi Germany and Italy in November 1938, when forfeited lands where ethnic Hungarians lived were recaptured, namely southern Slovakia and southern Carpathian Ruthenia. With his near phobia of Russia, Nazi Germany for Horthy was also a safeguard against Russian aggression.

For all their common bonds with Germany, however, László, like certain Hungarians, grew uneasy at the rise of fascism in the 1920s and 1930s. An outspoken anti-Semitic, Gyula Gömbös, had become prime minister in 1932. He cleverly negotiated an economic agreement with Germany, which in turn bound the two countries more closely together, making Hungary dependent upon Nazi Germany. This move made Gömbös popular among László's countrymen and women. It saved many families from unemployment and destitution, which László and others could plainly see. However, Gömbös's anti-Semitism caused outrage and led Regent Horthy to warn him to moderate his anti-Jewish rhetoric.

The deeply fascist Arrow Cross Party, set up in 1935 and led by Ferenc Szálasi, was particularly troubling for László. After all, László embodied a spirit of love and compassion towards all humankind, regardless of race or ethnicity. Regent Horthy held conservative old-empire views and was not zealously anti-Semitic. If anything, he favoured multi-religious, multiethnic and multilingual cultures and allowed them to flourish. Many Jewish people and others from outside the country found refuge within Hungarian borders during the early war period and were welcomed. Several of them were musicians known to László. Unlike in Nazi Germany, there was little legislation in Hungary that curbed the rights of Jewish people, although that slowly began to change during the war years.

The prime minister in 1939, Béla Imrédy, was forced from office because of his Jewish heritage and replaced by Count Pál Teleki. To Horthy's credit, he refused to allow German troops to use Hungarian railways and roads in its attack on Poland at the onset of war in September 1939. Desperate to spare his country from war, Teleki was in contact with British and US governments, urging them that the small countries of Central Europe needed to form some kind of alliance if they were to avoid being swallowed up by the more powerful nations. It all would be to no avail, however.

At first, while the war raged outside Hungarian borders, life continued fairly normally for László. It was common practice in the Royal Hungarian Army that once military service was completed, soldiers were transferred to the Military Reserves. It is unclear how often László was called up from the Reserves to perform in the military band. From army records, it would appear that it occurred from August 1939 and into 1941. National conscription was also introduced in 1939, so there would be no escaping military service for his younger brothers, István Jnr and Zoltán, still living in Debrecen. Before the onset of war, István had graduated from a business college and had worked in a bank, while Zoltán had attended a trade school and qualified as a carpenter. When István Jnr enlisted, he trained as a reservist officer at a military school and later became a quartermaster officer at the military airbase in Ungvár, today known as Uzhhorod in Ukraine.

By now László was firmly established as a musician in his own right and, as I later learned, much more besides. When researching his life in Budapest, searching for what he wished me to find, I made an extraordinary discovery. During those early years he had fathered a child at the age of twenty-four. His baby daughter Lívia was born in January 1940. I have little knowledge about his wife Etelka Nagy, whom he subsequently married in 1941, neither about their courtship nor life together. I believe they lived in an apartment on Madách Imre Square, a small arcaded square with a huge arched gate off Károly Boulevard, situated on the Pest side of the river. The location would have suited László, being relatively near the musical hub of the city.

It would appear that László's father István did not attend the wedding, but was keen to meet his son's wife and their daughter nonetheless. Family ties were particularly important to Hungarians, especially in those days, and while László was an ardent letter-writer, he seldom made trips home. Even so, when Lívia was two years of age, László and Etelka journeyed to Debrecen to meet István Gede. I have no knowledge of how the reunion went or László's thoughts on the matter. I can only surmise that István was pleased that László was doing well for himself and now had a family.

For whatever reason, the marriage sadly broke up shortly afterwards. László and Etelka separated and Lívia lived with her mother. In her teenage years the daughter discovered a most beautiful and touching farewell letter written by her father to her mother, lamenting how their life together had come to an end. By today's standards, László would appear rather old-fashioned. Giving his family name to a woman upon marriage was seen as an honour to bestow on her – perhaps it was a throwback to the chivalrous customs of Austro-Hungary. I have no doubt the separation grieved him greatly and their divorce was eventually finalised around 1949. I learnt from László's papers that he considered the union a marriage of convenience, or so the translation read. The one thing I do know, however, is that László was an honourable man who would have wished and wanted the best for his child. He would have done his best to provide for his wife and child given the circumstances. Clearly, he was a very young man trying to do the right thing. The loss of little Lívia as a result of divorcing his wife left a great unspeakable void in his heart. It was a secret he harboured for the remainder of his life. No doubt László had his own reasons for keeping Lívia a secret from me and others. Perhaps the pain and sense of failure it engendered prevented him from disclosing it to me. There was also his habit of compartmentalising people in his life – chapters once read were firmly closed.

* * *

As the war continued Hitler appeased Hungary by granting more territory lost under the Treaty of Trianon. In September 1940, the northern half of Transylvania was returned. For Hungarians, even the Gedes, it felt like one of its severed limbs had been restored. The country was not to be spared the barbarity and full horrors of Nazism, however. It entered the war in April 1941 when forced by Nazi Germany to join the invasion of Yugoslavia and allow the Wehrmacht to march through its territory. Prime Minister Teleki had failed in his endeavours to keep his country neutral and out of the war. The friendship and peace treaty signed with Yugoslavia in December 1940 had ended before it had hardly begun. The former lands in Vojvodina, Yugoslavia were soon back under Hungarian control.

Doom and despair were all around, not only for László and his family, but also its leaders. On 3 April 1941, the prime minister took his own life. In a suicide note to Regent Horthy, he wrote:

> We broke our word, out of cowardice, with respect to the Treaty of Permanent Peace …. The nation feels it, and we have thrown away its honour. We have allied ourselves to scoundrels … we will become body-snatchers! A nation of trash…

Indeed, in taking his own life, it must surely be looked upon as an act of unimaginable courage in protest against a Nazi regime of horror. Count Teleki possessed a noble mind, in my view, and today is held in great esteem in the Hungarian heart. However, it was with a cold heart that László and his fellow band members struck up lively marches to see regiments off to the Eastern Front in the months that followed.

Worse was to come. Jews in ever-increasing numbers were deported to work camps. It was a shameful day in the nation's history when Hungarian troops massacred thirteen hundred Jews, Serbs and Magyars in Újvidék (present-day Novi Sad) in January 1942 and threw their bodies into the River Danube. All done as reprisals for resistance activities. Although the perpetrators tried to suppress the entire matter, it eventually reached the ears of Regent Horthy, who had the men captured and punished. Death and destruction loomed on the horizon over the following months – the Battle of Stalingrad would annihilate the Hungarian Second Army and Third Army. László's father and others of his generation knew only too well the horror and agony the soldiers must have endured.

By now László and his friends could see the pervasive effect of Nazism spreading throughout Europe. He had a great many Jewish friends, not just musicians but those from other walks of life as well. He held a sincere respect and love for them and felt a great sadness for the pain, suffering and slaughter they now endured as a race. Mr Weisz, who had given him a lucky break when he first came to Budapest, instantly came to mind. He hoped and prayed the man would come to no harm. Since the onset of war, anti-Semitic legislation had been gradually introduced in Hungary that restricted the rights of Jewish people and caused them considerable hardship in earning a living. More so, thousands of Hungarian Jews had been forced to join labour battalions that were sent to the Russian front in June 1941 after Hitler declared war on the Soviet Union. Some of them had been gifted musicians like László. With the borders of Europe now closed to Hungarians, László wondered what the fate of his friends and their relatives would be. Would Horthy be strong enough to resist Hitler? The death of László's ailing Goose Grandmother in those early years of the 1940s filled him with sadness. However, it was a merciful release when he thought about what lay in store. Her husband, also in his eighties, still battled on in good health.

Brutal and barbaric, Nazism preyed upon people's fears, as László observed. If found uncooperative or obstructing the authorities, people would face torture or perhaps death. The system was aided by informers, where even among friends and family members, trust was slowly broken down. The Nazi thirst for power and control knew no bounds, even in Hungary; anyone different culturally or ethnically was wiped out, such as Jews, Roma or gypsies, those of differing sexual orientation, of low intellect or with physical disabilities. Many of these people were deemed unfit to live and mutilated in some form or exterminated. Even Christians were not spared Nazi vengefulness. I am especially mindful of Dietrich Bonhoeffer, a German Lutheran pastor and anti-Nazi. Captured in 1943, he was put to death by hanging in April 1945 after heroically opposing the persecution of Jews. How Hitler could hypnotise or brainwash and bring so many minds under his control still defies logic even today.

* * *

Against the backdrop of war being raged on several fronts, László's career miraculously thrived in some ways. A lifetime's ambition was achieved when he embarked upon a course of study at the Liszt Academy of Music, beginning in 1944. Many years had passed since Uncle Bara had pressed a gold watch into his hand to make his dreams a reality. Now finally he had made good on that investment. The academy, founded in 1875, consisted of a splendid concert hall and music conservatory located on the corner of

Király Street and Liszt Square in the cultural heartland of the city. It was certainly a beacon for someone like László. Then, as now, its prestigious Art Nouveau-style building was a prized jewel for musically talented Hungarians. The huge seated statue of Liszt that adorns its façade makes it almost like a temple or religious shrine.

The admiration and reverence towards Liszt was well justified. The man was different from many other famous composers in that he actually founded his own academy. Not only did his music appeal to László, but also Liszt's vision and generosity. *Génie oblige!* was Liszt's motto, in that he believed each artist had a moral duty to use his gifts for the benefit of humanity and to foster genuine talent. And Liszt certainly did that, not only as one of the greatest pianists of his time, but also as an innovative composer, conductor, influential teacher and theorist. The Liszt Academy was renowned for its highly trained professors, who lived up to Liszt's credo, and for its teaching methods.

In this milieu László studied the clarinet in great depth under the tutorage of Professor Károly Váczi, a brilliant clarinettist. Chamber music and the art of ensemble playing were a particular focus of teaching in the academy. It was something that László could appreciate given his work with the Goldwin Gede band, even if they indulged in jazz and swing! László always held Professor Váczi in high regard. He respected most of his teachers and they in turn seemed to have returned that respect and were fond of him. Walking through the interior of the building decorated with frescos, stained glass and mosaics, and graced with statues of Bartók and Chopin, it must have been a wonderful experience for László. A mural of Károly Váczi can be found today along the corridor leading in from the artists' entrance to the State Opera House – as indeed can a mural of László Gede!

Speaking of jazz and swing, they had long fallen out of favour in Nazi Germany. Hitler had an aversion to such music, believing it to be subhuman and degenerate, created by Jews and performed by black people. Joseph Goebbels, Hitler's propaganda minister, had banned it but at the same time was not above using it for propaganda purposes when the occasion demanded. It was yet another reason for László to despise everything the Nazis represented.

* * *

The year 1944 also saw a savage turn of events for László and his fellow Hungarians. War drew ever closer to home. During those turbulent war years Regent Horthy became exasperated by continuing to collaborate with a tyrannical Nazi regime. His allegiance was faltering and on several occasions he tried to pull out of the Axis Powers. With the might of Nazi Germany on one side and the force of Russia on the other, it was like two Rottweiler dogs bearing down on Hungary. Regent Horthy was doing his upmost to protect his people, but against such military power it was impossible. When Hitler became aware that the prime minister of Hungary, Miklós Kállay, was in secret negotiations about an armistice with the Allies, the Nazis swiftly occupied Hungary in Operation Margarethe in March. The occupation was bloodless and took everyone by surprise. A new prime minister, Döme Sztójay, was installed in a puppet government almost immediately. But worst of all, Jewish deportations to death camps in Poland began, notably to Auschwitz, with the aid of the Arrow Cross Party. Until this point, Hungary had steadfastly refused Nazi Germany's demands that it participate in the Final Solution. By the end of June, almost the entire Jewish population outside Budapest had been deported.

László and his friends could not stand idly by any longer. Like some of his countrymen and women, he joined a small local resistance movement. He was a small cog in a small group, as he put it. Since March 1944, when the Allied bombing raids began in the city, Dr László Lajtha of the National Music School had become actively involved in resistance activities. This was the school where László had once studied, and Dr Lajtha now recruited other senior staff members there. His own two adult sons also joined and were under his command.

Dr Lajtha was no stranger to military action himself having served as an artillery officer during the First World War. Under Dr Lajtha's command, the group obtained access to a supply of military uniforms, courtesy of László's army connections, and thus on occasion was able to get about unnoticed, even ignored. At that time it was common to see troops parading from one barracks to another in the city. Dressed as soldiers was a perfect cover for underground resistance activities. They often hid

36

Jews and those escaping from the clutches of the Arrow Cross Party and supplied them with false papers.

László had excellent handwriting, an elegant cursive script, which came in handy when forging documents. I recall him saying how the unit was able to obtain blank baptismal certificates through the assistance of a local Catholic priest. László would then write out the names of various people on these certificates that were in turn given to Jewish families to disguise their own ethnic origin and religion. In this way many young Jews were able to live without fear of being taken away; some opted to move to the countryside where they could live in relative safety among the farming communities, while others, if they wished, could leave Hungary in absolute security. After László's death, my deep pride in him urged me to write and inform the Simon Wiesenthal Centres in the United States and in France of these activities.

Chaos followed in September 1944, when Russian troops crossed the country's eastern border. László was immediately called up and ordered to travel to Debrecen and report for duty as part of a military band. The Royal Hungarian Army was now pushing towards the Eastern Front to bolster an offence by the Red Army. The move was considered almost certain death for these soldiers; László in all seriousness referred to the Eastern Front as 'The Dock'. It was thus with a heavy heart that he reported for duty. The only music that now seemed to ring in his ears was a death knell. While marching eastwards, he remembered they would on occasions stop for a short break. Some fellow soldiers would sit or lie about on the ground, whereas László could only find rest by standing against a tree or some such support, fastidious as ever about hygiene. Tension and dread hung in the air and László began to fear his luck might have run out.

Help came in the form of his friend and mentor Dr Lajtha, however. By all accounts Dr Lajtha got in touch with the army authorities and complained irately that László Gede was one of the leading artistic voices in Budapest and clarinet player for official government functions, and could therefore not possibly be called to the Front. Soon after this protest, the young László was dispatched back to Budapest. No doubt some ranked official did not want to be blamed for the loss of an accomplished musician! László could never forget Dr Lajtha's great act of kindness and often spoke of him with much gratitude and affection. After this narrow escape, László went into hiding to escape the many wartime dangers and to avoid being called up.

Though László had evaded disaster, the same could not be said for the city of his birth, Debrecen. For most of October the Battle of Debrecen raged in the east. The Red Army together with Romanian Divisions – Romania had now swapped allies – battled against the joint forces of the Hungarian Third Army and German Panzer Divisions. It was one of the bloodiest battles of the war. László feared for the safety of his family and relatives in the city and in Monostorpályi, but miraculously they escaped harm. The city was almost destroyed, with nearly three-quarters of its buildings damaged while half were completely in ruins.

Meanwhile his brother István Jnr found himself in a perilous position. While advancing westwards and reaching Hungary, the Red Army had taken over control of Ungvár military base, where István was posted. The German-Hungarian forces managed to defeat the Soviet-Romanian onslaught, but it would only be a matter of time before the Soviets would invade Hungary with a vengeance. As a result, the Hungarian military aircraft fleet in Ungvár along with its staff stationed there were all transferred to the city of Pápa in western Hungary.

Regent Horthy, having temporarily halted the deportation of Jews, also negotiated a ceasefire with the Soviets and ordered Hungarian troops to lay down their arms. It was a move that had dire consequences. When the news reached Hitler's ears, he launched Operation Panzerfaust to depose Horthy and replace him with Ferenc Szálasi, leader of the Arrow Cross Party. Szálasi had Horthy's son kidnapped and informed Horthy that his son would be killed if he did not resign from office. The regent had no choice but to obey and did so on October 17. Soon afterwards he was placed under house arrest in Castle Hirschberg in Bavaria for the remaining duration of the war. It was one of the darkest days in Hungary's history. At this memory, László would utter over and over again: *poor Hungary, poor, poor Hungary.* Horthy was in fact too old to lead his country. He was seventy-six when he abdicated and set in his ways; he lacked the strength and courage to pull out of the war sooner and dithered instead.

The sad fact was that Hungary was now thrown into the arms of a madman. Szálasi and the Arrow Cross Party had seized power. Szálasi now looked to only one leader – Adolf Hitler. Hope was failing fast for Hungarians. The Russians and Germans were at the gates and Budapest within their sights. The ranks of the Hungarian Army now swelled with men desperate to defend their country. But László was careful not to get called up again. His resistance work became all-important, though he and his compatriots ran the risk of being captured and arrested if found to be helping Jews. Jewish ghettos and mass deportations became the order of the day. Thousands of Jews were tortured, raped and murdered in the last months of war and their property looted or destroyed. It was never recorded how many Jews were helped by László and the unit led by Dr Lajtha. Many foreign diplomats, such as Swedish emissary Raoul Wallenberg, came to the rescue too, saving thousands of Jews in Budapest by arranging passports and visas, false papers and safe houses.

* * *

Josef Stalin had his eye on the political prize of Budapest and within weeks the Red Army had reached the city's eastern suburbs in low-lying Pest. The city was thrown into panic. On Christmas Day the trams ground to a halt and Russian tanks and troops encircled the city. The Siege of Budapest had begun. Over the next seven weeks the German and Hungarian armies, amounting to 180,000 men, fought to defend the city and weaken the Russian and Romanian lines, numbering 500,000 men. László, like most of the city's inhabitants, had chosen to remain in the city, at first thinking it would be swiftly taken and the danger would pass.

Normality of a strange kind prevailed for a short while. Coffee houses like Café Gerbeaud and the New York Café were full as city-dwellers celebrated a rather low-key Christmas. But for László it was no time for music. Goldwin Gede had ceased to exist. Soon the fighting intensified and bombs rained down on the city. The night sky was ablaze with red and purple colours and the clatter of machine guns a constant refrain. László recalled taking great care on occasions as he drove from the Buda hills and across the Danube to the Pest side of the city, avoiding danger as planes flew overhead, sometimes menacingly. Driving was not always possible or safe as barricades were everywhere. The city was soon in chaos. Russian troops spread their tentacles out across the city like an octopus. Many magnificent buildings that had made Budapest the Paris of the East lay in ruins, and rubble began piling up everywhere.

Early on in the siege, the Russians had cut off both water and electricity supplies. Food was scarce and all the basics slowly vanishing. An added misery was that it was an exceptionally cold winter. By mid-January most of the city's one million civilians, including László and his family, crowded into cellars, ground-floor apartments and tunnels throughout the city, especially those bored into Castle Hill in Buda. Most were starving and thirsty. Many of the once fine cavalry horses were left to die on the streets and had their carcasses stripped bare. With the constant bombing, it was not safe to go outside in search of water or even light up a cigarette. There was no electricity, no trams, no public transport, no fuel, and schools and public buildings were closed.

On 17 January, Hitler agreed to withdraw the remaining troops from low-lying Pest to try to defend Buda, the hilly bastion on the other side of the Danube. When word got out, all of the five bridges spanning the Danube were congested with traffic, evacuating troops and panicked civilians. The next day the Germans blew up the bridges, despite protests from Hungarian officers. The destruction of the much-loved Chain Bridge and Elizabeth Bridge was another blow to the people, now that the defence of Pest had collapsed. Built in 1849 and the first permanent bridge across the Danube as well as a marvellous feat of engineering, the Chain Bridge had become a symbol of national progress and pride. It was a link between East and West. László and his fellow Budapestians felt cut off and left to survive among the bomb craters, trenches and barricades that littered the city. Cries and wailing were as regular as the artillery fire and drone of warplanes.

The siege finally ended when all the defences protecting Buda collapsed. An orgy of violence then ensued. Seeing Russian soldiers at close quarters was an experience László would never forget. They reminded him of wild animals, somewhat barbarian and savage, devoid of any humanity.

Aside from executing innocent civilians, they took to raping and plundering with abandon. He was astounded when they looted homes and drank perfume believing it to be some fancy or expensive alcohol.

The city unconditionally surrendered on 13 February 1945. The siege, as brutal as the Battle of Stalingrad, had left 40,000 civilians dead, not to mention the hundreds of thousands of soldiers dead, wounded or captured. The ending of the Nazi regime brought relief to the weary war-torn citizens, who were only pawns in the hands of those in power. László now fully realised why his father had preached peace after his return from the First World War. There were no true winners in war. István Jnr would soon become a prisoner of war and be banished to a labour camp in Siberia.

To this very day, the loss of territory remains a great sadness deep within the heart of some Hungarians, who still try to fathom why and how this tragedy happened. With my fascination for history, I have wondered from time to time, if the Entente Powers or Allies, especially Russia, had not been so quick to carve up the Hungarian territory and strip it of two-thirds of its land, there might never have been a Second World War or, for that matter, the Balkan Wars of the 1980s and 1990s.

Sadly, we shall never know the answer to this question. László had no answers either, just deep deep sorrow.

4.

COMMUNISM AND INCARCERATION

Somewhere, I know, there is a heart,
shattered and saturnine,
slain by desires and ecstasies
the very same as mine.
They listen to each other's tick,
night spreads a winding-sheet,
and in one moment of vast night
they both will cease to beat.

From 'Hearts Far Apart' by Apart Endre Ady

AMID the carnage and destruction of war there was one glimmer of hope for László. Shortly afterwards, on 1 April 1945, he was appointed an orchestra member of the State Opera House. The position was in their wind instrument section playing the clarinet. The audition took place at the Opera House in front of the music director and various other directors on the staff. From László's recollection, it was a big moment for him, as he attempted to control his nerves and put in the best performance he could muster. He grasped the clarinet and began playing, gliding deeper and deeper into the piece, inhabiting every note as though breathing it. When he had finished, the sheer strain of concentration broke him and tears flowed freely. The music director approached him and placed a hand on his shoulder.

'My son, my son…'

László's performance had far surpassed his own expectations and the director now congratulated him. All of the other directors gathered around to praise him, except for one who had taken an odd dislike to him. It didn't deter László, though recovering from the emotion of the audition took a few days. Another dream held so dear to his heart had been fulfilled. Like the wood he worked upon, the path he carved for himself was taking shape and opening up before him. The sooner the music establishments were reopened and performing concerts and recitals once again, the better for all.

Music would be a healing balm on the wounds of war for the national psyche. It would soothe, stimulate and invigorate, as a kind of therapy on traumatised minds. Music, he knew, worked in mysterious ways and had healed people since antiquity. Many Hungarian musicians could vouch for that. Zoltán Kodály, a composer and collector of Hungarian folk songs active at the time, thought that some parts of the soul could only be reached by music. Now László would have an opportunity to reach out to souls in the magical place that was the State Opera House once its doors reopened. The appointment also brought the added hope of touring abroad.

Hungary boasted a three-hundred year tradition of opera. The State Opera House dominated Andrássy Avenue, the boulevard often dubbed Budapest's Broadway. This was the exalted place where every music-loving Hungarian wanted to be. Handsomely funded by Emperor Franz Joseph of Austria-Hungary, the Opera House opened its doors in September 1884 in all its neo-Renaissance splendour. It was said that its designer, Miklós Ybl, was given strict instructions that the building could not outdo the Vienna opera house, the Ringtheatre, in opulence but that it could surpass all others. And opulent it certainly was in its vibrant red and gold colours.

Nothing much had changed by the time László walked through the hallowed building, a kaleidoscope of grand staircases, state rooms, royal boxes, marble columns, arches, frescos, mosaics and statues. The building had miraculously escaped serious wartime damage. The horseshoe-shaped auditorium, all three storeys, was decorated with more than several kilograms of gold and boasted a three-tonne polished bronze chandelier from Mainz. But from a performer's point of view, it was the acoustics that impressed László the most. The auditorium is said to have the best acoustics in the world, after La Scala and the Palais Garnier. A dizzying sight to behold, all the more so when playing to capacity audiences of around twelve hundred. A favourite composer of László's, Gustav Mahler, had been a director of the Opera House in the late 1880s and had memorably directed the operas of Puccini and Wagner as well as Mascagni's *Cavalleria Rusticana*. László now felt his own golden age had arrived.

Budapest was now a different place. Many cafés, restaurants and hotels were reduced to shells or in ruins. All the grand hotels overlooking the Danube had been deliberately targeted by low-flying Russian bombers as a strike against the upper classes. Afternoon tea dances seemed a thing of the past as did the Bentwood chairs and marble-topped café tables, where people drank coffee, smoked and read newspapers in bamboo frames. Rubble now lined the streets and boulevards, while people like ghosts wandered in search of relatives, food, fuel, often dragging carts or bundles on their backs.

Food and fuel were scarce, with rationing and escalating prices commonplace. Hyperinflation, another byproduct of war, hit the country like an express train. The street market was now where trade was conducted. Cigarettes, if you possessed them – not that László did – were evidently the best currency at the time. They could buy you anything, whereas cash in the form of the Hungarian pengő soon had little or no value. Over the next year basic staples, like bread and milk, would cost millions of pengő. The country's economy had virtually collapsed with the burden of war and reparations. The government's answer was to keep printing money and at ever-increasing denominations. The 100 million billió-pengő banknote was the highest denomination ever issued, worth about a trillion pengő. It scarcely seems imaginable that it would only buy you a cup of coffee and cake at a city café. Employers began paying employees in goods as well as money, which were used to barter. This was fine if you worked for a wine exporter or a baker, but not good for musicians at the State Opera House.

László was nothing if not resourceful and his survival instincts kicked in. Like many others, he started to exchange rings, watches, gold chains and other valuable jewellery pieces, precious stones, clothes, and whatever wine or spirits he had. An open-air currency market soon began trading in Nádor Street behind the bourse on Liberty Square. The trading was essentially the black market, but people were desperate for food and supplies. Money changing was also part of the scene. American dollars and gold were king. Gold chains, for example, were traded at one dollar per gram. In particular, gold in the form of French Napoleon coins was very easy to trade as their quality was indisputable.

Some traders, particularly jewellers, discovered that the gold content of the Napoleon coin was valued at eleven or twelve dollars but the coin itself could sell for sixteen dollars. As a result, some began to create a restrike of the coins, which incurred costs of about eleven dollars, and then sold them for sixteen or so dollars, making a tidy profit. This meant there was always a demand for gold on the black market. The black marketeers continued to make large profits in dollars, gold and goods throughout the inflationary period.

While László did have a certain flair for marketeering, it was never done dishonestly or exploitatively. His needs were simple and his ways frugal. Over the years, with all his multiple jobs, he accumulated money quite quickly to finance various projects. He was always motivated by a dreadful fear of poverty, not having a roof over his head and not being able to provide for his family. Many of his fellow musicians at the Opera House struggled to maintain even a basic standard of living and now resignedly parted with their jewellery. Their salaries had plunged from prewar times. Out of a sense of humanity, László no doubt offered advice and helped his colleagues to get the best possible price for their gold.

The black markets and bartering continued as the city got back on its feet. More food became available, the street rubble was cleared, bridges repaired, schools and universities reopened, and importantly for László, theatres and cafés threw open their doors once more. The collapse of Hungarian currency was at its worst in July 1946, however, when prices doubled every fifteen hours. There was no way the country could survive, and so a new currency was introduced in August, the forint, which stablished the financial situation. Once the official currency was introduced, László stopped his gold-purchasing activities. There was now no longer a demand or supply for gold as a commodity.

* * *

Ambition burned bright in László. So many different projects were juggled at the same time. He was busier than ever with all his new posts, but had not relinquished his connection with the Ganz Orchestra, by now in the role of conductor. Training the workers to become successful orchestral members brought tremendous satisfaction to László. From time to time he would come across a truly gifted worker that brought László a special feeling of contentment and fulfilment. He was also offering private tuition to those wishing to perfect or learn a musical instrument. With such a workload there were clearly not enough hours in the day! Around 1945 László moved from Madách Imre Square to Ó Street, a narrow elegant street of apartment buildings close to Andrássy Street. There was also the matter of a small weekend house he was building on Napsugár Street in the forested Buda Hills. How he came by the plot of land, possibly two acres, sometime during the war I have no idea – no doubt made possible by his savings and frugal lifestyle. I remember him saying that he always wanted a detached house with a garden as he couldn't abide living in city apartments.

He threw himself into building this small dwelling in the hills and acquiring the necessary materials. Naturally, money and materials were scarce given wartime conditions but László was resourceful and very determined. Brick by brick, he constructed the building, sometimes with a little help from friends. With extraordinary ability and creativity, he had taught himself construction skills in addition to those of woodwork and metalwork that his father had taught him. He had the most creative hands I ever encountered. Tools in his hands were as adroitly handled as his beloved clarinet and saxophone. He had the precision of a Swiss clockmaker combined with extraordinary strength. There were no half measures, no corners cut, no shoddy work. He took pride in his work, endowed as he was with a sense of permanence, ensuring things were built to last, to continue, there for posterity. The one-storey, flat-roofed house was built on an attractive stone foundation to offset the sloping ground. László also shaped a verandah space over the stone cellar at the front large enough to fit a wooden bench. Inside the house were several rooms and a dining-room where László placed his piano. The design of the house was simple but the stonework and corner bay window gave it unique touches.

At the time Napsugár Street was rather a quiet lane with a dwelling here and there and a far cry from the many affluent villas that now nestle there. The area in the Buda Hills was called Pálvölgy since at one time a monastery dedicated to St Paul was situated there and gave the limestone and dolomite valley its name. The lungs of the city, as the hills were called, with woodlands and wildlife became a mecca for László. It was also a fascinating place to explore. Beneath the hills were a series of underground caves with one of the largest at Pálvölgy boasting curious pearl-like stalactites. Napsugár Street was certainly a place where László could be close to nature and close to the city. As he grew older, peace and quiet had become more and more important to him. His forays into domesticity had not been entirely successful. High above the city, the sensitive soul could feel at peace with himself, gain respite from the ravages of war and the upheavals of domesticity. I'm sure as he watched the sunrise over Pest on the far side of the river, it must have been a perfect start to each day. I later learnt that *napsugár* in Hungarian meant sunshine or sunbeam. The street clearly must have been a suntrap that László no doubt relished.

László was also mindful of his status in society now that his musical career was blossoming. Hungarians as a nation prize individuality and value personal achievements highly. László was no different. By June 1946 he finished his studies at the Liszt Academy, receiving a music artist's diploma and adding to his qualifications and credentials. His driving licence was renewed in June 1946, so driving was now his main mode of transport. In his eyes, building a two-roomed villa in such a private residential spot as Napsugár Street would befit a successful musician. The following year, in 1947, he was appointed a professor of music for clarinet and a member of the National Music School on Nagymező Street. He may have had some luck on his side along with his abundant talent. Dr László Lajtha had become director of the school around this time.

His new post gave László tremendous joy. Being able to pass on all that he had learned about music and nurture the talent of others was something he deemed an honour and a privilege. It was no less exhilarating at thirty-two than it was for the baby who had clapped his little hands at the sound of military bands. László's single-mindedness, not to mention his talent, was reaping dividends.

* * *

Though the war had long ended and the economy was stabilising, the political scene was as turbulent as ever. Another darkness had engulfed Hungary with the occupation of the Russians, who wove a web of steel around the perimeters of its newly captured territories. Once again the streets of the capital were carefully monitored and Russians became the new enemy. Their troops occupied the entire country and gradually, through electoral fraud and brute force, the transition to communism was complete. By 1948, Hungary had become a satellite state of the Union of Soviet Socialist Republics (USSR). The forint's success was exploited for political gains, contributing to the takeover of power by the communists.

The old way of life in Budapest started to disappear in keeping with communist ideals. Land reform took place almost immediately and large estates were broken up and divided among the peasantry. The old social classes were soon no more; the old Austro-Hungary culture no longer dominated. Gone were old wealth, old mores and notions of chivalry and personal integrity. However, through it all music was still important and had high prestige. Luckily for László that meant employment. With communism, however, there was an emphasis on folk music with the government controlling the type of music that should be performed. It was to be festive and optimistic, and anything else was distrusted. After a while this grew rather sterile, not least to László and his colleagues but also to the general public. After all, music for every mood and occasion had been at the heart of Hungarian expression for centuries. And, disappointingly for László, there was less and less room for classical jazz; the good old days of the Goldwin Gede were most definitely gone.

Another problem befell some of László's fellow musicians. Many of their families were of German origin and had lived in Hungary for several generations, if not centuries. Under the Potsdam Agreement in August 1945, the Hungarian government began to forcibly expel those of German nationality or German-speaking citizens – the so-called ethnic Germans. The deportations continued for about four years, with families having their homes and personal assets confiscated. The threat of deportation also hung over many families for a long time. Many of the deportations were conducted by the state security police. The relatives of László's colleague Iván, a cellist, for example, were eventually forcibly resettled in Germany. Knowing that László had once dabbled in gold and foreign currency, it appears that Iván offered to sell László gold belonging to his family in order to help them in their plight.

László's success was always tempered by the sadness he felt at his brother István's incarceration in Siberia. The family prayed that he would survive the ordeal and not die in the snowy wastes of the region. To their utter relief István did return home on 20 June 1947. It had been an inhumane experience; there had been no escaping the brutality of Stalin for him as a Hungarian officer, enduring great hardship and deprivation. Often beset with frostbite, the prisoners were worked nearly to death and starved into the bargain. At one desparate stage, hunger had forced István to eat grass and weeds.

László, like many other citizens, was devastated to find his beloved Hungary once again in chains, where the intelligentsia was suppressed and poets and artists could not flourish freely. Perhaps given his dealings at the fringes of the black market, László himself became a marked man. Like many a secret police force in communist states, they trapped people into spying on their neighbours, colleagues and friends. Betrayals could result from mere whim, envy or disgruntlement. That László and his colleagues could travel abroad to concerts and smuggle back dollars rankled with some at the Opera House. Most likely László was a watched man.

Around this time a certain Hungarian musician came to the attention of the communist authorities, one with an international reputation. László grew concerned at the fate of Dr László Lajtha. The composer's career over the years had soared into the stratosphere – with works regularly performed in Budapest, Paris, Vienna, Prague, London, New York, Washington and Moscow – but would soon come crashing down like a meteorite.

It began when Dr Lajtha was invited to London in 1947 to compose music for a film version of T.S. Eliot's verse drama *Murder in the Cathedral*. The film was directed by George Hoellering and stared John Groser as Thomas Beckett, Archbishop of Canterbury. Dr Lajtha's family had accompanied him there, relishing their time in the West, all the more so when the project dragged on for over a year. This state of affairs caused much displeasure to the communist government back home. Nonetheless, Dr Lajtha wrote three important concert works to critical acclaim, extracts of which were used in the film. In late 1948, he returned to Budapest without his two adult sons, who had chosen to remain behind in London. Dr Lajtha's overstay and his sons' effective defection resulted in his passport being confiscated and his dismissal from all the posts he held. He was no longer director of the National Music School where László taught, director of the Museum of Ethnography, musical director of the Hungarian Radio, and a host of other positions.

With no work and no pension, Dr Lajtha now faced a future of constant harassment, scrutiny and penury. László and close friends dared not visit him openly but only seldom and in secret. Because he had enjoyed an international reputation, Dr Lajtha had seemed beyond the reach of the communists. It was a sobering lesson for László and his fellow musicians – no one was safe in the brutal and oppressive regime. The ban on Dr Lajtha travelling and performing abroad, having been denied a passport, brought a premature end to a wonderful career.

For his part, László had enjoyed performing abroad whenever possible. Tours by the State Opera House were made to Berlin and Vienna and possibly Italy. In the company was a magnificent soprano singer from Brazil that also toured with them; it was reputed that she had even sung for Hitler during the war, although I cannot recall her name. In the late 1940s and 1950s touring proved more difficult and travelling visas were often denied them. It certainly was something that László did not speak much about in later years.

His brother István soon fell foul of the communist authorities too. With no prospect of meaningful work, he and a friend tried to escape to Western Europe in 1948. The information was reported to the secret police, the ÁVH, by a person unknown, a 'well-wisher', you could say. As a result, both of them were arrested at Keleti train station in Budapest and taken to 60 Andrássy Street, then the headquarters of the ÁVH. Today it is known as the House of Terror. It had once been the party offices of the fascist Arrow Cross Party, so the building held particular menace. Owing to the extensive work of the ÁVH, the organisation occupied an entire block on Andrássy Street – filled with an underground labyrinth of cells, torture chambers and gallows. It seems ironic that Andrássy Street, the scene of such high points in László's life, would be one of the lowest in his brother's life. Armed ÁVH men stood guard outside interrogation rooms in sand-coloured uniforms and service caps bearing a red stair circled somewhat by a sheaf of corn. Mercy and justice were in short supply. Prisoners were usually interrogated at night in the full glare of bright electric lights and after being deprived of sleep, food and water.

The two men were convicted and sentenced to two years of imprisonment as political prisoners at Andrássy Street. Some prison cells in the building were 'wet cells' where prisoners were forced to sit in water, others were dank 'foxhole cells' where they had to crouch for hours on end. Windows, such that existed, were blackened out so a prisoner was denied daylight and the pleasure of seeing the sky. There was no regard for personal hygiene and beatings were commonplace. Instruments of torture ranged from nail presses to whips to limb crushers. Their daily diet was a cup of bean soup and a slice of bread.

Fortunately, István survived the inhumane regime for the duration of his sentence, but was transferred to an internment camp north of Budapest called Kistarcsa for six months. This camp was typically used to 'rehabilitate' prisoners and involved forced labour. When finally released from captivity, though a young man not yet thirty, he was in a debilitated state, very delicate and suffering from rheumatism. There was little trace of the young handsome man with the fine Slavic features. His hair, once as dark as László's, had turned white! Nonetheless, though his family were shocked at István's condition, they were overjoyed to see him free from captivity.

By the late 1940s, the house in the Buda Hills was also complete. László had taken up residence there, possibly as a weekend home at first. Constructed with cement blocks and bricks, the modest dwelling contained a living room, kitchen-cum-dining room and a bedroom. The surrounding land was cleared and, seeing that the soil and aspect were suitable for peach trees, he planted two hundred. László did nothing by half measures! Each day he made the journey down from this idyllic setting, across the Chain Bridge and on to the State Opera House.

László sometimes mentioned that as a young man he employed Zsófia, a hardworking young woman who kept house for him. By all accounts, she was absolutely charming and a real treasure. In fact, everything was spotless and shipshape under her care. His reminiscences of her in later years would always bring a smile to his face. Zsófia clearly took great pride in working for the young professor and was not slow to show it. Upon opening the door to music students arriving for their piano lessons, she adopted a formal demeanour, if not a little haughty.

'Professor will be with you in a moment!'

László's greatest joy, however, came when his father visited his home at Napsugár. István Gede was impressed with his son's handiwork and all that he had achieved. No doubt István too enjoyed the spectacular panoramic views of the Danube and magnificent city below. On that occasion, with justified pride, László took his father to the State Opera House and was delighted to show him the magnificent building. István was, understandably, overwhelmed at the splendour all around.

It was all surpassed, however, when they entered a long narrow hallway leading in from the artists' entrance and viewed the murals of hundreds of Opera House artists from musicians to singers to composers all along the corridor. László paused as he approached one mural and turned towards his father. On the wall, István beheld a small mural of his own son. There was no mistaking the brown hair, high forehead and clear symmetrical face of László. He took his son's hand and the earlier reticence shown towards his musical career melted away.

'I am most proud of you, my son.'

László grasped his father's hand and kissed it tenderly, a dutiful and delightful Hungarian tradition. Both men had finally made their peace. László's portrait is one of six hundred artists that were painted on the walls of the former smoking room, near the artists' entrance. The practice began in the late 1800s and continued until the 1950s when I believe it ceased under communism.

* * *

Following his divorce from Etelka, László had quickly embarked upon a second marriage in 1950, as I later came to learn. His new wife, Anna Gerzson, was a ballerina at the Hungarian National Ballet and a most beautiful young woman with stylish dark hair. With Anna's exquisite beauty and poise and László's handsome features they must have made a striking couple. At that time the National Ballet stood on Andrássy Avenue in a rather majestic building directly opposite the Opera House. I'm sure Anna and László's life together had been exciting, first going on tour together and then making trips to the renowned Lake Balaton at the foothills of the Bakony Mountains. It was the summer and party capital of Hungary, about an hour's drive from Budapest.

László and his colleagues from the Opera Houses regularly performed in a grand hotel possibly in the resort city of Siófok on the shores of the lake. The magnificent lake was a popular tourist destination and, at eighty kilometres long and the largest in central Europe, it was dubbed the Hungarian Sea. The place was attractive too for László with his deep appreciation of nature, gazing upon the alluring opalescent lake, its freshwater supplied and replenished by the Zala River. There he felt at one with nature and at peace with himself.

Though I believe that László's Napsugár house was constructed in the late 1940s, he may have lived elsewhere with his second wife.

László, and possibly Anna, lived in an apartment on 3 Szilágyi Dezső Square, overlooking the Danube on the Buda side. Perhaps the fact that the composer Béla Bartók had lived in the house next door, number 4, during the 1920s had appealed to László. The centre of the square was dominated by a large redbrick Calvinist church, the first in Buda, and built surprisingly in a neo-Gothic style. Though László was no longer a practising Calvinist and eschewed religion, he could still appreciate the beauty of the building. His newfound talent for construction made him an avid observer of buildings.

The embankment beside the building held dark memories, however. The Hungarian Nazis in the Arrow Cross Party had thousands of Jews massacred there in 1944 and 1945, as the war came to a bitter end. Hundreds were bundled into small groups and handcuffed together before being cast into the freezing river and left to die. Everywhere in Hungary the sacred and sublime seemed entwined with death and destruction. Yet life must go on.

While residing at Dezső Square, László also had a small garage on nearby Csalogány Street so he could have somewhere to park his car. There he also kept a workshop to indulge his passion for creating, repairing and fixing things. Tinkering with machines and motors had become second nature to him. In fact, he always needed a workshop and, wherever in the world he found himself, it was a chief prerequisite. On Csalogány Street, in a bench drawer he placed valuables that he would trade on the black market during 1951 and 1952. These were concealed within a Gerbeaud package – the famous confectionery and coffee house in Budapest. Later he moved these valuables to a garage located at 16 Donáth Street in the Buda Hills.

I have no knowledge whether or not Anna knew about his ex-wife and child. It would appear that László had no contact with them at this time, other than providing financial support. His daughter in later years revealed that when she was ten she was taken to a concert at the Opera House by her mother. Etelka pointed out a man in the orchestra pit playing the clarinet and told Lívia that he was her father. Lívia instinctively waved to the man, knowing that he was a wonderful musician. László, by now remarried, played on unawares. His marriage to Anna was not to endure, however, due to frequent quarrelling and they divorced in 1954. Their break-up seemed acrimonious, not least due to financial matters.

That both of his marriages should end so quickly in divorce set me thinking. László was certainly no saint; he had the same faults and failings as myself and the rest of humankind. Firstly, he was undoubtedly a workaholic and totally wrapped up in his music and in furthering his career. It's possible too that he was spending far too much time in the Buda Hills. It seemed like a retreat from the trials of domesticity where he could devote himself to music and giving lessons. There were also the various projects he threw himself into. In fact, his workshop bench most likely consumed much of his free time.

Secondly, being extremely cautious and frugal by nature, he had great difficulty with regard to spending money, perhaps to a fault. With his incredible good looks and talent, women were drawn to him and perhaps expected him to shower them with gifts. It was just not in his nature. That said, he had good cause to save his money: the poverty he witnessed and experienced during those early years must have seriously hardened him.

For all his faults, family was still important to László. The years had taken their toll on his father back in Debrecen and in the early 1950s he retired from the Hungarian State Railways as locksmith. For all László's earlier animosity towards his father, they were very much alike. István Gede Snr had struggled hard to provide for his family, even into adulthood, and now had three apartments reserved for his sons beside the family home on Hajnal Street. All these dwellings were set off a large courtyard behind a large imposing gate. However, László in his heart could not accept such a gift and instead ensured others benefited from his share. The Gede family certainly knew how to accumulate property through sheer hard work, prudence and thriftiness.

László's two brothers, István and Zoltán, were never far from his mind either. Not much is known about the youngest, Zoltán, other than that he married a woman called Julianna Kiss around 1950, and that László had attended his wedding in Debrecen. Seeing that Zoltán adored his elder brother, there was no way that László could miss his big day. The newlyweds lived in the Goose Grandmother's house on Szív Street, and in January 1955 Julianna gave birth to a son, László, who inherited his uncle's musical talent. That no doubt pleased his father immensely.

Finding employment after imprisonment had proved difficult for István Jnr given his state of health and any medications administered were of little help. Returning to the army was also out of the question. Now back in the family home on Hajnal Street, he worked for a time as a labourer at the Hungarian State Railways before training as a locksmith like his father. Despite being in poor health, István married in March 1951. His wife, Éva Szép, was the daughter of a successful lawyer in Debrecen. For whatever reason, it fell to László – in a kind of loco parentis – to ask Mr Szép for permission for István to marry his daughter. Perhaps László's father was indisposed at the time and suffering from the infirmities of old age. And it was also László who represented his father at the wedding, thus acting as a witness. The bride joined her husband on Hajnal Street, which became the birthplace of their two children, Éva and István, bringing great joy to the parents. In a sign of the close family ties, Uncle Zoltán and Aunt Julianna became godparents to little Éva. László's brother István later recovered his health somewhat and completed a machinery course at a technical school and began working in an office.

It was in the late 1940s that Irén Matlag came into László's life. At the time she was married to Jószef Lengyel and had a young daughter called Marie. Irén, then in her early thirties, was a handsome woman who took to László immediately. They had much in common, not least a passion for music but also unhappy marriages. Small in stature with dark hair, her face was round with typical Slavic features. Irén was fastidious about her appearance and, regardless of economic conditions, always dressed in the latest fashions. In Budapest that was made possible by the life of privilege she had enjoyed as the daughter of a wealthy baker. József Matlag was a Baptist whose establishment, the Matlag Bakery, was renowned throughout Budapest for its finest breads and confectionery.

Boasting a baby grand piano in her luxury apartment, Irén delighted in opera and concerts and was enchanted by the world of music. She also sang in a choir like a great number of Hungarians. As a regular patron of the State Opera House, it was not long before she made László's acquaintance.

It was her common practice to head down to the orchestra pit and converse with the various musicians during the interval. This led on to meeting László after performances. László – with no hint of bias on my part – had a most charismatic and magnetic personality. Women found him incredibly attractive. László too, no doubt, relished her company, especially for the fact that Irén was able to appreciate music and share opinions on composers and musical arrangements. As time went on, Irén confided in him more and more about the state of her marriage. Highly intelligent, József Lengyel had been an employee at her father's firm, whom she had married at an early age, but irreconcilable differences now set them apart. Their daughter, Marie, on the brink of adolescence, was no longer a reason for staying together and Irén wished to file for divorce. I'm not sure if Irén and László enjoyed a dalliance before their divorces were finalised but it seems likely they did.

There was also another reason that brought them together: gold and foreign currency. In the early 1950s gold had become an expensive commodity in Hungary, after all the earlier financial upheavals. László, if he ever needed to do so, now had to pay a higher rate, often seventy Hungarian forints per gram. Earning a living was still proving difficult for many Hungarians. By the end of the 1940s wages and salaries had fallen by one-fifth, and Stalin's attempt to make Hungary a land of iron and steel did not bring the much-trumped benefits. The communists' abolition of private ownership meant that Irén's family business was doomed. Small enterprises, where they existed at all, suffered the most. Rationing of bread, sugar, flour and meat was reintroduced in 1951 and long queues and food coupons became the norm once again. Under these circumstances the Matlag Bakery collapsed. The Matlags would go on to lose much of their fortune, a tragedy that affected them deeply, causing tension within the family. Ever resilient, Irén turned to László to procure gold for her at a reasonable rate, which he did.

László's busy lifestyle continued in his beloved world of music: as clarinet player and member of the State Opera House, teaching and conducting the two amateur orchestras, and member of the National School of Music, as well as his countless private students. As mentioned before, he was a workaholic and his deep-seated fear of poverty remained a constant companion. It was no irrational fear on his part. He knew that life had become precarious again under communism. Letters and phone conversations were monitored by the secret police, the ÁVH, and battalions of informers under their control. They had invaded all parts of society from factories and offices to churches and theatres. Even the Opera House had inhouse spies. To succeed in Hungarian society, indeed to have any decent standard of living, you also had to be a member of the Communist Party. László would never consent to join up, cherishing his ideals and freedom too much. His fears soon came to pass.

He received a mighty blow when he was summarily dismissed from the State Opera House on 15 July 1954. It was claimed that he had lent money to fellow members for a small charge or fee. Though he had admittedly sold gold and currency to orchestra members, László was no crook or shady character. The amounts involved were small and insignificant. When asked, he certainly would help people out – but not at allegedly exorbitant rates. Granted, he had a head for business and making a profit, but not at the expense of others. Every Hungarian was trying to survive in a world where normal society just did not exist. Under communism, every trivial indiscretion or misdemeanour was elevated to the ranks of serious crime and treason. It speaks volumes that, when I sought information after his death about his time at the Opera House, all traces were expunged from official records, other than when his employment commenced and ceased. At least his mural in the artists' entrance showed that he had some standing in that august building.

In all our life together László never once told me about his dismissal. Perhaps he found it hard to explain, given the circumstances of the time, or maybe it was too painful a loss for him. What he had worked so hard to achieve, reaching the pinnacle of his career, had been snatched from him. Then again maybe he was just compartmentalising his life again. But László was a survivor and, though subsequently unemployed for three months, he never gave up hope. Following this period, he went to work for the Budapest Handicraft Cooperative as a purchasing agent. While employed there, he also taught and managed the cooperative's orchestra

58

for which he received a separate stipend. And, ever the workaholic, he also conducted the State Electrical Works Orchestra during this time. I am unsure if he was still engaged with the Ganz Works Orchestra by then or the National School of Music.

* * *

László and Irén married on Monday, 29 August 1955. His own divorce had been finalised the year before and hers shortly before their marriage. The end had been bitter for László and Anna. No doubt it centred on money and the division of assets. I later learned that the valuables he had kept in the Gerbeaud package in the Donáth Street garage had been taken by Anna and her older brothers. However, Anna's mother had clearly been an honourable woman, and had requested in her last will and testament that the valuables be returned to him. Not long after her death, her family duly complied with her request.

Irén and her twelve-year-old daughter Marie came to live with László in his house in the Buda Hills. By then the house had been extended and Irén started to enhance it, adding more comforts. The house, though small, had extensive grounds, and so for Irén held massive potential. She was a most caring wife to László, who years later spoke of her good head for business, no doubt a family trait. She had taken charge of the finances and ran the family home with aplomb. László, mindful of his life's savings, also retrieved the gold jewellery he had stored in the wake of Anna's exploits. He and Irén took the casket to their home for security. At the time they also pawned about 250–300 grams of the gold jewellery. For young Marie, it was a whole new life too. The adjustment must have been difficult for a girl just entering her teens. However, what followed was to change all their lives irrevocably.

* * *

In January 1956, the police were contacted and informed that László held gold and foreign currency in his house. This information propelled the police to swiftly raid their home. Both László and Irén were arrested and taken to the public prosecutor's prison on Markó Street. László was basically accused of having unlawful amounts of gold and foreign currency in his possession. At the time citizens could legally hold only about five hundred grams of gold. The official charge was of having a deliberate plan to destabilise the status of the country's foreign currency exchange and of engaging in usury. It seems outlandish and far-fetched when you knew László as I did.

If the state archives are to be believed, his interrogation began at nine o'clock on the evening of Wednesday, 18 January, and lasted until midnight. It seems more likely that it took place at night after he had been deprived of sleep and food, as was often the case. The interrogation papers contain László's own account of his personal history, in which I learned of the existence of his daughter and former wives. There are errors in the account, notably in his military record, though he may have been under pressure to remember exact dates, or perhaps they were falsified.

The police claimed to have seized 823.6 grams of gold pieces, 270 grams of gold pieces held in a pawn shop, a significant amount of foreign currency and 1,400 forints from the Gede home. They furthermore claimed that this gold could not be accounted for by László's regular salary, some 1,290 forints per month for his post of purchasing manager with the Budapest Handicraft Cooperative and an additional 1,600 forints for his musical conductor fee. Though László was entitled to engage a lawyer, it was stated that he deferred having a lawyer represent him at that stage. Under the circumstances, László would most definitely have wanted one, but civil rights counted for very little under communism.

The interrogation papers give details of those with whom he allegedly dealt in gold and foreign currency since 1945, from mechanics to stage managers to musicians. There is no way of knowing if all these were true or fabricated to make a case against him. Several of the signatures – each page of the document required László's signature – often bore no resemblance to his signature or rather looked like clumsy attempts to forge it. It was claimed that the first time László purchased foreign currency was in 1945. It came about due to him exchanging his flat on Madách Square with that of the stage manager at the Opera House at the time. This man's flat was located on Ó Street near his workplace.

The exchange also required László to make an additional payment of one hundred and fifty dollars as well as supplying the man with a small radio and mail-ordered clothing from America.

László also allegedly sold thirty dollars in his possession to a jeweller who had a shop on Kazinczy Street. With this cash, László supposedly purchased some gold and thereafter would buy small amounts, for example twenty to thirty grams, on a daily basis from staff at the Opera House. He would then sell it at the jewellery shop or to an auto-mechanic who had a large shop on Liszt Square.

There were many others in the orchestra that seemingly came to László for help. The interrogation papers mentioned the concert master at the Opera House, who brought him a signet ring. László bought a bracelet weighing about twenty-five to thirty grams from the bassoon player. Around the same time the tuba player sold him twenty or thirty dollars. Two pairs of earrings were also purchased from a fellow clarinet player.

Selling gold to Irén around 1950 was also on the record. László allegedly took her to a schoolteacher who was an acquaintance of the mechanic whose business was next door to László's garage then on Csalogány Street. Over five months Irén supposedly purchased several pieces of gold jewellery in small increments, totalling around two hundred grams in weight. It was also recorded that László gave her about forty dollars. Around this time, László supposedly also came to the aid of a much-acclaimed soprano at the State Opera House who fell on hard times during communism. László seemingly sold her about one hundred and fifty grams of gold jewellery and one hundred dollars.

It was recorded that the man involved in the flat exchange back in 1945 also sold gold jewellery pieces to László. It seems that the man offered several smuggled watches to other staff members in the Opera House, but that László only purchased one Swiss-made Doxa watch from him at that time. Thereafter, László supposedly purchased about forty grams worth of gold pieces in small increments as well as thirty or forty dollars. The trading in gold and foreign currency swiftly came to an end when the authorities arrested the teacher in July 1952. After that László apparently dared not purchase gold or foreign currency from anyone.

László was also required to list where he had placed the gold and foreign currency over the years, which was usually in garages. Finally, he was forced to admit his 'guilt' and had his case heard by a judge on 30 January. His defence was also on record:

> During the years of my growing up, I was able to observe over a thirty-year period that making a living was quite difficult. I was also always told to plan for my retirement and do what is necessary to achieve this. This, and only this, was the motivating factor for my purchasing (more than permitted) gold and bringing back foreign currency acquired during my stays abroad.
>
> Please believe me, I had no other purpose in doing so but to help support my family and myself during our eventual retirement years. My wife had no knowledge of how much foreign currency I possessed considering that this was my own which I had acquired before our marriage. I would like to raise my child and properly support my family.
>
> I shall never have any more dealings with gold or foreign currency from this day on.

It was difficult for me reading all these official documents, knowing how honest László was. There was no way of establishing if the allegations against him were true or not. I believe they were exaggerated at the very least. At that time the police had a way of falsifying documents, distorting evidence and making people confess to crimes or misdemeanours they had not committed. It was interesting that when I searched, all traces of him had been expunged from official records.

The allegations seemed so over the top when you knew his actual character. His colleagues trusted him, knowing that he would pay the black market rate and not extort them. He was universally loved in the Opera House, with the possible exception of the one director who originally had not wished to employ him.

Motivated by altruism, László could see that his colleagues, who had strived and struggled for years, trying to rebuild lives and homes, were facing ruin and he could not stand idly by.

The Gede family (left to right), István Snr, István Jnr,
Zoltán, László and mother Zsuzsánna in the 1920s

Julianna Kálmán Gede,
known as Goose Grandmother

László's grandfather, István Gede

László Gede in 1933 at the age of eighteen

Professors of music at the National Music School, 1947–1948, including László Gede (second row, third from left)

László tutoring musicians in Budapest in the 1940s

László conducting the Ganz Works Orchestra
at an outdoor performance in Budapest in the late 1940s

A mural of László Gede in the Hungarian Opera House

László's Hungarian identity card from 1947

László as conductor of the State Electrical Works Orchestra at a 1952 performance

HUNGARIAN IMMIGRANTS: From Budapest come four charming Hungarians to settle in South Africa. Arriving on Sunday morning early they are already anxious to find work, and stand on their own independent feet. Only one of the above Mrs. Irene Gede (first on the left) is not looking for a job, and that is because her husband, who was a member of Hungary's famous Philharmonic Orchestra in Budapest, has already found one. Next to her is Irene Kovacs, who has been the confidential secretary of an industrial technician. Second from the right is Miss Emoke Vass, a technical draughtsman, and on the extreme right, Miss Elizabeth Nagy, an architectural draughtsman.

Irén Gede (far left) pictured on arrival in Johannesburg, in
The Rand Daily News, 15 January 1957

László pictured playing the clarinet in
Johannesburg's *The Star*, 6 June 1959

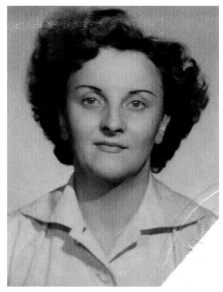

László's 'stateless' status on his South African identity documents

Irén Matlag Gede, László's third wife

László enjoying an evening of jazz
in South Africa in the 1960s

The judge found László guilty and sentenced him to two years' imprisonment. It must have been devastating for him knowing full well his brother István's experience in captivity. Irén was also found guilty and at first received a prison sentence of one year and two months. From what I learned from László, he pleaded with the authorities that he had acted alone and that Irén was entirely innocent. Fortunately, his pleas were heeded and she was released and served no time, returning to their home. During Irén's detention in Markó Street, her daughter Marie had been cared for by her mother Marianna and sister Etelka. It had been an anxious time for all. László's valuables were confiscated by the Hungarian authorities, though he was left with his house, land and some furniture. To this day, the identity of the informant remains unknown but widely surmised to be someone who knew László well. Indeed, László had his own suspicions but kept them to himself.

Once convicted, László remained in the prison on Markó Street. This prison housed many convicted of common crimes under communism and was renowned for showing no mercy. I dread to think what conditions he endured during his incarceration and the effect on his mind and body. He never spoke much about that time, though he did admit to spending time in solitary confinement. Often the wardens would insult him but if they ever meted out harsher penalties, of these László was silent. Whether or not his family and Irén were permitted to visit him, I never found out. Irén, who had neither job nor profession of her own, relied heavily on her mother's assistance during this time. How László managed to feed himself, knowing how pernickety he was with regard to food, I do not know, but probably had no choice under the circumstances.

No matter how delicately I tried to broach the subject over the years, I very quickly realised it was not a topic for discussion. László could not bring himself to reveal details. Stories emerged many years later of similar prisoners being in chains and heavy iron balls attached to their feet. Whenever I think of László in prison, Wordsworth's poem 'The Affliction of Margaret' always comes to mind. *Perhaps some dungeon hears thee groan,/ Maimed, mangled by inhuman men…* The imprint of such a reign of terror in his homeland was forever on his mind. During our married life, on two occasions something triggered the painful memories and he broke down, sobbing quietly. Immediately, I would wrap my arms around him and hush him. *László, László, I am always with you.* I shudder each time when I think of what he might have had to endure.

The slightest wrongdoings in Hungarian life were classed as major crimes against the communist order. Those arrested were dubbed enemies of the people. László was not alone, however. During 1956, history records that nearly two hundred thousand people were locked up in prisons or work camps throughout Hungary. Being deprived of music must have been difficult for László, though. While in prison he must surely have thought about Dr Lajtha too. For overstaying his visit to England, he was now silenced and classified a political insurgent. But at least Dr Lajtha had been saved from imprisonment. For such a talented composer to have his compositions barely played in Hungary was indeed a bitter pill to swallow.

* * *

However, all was not lost. Hope was on the horizon. While in prison during 1956, unbeknownst to László, events were taking shape outside. In Moscow that February at the Twentieth Congress of the Soviet Communist Party, the new Russian leader Nikita Khrushchev launched a sharp attack on the rather recently deceased Stalin and his oppressive policies. It was hard to believe it happened yet it did, and more so it was to have an impact on Hungary. The Hungarian leader, Mátyás Rákosi, installed by Stalin and overseeing a disastrous economy, was forced to resign in June. László's family and fellow Hungarians continued to grow more and more discontented with falling living standards, failed harvests, fuel shortages and not least living in a police state. For encouragement, they looked to Poland staging its own street protests against totalitarianism and their small victories.

On a bright sunny day on 23 October, the courageous Hungarian people spontaneously rose up against the communist regime. Rioting students and workers pulled down statutes of Stalin and demanded radical reforms such as more personal freedom, more food, the disbandment of the secret police and removal of Russian control. Crowds were chanting 'Russians go home' and 'Now or never' and waving national flags stripped of the Soviet red star. In an effort to quell the rioters, Imre Nagy, a liberal and reforming communist, was appointed prime minister the following day and martial law imposed. It appears that Nagy was a music lover, who admired the composer Kodály, and was a regular at the State Opera House. Indeed, he counted many orchestra members among his friends. On learning of his appointment, it inspired hope in László and others.

However, many people at peaceful demonstrations throughout the country were shot and killed by Soviet troops garrisoned in the country and by the ÁVH. The Hungarian Uprising soon became a national insurrection. The Hungarian insurgents, about 3,000-strong, bravely fought Soviet tanks using Molotov cocktails and handguns. By 29 October Nagy had disbanded the ÁVH and was pushing through more reforms such as restoring the multi-party system. Though many in number, the Soviets troops suffered heavy losses and by 30 October most had withdrawn from Budapest to garrisons in the Hungarian countryside. Meanwhile the fighting continued fiercely in Budapest. The memory of the Siege of Budapest had not dimmed in the minds of the city dwellers, who prayed that this time it would be brief. It was soul-destroying to see city buildings in ruins, crater-filled roads, debris-laden streets, burnt-out trams and barricades everywhere.

During the first week of the Uprising, prison doors were thrown open by the insurgents and thousands of innocent prisoners set free. László was luckily among those numbers and soon was reunited with Irén and Marie. Though overjoyed to have regained his freedom, there was no way this time that he could take part in the Uprising. As for Dr Lajtha, he found himself in the city of Sopron on the Austrian border when the Uprising began and took some time to return to Budapest, where he promptly had a heart attack but fortunately survived.

Seriously debilitated and frail, László could barely walk and eat. He was in need of much care and nourishment and Marianna Matlag, Irén's mother, played a big part in nursing him back to health. His property proved a great consolation to him now that he could sit on the modest verandah and observe his garden of peach trees. Free again, he could appreciate nature, taking in deep lungfuls of fresh air and surveying the surrounding hills and the beauty of its wildlife. For the first time in a long while, he dared to hope that his suffering was at an end. He felt confident that Imre Nagy could stand up to the Soviets and restore Hungarian society to its former self. The period of tranquillity was short-lived, however.

On 1 November, a dramatic moment came when the reforming Nagy announced the country's withdrawal from the Warsaw Pact and declared its neutrality. He also contacted the United Nations in the nation's hour of need and looked for support. But it was all a step too far for the Soviets. They retaliated and before long Soviet troops were storming towards Budapest. Early on the morning of 4 November 1956, László and all of Budapest were awakened by the thundering sound of over a thousand Russian tanks rolling back onto their streets. It must have been a terrifying moment. Startled and anxious, László had a deep sense of foreboding. The government and his country were doomed. Within hours Imre Nagy was forced to seek refuge in the Yugoslav Embassy and would in time be executed. The horrific battle that ensued on the streets of the capital left thousands dead and thousands more wounded. Help from the West had not come, especially since the Suez Crisis had erupted in the meantime.

By 14 November, the Soviets had restored some kind of order and reinstated a hardline communist government. Once again the tide of European history engulfed László. He quickly realised that he could not stay in Hungary any longer. The prisons would soon be filled again with those accused of dissenting against the state. For László, it would mean a most definite return to prison at best and death at worst. Mass arrests and deportations had already begun.

To her credit, Irén's mother Marianna came to his assistance, hiding him in the cellar of her home while he made preparations to flee the country. He quickly met with his lawyer at Mrs Matlag's house and there plans to dispose of a portion of his land were effected. The money from the sale would pay for the lawyer's fees, cover the cost of his and Irén's escape and enable them to set up a home beyond the border. Trusting as he was, for reasons unknown, László agreed to sign a blank sheet of paper in the hope of securing the rest of his property when times were favourable. The lawyer was to fill in his instructions later. I can only surmise that László was ill, physically weak, vulnerable and under tremendous stress. Indeed, I would say he was under duress and in no fit state to sign any legal document.

László and Irén planned to escape to Austria and naturally Marie figured in their deliberations. Fleeing across the border would be dangerous, especially as László was not in the best of health. It would take all of Irén's energies to make sure that he could make it. As in the case of so many other refugees, it was decided to leave the young girl behind for the time being. They would send for her as soon as they had settled in their new location. In the meantime, Marie was entrusted to the care of Irén's sister Etelka, who was married with a child of her own, and Etelka now took over the running of László's house.

For me, those oppressive times in European history bring to mind the Jesuit spiritual writer Anthony de Mello and his book *Awareness*. In it, he mentions the Jesuit superior general, Father Pedro Arrupe, who responded to a question on the relative value of communism, socialism and capitalism. His answer was that 'a system is about as good or as bad as the people who use it'. De Mello adds in his own words that 'people with golden hearts would make communism or socialism or capitalism work beautifully'. Human nature is flawed for sure.

5.

ESCAPE AND STATELESS

It's easy to cry that you're beaten – and die;
It's easy to crawfish and crawl;
But to fight and to fight when hope's out of sight –
Why, that's the best game of them all!
And though you come out of each gruelling bout
All broken and beaten and scarred,
Just have one more try – it's dead easy to die.
It's the keeping-on-living that's hard.

From 'The Quitter' by Robert W. Service

I T was in the latter half of November that László and Irén put their plans into operation. The winter had set in with a vengeance and temperatures had plummeted. Soon the Hungarian landscape disappeared under a cover of pristine snow. László and Irén were nervous about what lay in store. Thousands of their fellow citizens were fleeing across the border to Austria, who offered a warm welcome to the citizens of its one-time sister nation. What help Austria could not supply militarily as a neutral country, it more than compensated for with humanitarian aid. They had read in the newspapers that Oskar Helmer, the Austrian Minister of the Interior, on 26 October had offered asylum to all Hungarian refugees, regardless of why they left their home country. Austria then was seen as their only hope.

They realised their planned escape had to look quite casual, under the guise of a day's outing or a visit to a friend. Hence, no luggage or baggage was taken; nothing but the multi-layered clothes they stood in, which had to be thick and warm and their boots fur-lined and stout. Their only concession was László's treasured clarinet. Whether or not László got an opportunity to send word to his family in Debrecen that he was defecting or indeed had escaped from prison, I do not know. Chances are he thought it better to keep quiet until he was safely out of the country. A person caught fleeing faced prison time and hard labour, professional ruin and possibly execution.

Having bid Marie goodbye, a heavy-hearted Irén and László made their way as calmly as they could to Budapest-Déli railway station in the south of the city. László's encased clarinet hung tightly around his neck. Soviet tanks were to be found at every major intersection in the city and soldiers were everywhere. At the station, some carriages had been damaged during the Uprising but the trains were still running. The area had been the scene of fierce fighting for weeks. Over two hundred students and factory workers had built barricades in nearby Széna Square using upturned railway carriages and had taken on the might of the Russians. Many were to die as martyrs. The station was now crowded with Budapestians intent on making their escape.

Vienna, three hours away, was László and Irén's hoped-for destination. By now the main roads to Austria were clogged with the traffic of fleeing Hungarians. Soviet troops stationed along the border were guarding most exits and the borders were well closed. Hungarian citizens were promptly being turned back and told to return to their homes. Driving to Austria was therefore out of the question. The plan was to take the train bound for Vienna and to disembark before reaching the border station of Hegyeshalom and then make their way across the border on foot.

It was time to bid farewell to the city that had become László's home. His heart must have been truly heavy. He was now leaving behind his work, the house he had constructed brick by brick, the life built from scratch through sheer hard work, and closing the door on friends, colleagues and family, perhaps forever. Everything had turned pear-shaped.

Everything was gone. He must have cursed his own nature for some of his misfortune, being too trusting and only believing in the goodness of people. And through it all there was a touch of naivety.

Years later, when no doubt referring to all the aforementioned ups and downs in Budapest, both personal and professional, he would sigh at his perceived flaw.

'Oh Pixie, I was such a stupid monkey.'

All that loss must have been unbearable. Even so, László was lucky to possess a fearless and determined self that enabled him to cope with every peril he faced. He had reserves of strength far beyond the average man.

Once aboard, László and Irén suspected that some of their fellow travellers were in similar circumstances to themselves. Finding vacant seats in one carriage, they sat down trying to make themselves look as inconspicuous as possible. ÁVH men were also aboard and constant inspections took place throughout the journey, yet László and Irén were careful to hide their irritation as they handed over their tickets and identity papers each time. As they headed west towards freedom, they could not afford to let their guard down. To his surprise, László recognised someone from the world of music on the train. His colleague, an oboe player called Tamás, was accompanied by his wife Erika and their two young children, Melánia and Lilla. László discreetly nodded in his direction, while his friend reciprocated. Neither made a move, deciding instead to bide their time.

Meanwhile Irén worried about László's health and fitness, as he had not yet recovered his physical strength. Yet what worries she had she kept to herself. Onwards they went, passing the towns of Tatabánya, about an hour into the journey, and then the industrial town of Győr. Gradually the train shed much of its load, some no doubt wanting to make an early bid for freedom. From Győr, it would be about a two-day trek to the border. Fear was rife that, as the train neared the frontier, there would be reinforced security guards and troops deployed at every station that would capture those not local to the area. I had read that some passengers in those days took advantage of the train slowing to almost a halt – often by an obliging train driver – to jump off and take their chances in the open countryside.

Most escapées, indeed thousands, had headed for the main crossing points around Lake Neusiedl, or Lake Fertód as it was called in Hungarian, and Andau. One of the focal points was the Andau Bridge, a narrow wooden footbridge over the Einser Canal in northwestern Hungary. This marshy ground was in the hinterland of Lake Neusiedl, a skinny lake just inside the Austrian border about thirty-five kilometres long. However, the Andau Bridge had been blown up on 21 November by Hungarian border guards. Even so, makeshift rafts were cobbled together and people still managed to get across.

Eventually, Tamás and his family linked up with László and Irén. Birds of a feather, I imagine! They talked quietly among themselves and decided to remain together, thinking safety in numbers. Being together might also give them a greater chance of actually crossing the border. The train ploughed ever westwards as the two little girls slept oblivious beside their dozing mother. Irén too fell into a slumber after a while, but both men remained awake and alert with their thoughts firmly fixed on the future.

* * *

As the group approached the station of Mosonmagyaróvár, they anxiously prepared to leave the train. This medieval town was the last stop before the border station of Hegyeshalom. László and Irén were now on the margins of freedom, the border being about twenty-five kilometres west of the town. The next stage of their flight would be the most dangerous, however. Armed border guards and Soviet soldiers controlled all the roads and railways out of Hungary. Knowing this, the two families alighted with László calmly carrying one little girl, while Tamás held the other. Irén and Erika followed behind doing their best to appear relaxed and unruffled. They duly presented their tickets to the guards and fortunately no questions were asked.

Before long the little group put the station behind them and faced into the fading light of the late afternoon. Night-time curfews had been imposed so they were anxious to get off the streets as soon as possible. Shortly afterwards, they were met by a small, dark-haired stocky individual named Maté, who greeted them.

71

'Gede? Gede László?'

László nodded. The man was a local insurgent and communication had been made through László's former contacts in the wartime resistance. The town of Mosonmagyaróvár had its fair share of suffering during the Uprising. It had witnessed much bloodshed when ÁVH men had opened fire on peaceful demonstrators, killing over a hundred and maiming hundreds. It was not safe to be in the town now crawling with Soviet soldiers.

Maté led the little band away from the station, situated at the edge of town and headed towards nearby farmland. They would look conspicuous on the main road amid Soviet tanks and local farming folk on horse carts. Instead they travelled down laneways and across fields, taking in their surroundings. Large collective farms had become typical of the area under communism, though many farmers were permitted to have pigs, poultry and rabbits for their own sustenance.

The group was fortunate that the snow was not as deep as expected and weather conditions less treacherous. Their progress was slow, however, as László could not maintain a quick pace. After what seemed like hours walking, they came upon a farm. Maté told them to stay together while he made his way to the farmhouse. After a short while, Maté returned with a farmer who appeared friendly and reliable, and who gazed with deep compassion over the small group huddled together. Before long the farmer placed young Melánia and Lilla in a cart which Maté started to pull. The farmer beckoned them all to follow him. After guiding them through fields and down a long overgrown laneway, they eventually reached an outhouse on the farmer's land.

Once inside, to their amazement, they saw a simple meal had been hastily prepared for them. László realised they had been expected and marvelled at the efficiency of the men. A warm glow overcame him at the time. Rózsa, the farmer's wife, made them all feel welcome and apologised for not bringing them into the farmhouse given the unsafe circumstances. László felt very humbled at the kindness of these country folk, privileged to be in the presence of such goodness.

That night they slept fitfully but enjoyed a hearty breakfast the following morning. Afterwards, the farmer reappeared. Maté, sharp and alert, took

László and Tamás outside for a short stroll and there they discussed the situation and the best strategy to get to the border. It was not safe to be on the roads as they were subject to frequent patrols and hence they would have to stick to the fields, lanes and some woodlands. The land, being part of the Hungarian Lowlands, was rather bleak and flat open countryside. As it neared the border south of the Austrian village of Andau, it grew marshy and boggy and was drained by a series of canals. The terrain would not provide much cover for those fleeing.

Observing the group, Maté was anxious about the young children and that László was not the most robust, health-wise. His fear that the severity of the winter terrain might prove too difficult for them was evident. Nonetheless, Maté promised to take them as near as possible to the border, as he knew the lie of the land well and was also acquainted with several sympathetic farmers en route. The group soon bade farewell to the farmer and his wife Rózsa. László shook their hands and thanked them profusely.

They set off with Maté and Tamás carrying the two little girls part of the way. In their innocence the children delighted in the excitement of the big adventure, laughing and clapping. It took all their mother's strength to keep them quiet. Meanwhile László did his utmost to keep up with the group but still could only walk very slowly. The going grew tough as the thawing snow turned the land to mudfields. It soon became obvious to the men and to Irén that their walk to the border would take far longer than expected. The group took cover in woodlands whenever possible and rested there.

I'm not sure exactly where along the border that László and the group were heading for. I suspect they were aiming for somewhere near the two Austrian villages of Andau and Halbturn. The border near Halbturn was heavily guarded. So it would seem more likely that they skirted the villages of Mosonudvar and Újrónafő and the town of Jánossomorja before trying to reach the vicinity of Andau.

Now so close to the border it was best to travel by night and rest by day. The border was continually patrolled by armed frontier guards and Soviet soldiers, now intent on arresting any likely escapées. At least, in the heart of winter, there were longer spells of darkness in their favour. Soon Maté indicated another farm where they could take shelter. And as with the previous farm owner, the same graciousness was shown to them. They rested in his hay barn and were given bread and coffee. It was a memory that László never forgot.

'The Hungarian people could never in a lifetime show enough gratitude to the farming community,' he would recall emphatically, 'for all their heroism during the war and the Soviet occupation.'

It reconfirmed his faith in his countrymen and women.

After thanking the farmer for his hospitality, they marched onwards in darkness through the sleety rain and snowy plains. László never spoke about encountering other people who were fleeing but given the thousands that did so I'm sure he had. There was much they and other escapées now had to contend with in their bid for freedom. Soviet troops, stationed in huts along the border, were in the process of hermetically sealing the frontier. Landmines had been laid over large stretches of fields and barbed wire fences constructed. From time to time the soldiers set off flares that lit up the night sky and revealed those escaping. Gunfire rang out across the countryside. At the sight of flares or the sounds of vehicles, soldiers, barking guard dogs or gunfire, those escaping would dive to the muddy or marshy ground for cover.

Maté warned them to be alert and on the lookout for landmines. Finally, he gave them directions to a good spot to cross where the barbed wire was weak. Then wishing the little party well and with a last goodbye, he watched them take their final steps towards freedom. His kindness and heroism was never forgotten; he truly was one of many unsung heroes of those troubled times. As night descended, László and the group observed the lights of an Austrian village, possibly Andau or Halbturn, twinkling in the distance. It was a most welcome sight and indelibly sealed on his mind. With his sharp sense of hearing he could also make out the church clock strike. It was all so tantalising close. A field lay ahead of them, ending in a thick barbed wire fence. The Austrians, to their credit, had marked the length of their border with red-white-red flags and built fires to illuminate the border at night. It was a symbol of welcome and a sign they had not deserted Hungarians in their hour of need.

Cautiously, in those early hours of the morning, with neither border guard nor soldier in sight, the final move was made. Despite his frailty, László decided that he would lead the way. I can still hear his strong accented voice telling me how, very gingerly, he picked his steps on the field and focused his eyes ever downward lest he tread on a lethal landmine. With his tremendous powers of concentration helping his every move, he warned each one to take the exact same step as he had taken. It was an agonising trek for all but thankfully calmness prevailed. Once they had all reached the wire fence, László and Tamás found a place where it was weak, threw their coats over it and managed to climb over slowly before helping the others across.

* * *

László and the little group were now safely inside the Austrian border, though cut and torn from the barbed wire. Freedom finally was reached. They were welcomed with open arms by volunteers – men and women who had arrived in droves to help the Austrian border guards manage the tsunami of refugees – and Red Cross officials. Hungry, frozen and exhausted, they were quickly ushered over to a campfire and given a hot drink. Thankfully both László and Irén could speak German – László also had French – so communicating with the Austrians posed no problems. Then they were taken in a tractor pulling a hay cart to a village schoolhouse. There they were given hot food and drink, their cuts tended to, and dry clothes to wear. With a blanket in hand, they joined many other refugees sleeping on the floor wrapped in blankets.

Never would László allow himself to forget that crossing and the genuine warm and sincere welcome the Austrians gave them. He never once felt he was just a statistic. After all, within the space of two months, seventy thousand Hungarians entered Austria in the vicinity of Andau. The humanity of these Austrians was unforgettable. In one way it was not surprising that the people of the border province of Burgenland, containing the villages of Andau and Halbturn, helped out. After all, the region had been part of the Kingdom of Hungary for centuries until 1921 when, under the Treaty of Trianon, it was transferred to Austria.

Those people were kindred spirits. While no words could describe the ecstasy of freedom, there was loss too. A burden had to be borne – László would never again set foot on his beloved Hungarian soil.

After some hours' rest they were once again on the move. This time the International Red Cross transported them to a refugee, or rather transit, camp on the outskirts of Vienna. It was called Traiskirchen, a ruined and run-down former cadet school with a series of imposing buildings. Despite its forlorn appearance, they were warmly welcomed by good-humoured staff. Each received a parcel of fresh clothing and given all the essentials for living. Irén was grateful and for once could not care less about the latest fashions.

Thanks to the generosity of the Austrian people and the many European countries that had weighed in, food was plentiful. Meals of goulash, bread rolls, various casseroles, cottage cheese and sardines were regularly served in the mess hall. As for their sleeping arrangements, they each had an army camp bed to rest their limbs. László sought comfort in music and would remove his clarinet from its by now battered case. The sounds he blew at first were soft and tentative but gradually as he recovered his strength he played with renewed vigour. It gave Irén – and indeed their fellow refugees – pleasure to listen to the sounds of Mozart's Clarinet Concerto in A major echoing through the dormitory. Tamás too produced his oboe and together they tried to play compositions written for both instruments, such as Beethoven's Rondino in E Flat major.

In Traiskirchen, László and Irén were issued with provisional identity cards. Thousands passed through the camp and left as they were directed on to other destinations. Refugees were offered a choice of where to go. Many opted to go to Germany, Switzerland, Sweden, Britain and a host of other European nations, the USA, Canada, and Australia. Even Ireland too offered to take in a thousand refugees, but more of that later.

László and Irén were undecided, but for now wished to get in touch with musicians of László's acquaintance in Vienna. I well remember László saying that contact was successfully made with these musicians, many of whom performed with the Viennese Philharmonic. They certainly came to his rescue and found him an apartment in the city centre.

Shortly afterwards László and Irén bade farewell to Tamás and Erika and the two little girls. There was sadness in parting seeing that they had been through so much together. Now in freedom they had their separate paths to follow and they would never cross again.

By 28 November, László and Irén were issued with identity cards in Vienna by the city police authorities. Soon they were installed in 22 Weihburggasse in the heart of Vienna. Weihburggasse was an elegant street full of nineteenth-century apartment buildings, near the towering St Stephen's Cathedral, and located in the historic Biedermeier district. Both of them were grateful to have a place of their own so quickly. Money from the sale of the land on the Buda Hills enabled them to rent the apartment and try to build a new life for themselves. Vienna was a city familiar to both of them and took little adjustment. For Central Europeans, it was said that Vienna was the city to live in, Prague the city to see, and Budapest the place to have a good time in. The city now reminded them of a time in Budapest when life had been carefree and full of music.

The State Opera House was a short distance away as was the famous Café Sachar. And with nearby streets named after composers such as Mahler and Schubert, it must have been a salve on the wounds of the two music lovers. The end of their street opened onto a city park where they took short walks to rebuild their strength, stopping to gaze at the gilded statute of Johann Strauss II playing his violin. And if they felt stronger and the weather not too inclement they strolled further afield to see the monuments to Beethoven and Brahms. Regardless of their plight, they must have felt at home in this milieu.

Vienna was awash with Hungarian refugees, greeting and embracing each other in the streets. However, all of Austria seemed to have embraced the refugee crisis and went out of their way to help them. By today's standards, the refugee response was unprecedented. Both László and Irén were issued with welfare cards by the municipal authorities almost immediately. Bearing these cards they were able to avail of any essential items and so in early December they received a towel, raincoat and spectacles for Irén, to name but a few. These were dispensed by either the municipal authorities or Evangelical Relief agencies. Meals were supplied to refugees by the Viennese Public Kitchen Company, originally set up to feed children and vulnerable adults and pensioners, but now catering for refugees. László and Irén did avail of these meals at first but once on their feet looked after their own cooking.

The Christmas season was upon them, and the city blazing with twinkling lights. László and Irén were far from festive, as it was hard on Irén being separated from her daughter Marie at that time of year. By now the pair had sent letters home letting their families know of their whereabouts. The authorities at the Vienna Philharmonic were no less kind with regard to work. They gave permission for László to play in the orchestra as a substitute for any clarinet player on days off. In the run-up to Christmas there was plenty of work for talented musicians such as László. Because there were so many Hungarian refugees in the country, either in camps or with host families, the authorities tried to boost their morale by broadcasting concerts on Radio Wien with an emphasis on Hungarian music. László performed over a three-day period before Christmas and received 560 Austrian schillings from the Austrian Broadcasting Corporation for his efforts.

They spent a bittersweet Christmas and New Year and looked to the future. 1956 had been a tumultuous year for them, made more poignant by the death of László's grandfather living on Szív Street.

Their stay in Vienna was to last just over a month. During this time László got his Hungarian driving licence officially translated into German by the Austrian Automobile, Motorcycle and Touring Club. So he was possibly thinking of acquiring a car. But the question of how he was going to earn a living in the long run remained. He could not get by relying on just occasional work from the city orchestras. Fortunately, during this stressful period he was put in contact with two orchestras looking for musicians. The first was the New York Philharmonic Orchestra and the other was the South African Broadcasting Corporation, who was specifically searching for talented musicians in order to build up their own fledgling orchestra. Ireland, which would later become his home, was not on his horizon at all at this stage.

For his own reasons he chose South Africa. Perhaps given the ravages of war and his delicate health, he imagined the warm climate would favour them both. It was a major decision but a wonderful opportunity all the same. And so on 12 January 1957, he and Irén left for South Africa. However, the biggest heartbreak for László was his passport. Stamped across it in big bold letters read the word STATELESS. Loving his country as he did, it was an unbearable pain for him. For Irén, the temporary loss of her daughter was a heavy burden to bear.

6.

SOUTH AFRICA

I love the thought of his anger.
His obstinacy against the rock, his coercion
of the substance from green apples.

The way he was a dog barking
at the image of himself barking.
And he hated his own embrace
of working as the only thing that worked –
the vulgarity of expecting ever
gratitude or admiration, which
would mean a stealing from him.

The way his fortitude held and hardened
because he did what he knew.
His forehead like a hurled *boule*
travelling unpainted space
behind the apple and behind the mountain.

'An Artist' by Seamus Heaney

THE sorrow at what had befallen László and Irén lifted somewhat as their plane approached the then named Jan Smuts Airport in Johannesburg. It was a bright Sunday morning on 13 January 1957. László always smiled whenever he recalled the vision of beauty that greeted them. From the plane, he looked down over the airport situated on the high plains, or veld as it was called, and spotted a magnificent floral display in the brilliant sunshine.

'Look,' he pointed to Irén, 'Paradise!'

It only confirmed his belief that he and Irén had made the right decision.

On the plane were a number of refugees from Budapest, who like László and Irén wished to make South Africa their home. The story of the Hungarian Uprising still generated headlines around the world and Irén's picture along with three of her countrywomen duly appeared in the Tuesday edition of *The Rand Daily Mail* with the following caption.

From Budapest come four charming Hungarians to settle in South Africa. Arriving on Sunday morning early, they are already anxious to find work, and stand on their own independent feet. Only one of the above, Mrs Irene Gede is not looking for a job, and that is because her husband, who was a member of Hungary's famous Philharmonic Orchestra in Budapest, has already found one.

The caption listed the other women as Miss Irene Kovacs, secretary to an industrial technician; Miss Emoke Vass, a technical draughtsman, and finally Miss Elizabeth Nagy, an architectural draughtsman. They were joining a very small but grateful and proud Hungarian community in South Africa.

Before 1956, a community of about three hundred Hungarians was based in Johannesburg and the nearby Gold Reef, many of whom were employed in the mining industry. Almost all had fled Hungary to escape the terrors of Nazism or the early years of communism. Seeing that Hungary was a closed country, no embassy or consul existed in those days in the Union of South Africa, as it was known at the time. However, the country did respond to the Hungarian refugee crisis in Austria in late

1956 and offered to take in over one thousand refugees, much like Ireland. It was done, so they say, in an attempt to appease the United Nations for its condemnation of the country's apartheid policies.

By the time László and Irén arrived in January there had already been a number of refugee flights since mid-December. The Hungarian community had turned up in droves at the airport to welcome their fellow countrymen and women in a spirit of solidarity. It certainly lifted many a flagging spirit. A lot of the refugees were artisans or had specific qualifications, such as electricians, craftsmen, upholsterers, dressmakers, and were accompanied by their families. A number of employers came forward to offer them work, including the South African Railways, the mining companies and various businessmen and industrialists.

First the refugees were taken to a small industrial town called Vanderbijlpark on the banks of the River Vaal about sixty-four kilometres south of Johannesburg. Two modern hostels for workers had been hastily converted by the Red Cross to a reception centre. There they received any amount of food, clothes, shoes or medical supplies they required. There had also been an outpouring of generosity from South Africans, bombarding the centre with Christmas gifts and clothes, many of which were brand new.

With such a prominent welcome, László and Irén began their life in Johannesburg and looked forward to the day when Marie could join them. After Vanderbijlpark, their first home was on 338 Bree Street in the Queensbury Court apartment block. The location was right in the heart of the Central Business District convenient to the South African Broadcasting Corporation (SABC) headquarters then on Commissioner Street, a couple of streets away. With accommodation secured, the next hurdle was the language. It soon became apparent to László that English was the dominant language in South Africa, though neither he nor Irén spoke much English. In fact, most of the Hungarian refugees could not speak English at all. László and Irén now had a very different battle on their hands – that of mastering English, especially if László hoped to get a job with the SABC. Without further delay, English textbooks and dictionaries were acquired and language classes attended. They studied diligently and daily to accomplish their goal of fluency. László found learning a foreign language quite difficult at first, but with Irén's persistence he soon could partake in any conversation.

László's prospective job was put on a firm footing in April that year when he auditioned for broadcasting engagements in the English and Afrikaans Services of the SABC. This took place on 23 April and László was informed by letter the next day that he had been successful. Another hurdle thankfully surmounted. Before long László was introduced to his new colleagues at the SABC. Several of them, musicians and conductors, had received their training in Europe, so László felt in good company.

The orchestra itself, the National Symphony Orchestra, was in its infancy too, following the amalgamation of three studio orchestras of the SABC in 1954. Even so, it was fast gaining an international reputation. The musicians, some eighty strong, were still on something of a high after celebrating the seventieth birthday of the city of Johannesburg several months before. On that occasion, the London Symphony Orchestra had paid its inaugural visit to South Africa and La Scala Opera had presented three operas conducted by Guido Cantelli featuring the magnificent tenor Giuseppe di Stefano in *Cosi fan Tutti* and soprano Graziella Sciutti. Leading English conductor Sir Malcolm Sargent had conducted the SABC orchestra in Beethoven's Ninth Symphony with South Africa's own soprano Mimi Coertse as one of the soloists. And the list of stars did not end there! Violinist Yehudi Menuhin, guitarist Andrés Segovia, cellist Pierre Fournier, pianist Claudio Arrau as well as conductor Mantovani all came to town for the festivities.

The more comfortable he felt speaking the language, the more content László became in the orchestra. He liked his fellow musicians a great deal and felt tremendous relief in his newfound freedom. Though serious-minded musicians, they also had a keen sense of fun. Their bassoon player, Joss de Groen, for example, once told a music critic from *The Star* newspaper about the time his teenage son, also a bassoonist, joined the orchestra. The earnest young man asked his father for advice on what to do if he hit a wrong note during a performance.

'Always remember,' replied his father, 'that when you make a mistake look at someone else as if he were responsible.'

The son took the advice to heart and when in time he did strike a blue note, he looked straight at his father!

It was the start of a great period of contentment for László. Johannesburg had a thriving musical scene, as he came to learn, and could boast a number of orchestras and musical groups. László and Irén soon felt at home in this musical milieu. The SABC orchestra, under the direction of Anton Hartman, Edgar Cree and Gideon Fagan – at least during László's tenure – did much to enhance the musical life of the country. That said, it generally performed in front of white only audiences. The SABC conductors also introduced light music as well as ethnic Afrikaans music (Boeremusiek) to their audiences. Contemporary South African composers, such as Stefans Grové and Hubert du Plessis, were promoted and there was no shortage of broadcasts and gala concerts for the orchestra. Indeed visiting conductors and overseas musicians were always in great demand. Opera productions too became a feature when operas and oratorios were translated into Afrikaans by Anton Hartman and his colleagues. László, being able to speak German, could understand some Afrikaans, essentially a Dutch dialect.

* * *

László took to Africa as many of his countryman before him had. Hungary had never acquired colonies in Africa unlike other European nations, but nonetheless the continent had inspired Hungarian adventurers, ethnographers, mapmakers and geographers since the nineteenth century. Some were aristocratic like Count László Almásy, whose life story was fictionalised in the film *The English Patient*, while others, like naval officer László Magyar, lived among the natives for decades recording their customs and way of life. There was something enchanting and vibrant about the people and the land that László welcomed. Throughout the city there was colour everywhere. From the bright protea blooms – the national flower of South Africa – to vivid bougainvillea and lilac jacaranda trees, it was a kaleidoscope of colour.

One of the best things about living in Johannesburg was its dry climate, as László and Irén soon learned. No longer did they have to worry about grey cloud-soaked skies and freezing cold, harsh winters. The days of pawning great overcoats in summertime Budapest became a distant memory, at least where László was concerned. The most they had to endure were some cold nights in winter and some strong dusty winds and occasional rain in summer. Outside of that it was warm sunshine all the way and perfect for rehabilitating their tired bodies.

On first arriving in Johannesburg László and Irén really had no idea what to expect. They were accustomed to European cities yet found parts of Johannesburg surprisingly modern. It had followed the line of New York by building skyscrapers in the 1930s and was laid out in a rectangular grid pattern. László was forgiven for thinking that he had taken the New York job! Before long he acquired a driver's licence and car and grew accustomed to driving in the city. It was a bustling metropolis after all engaged in mining, manufacture and finance. Again the irony of gold surfaced in László's life. The city of Johannesburg had been founded after gold deposits were discovered in 1886, and it was known ever afterwards as Egoli – the City of Gold. Yet gold was the last thing on László's mind.

Even so, he never stopped thinking about how he could provide for Irén and for Marie should she resettle in South Africa. He put his head down and characteristically started to put money by for their future. The warm, sunny climate did both of them good and they regained much of their strength and vitality. Life was starting to feel secure again, despite the nostalgia they felt. For both their sakes, it was important that Irén's daughter join them as quickly as possible. During 1957 Irén wrote to her sister Etelka in Budapest to make her intentions known, in the full knowledge that her letter would be intercepted and read by the communist authorities. And so the process of corresponding with the authorities seeking permission for Marie to join her mother began soon after. Luckily for them legal emigration was permitted in Hungary on the basis of reuniting families. It came to pass sometime in late 1957 or possibly early 1958 and Marie finally put her feet on South African soil.

Around this time they moved to the eastern suburb of Yeoville. Their accommodation there was in a three-storey apartment building called Edwardian Court located on the corner of Hendon Street and

Grafton Road. Yeoville must have appealed to László seeing that it was about fifteen metres above Johannesburg and reputedly once known for its clean air. On one side, this high ridge had views of the city centre and its hundreds of suburbs and on the other the Magaliesberg Mountains, supposedly one hundred times older than Mount Everest. The neighbourhood at the time was broadly middle class with white South Africans and immigrants making up the mix. Many of the latter were Jewish, seeking a new life in South Africa after the war. In fact, Yeoville had a fair smattering of artists and musicians, much to the approval of Irén and László. It was especially pleasant strolling under the shade of the sycamore trees huddled beside the apartment building.

It was a significant time for the family. Marie was now in her early teens and on the verge of adulthood and got on well with László. He always remarked that she was a most intelligent and talented girl and deserved the best education they could afford. He insisted that she attend a good school run by Catholic nuns. At this boarding school, she soon established herself as an exemplary student. Recognising her musical ability, László also taught her piano and Marie possessed a fine singing voice. Much to his delight they occasionally took part in concerts together. He was always very kind to her and most understanding of the difficulties she had experienced in her young life. After all, the trauma of being separated, first from her natural father and then her mother, not to mention the upheaval during those oppressive years in Budapest, would inevitably leave scars. Indeed few people were left unscathed by the turmoil of those times.

* * *

The oppression they had experienced in Hungary made them hyper-aware of the oppression now on their very own doorsteps. Back in Europe they had hardly met a black person, but the segregation of white and black people in South Africa did strike László as unjust. He could plainly see that the orchestra was the preserve of white people. In March 1959, a city councillor in neighbouring Cape Town had called for other races to be employed in that city's orchestra but it had fallen on deaf ears. The law made it impossible for black people to be employed in certain posts and that included concert musicians. Seeing that South Africa had given him a home, László was in no position to object to its state of apartheid. Legally, both he and Irén were stateless and hence not entitled to hold a passport. In lieu of a passport, they were issued with a document of identity that had to be renewed each year. They could be deported if they ever ran foul of the authorities. It was a bitter pill for László to swallow every time he opened the document to see stateless, and *staatloos* in Afrikaans, inscribed. That said, they were given the opportunity to become South African citizens on several occasions; however, though they dearly loved the country, László and Irén did not feel completely comfortable or relaxed enough to accept.

Given his love for jazz music, László soon became aware of how vibrant the jazz scene was in Johannesburg in the late 1950s. It was another opportunity to play the saxophone. The South Africans over the years had taken to ragtime and Dixieland music with gusto and fused it with African cyclical harmonies and a rather trance-like rhythm. Swing music that László had performed back in Budapest with Goldwin Gede was just as popular. The suburb of Sophiatown was a place where black and white jazz musicians could meet regularly for the first time in South African history. Some of the black musicians would later go on to international recognition such as trumpeter and composer Hugh Masekela, singer Miriam Makeba and pianist Abdullah Ibrahim. However, with new apartheid laws in 1960 banning gatherings of more than ten people, within a few years it was no longer safe to visit or perform in jazz clubs. Some things never changed; oppressors always seemed to be suspicious of jazz music, whether it was the Nazis, Communists or Afrikaners.

Marie's arrival in Johannesburg was also a reminder of the life they had left behind and of the state of their affairs. Back in Hungary, in the aftermath of 1956, there had been a harsh backlash: over twenty thousand people were imprisoned, hundreds executed, and tens of thousands dismissed from their workplaces. Property had been confiscated wholesale. After László's sentencing in early 1956, an appeal had been lodged by Irén's lawyer against his conviction and hers, though she had in fact never served time. She desperately wanted the return of items that had been confiscated upon their arrest, namely money and gold jewellery. On 28 June 1957, the appeal was partially successful in that about fourteen hundred Hungarian forints were to be returned to them. The appeal court also agreed that 295 dollars should be returned to Irén herself as well as a 9.9 gram gold signet ring. The gold ring was returned since it was within the legal weight limits permitted at the time. Interestingly, Jószef Lengyel, Irén's former husband, was cited as another defendant in the case. It is not clear if he too had been convicted and sentenced like László. László never spoke about that aspect of the case to me.

The matter was complicated further by the fact that Irén and László were regarded as dissidents or defectors. In those days, any confiscated property belonging to defectors was treated as if the owners were deceased. Hence all their property and assets had to go through probate and all the headaches that entailed.

The fate of László's house on Napsugár Street was a pressing matter for him. On several occasions he had tried to make contact with the Hungarian lawyer who had looked after his affairs. However, all his attempts came to naught. Knowing László as I did, he certainly would have made a will and lodged it with this solicitor, identifying who would be the executor and beneficiaries. Given how stubborn, obstinate and strong-willed my husband was, if he wished to repossess his home, he most definitely would have done so. There was a suggestion that the solicitor had fled the country after the Uprising but nothing was known for certain. Either way, László was resigned to his fate and his natural kindness once again took precedence over monetary gain.

The property rights case came before the Hungarian courts in June 1958. At the heart of it was establishing who László's legal successors were: Lívia Gede or Marie Lengyel? His ex-wife Etelka Gede made a late submission pleading on behalf of their daughter Lívia Gede, while Etelka Fekete, Irén's married sister, pleaded on behalf of Irén's daughter Marie Lengyel. Etelka Fekete claimed the property had been donated to Marie because she was residing at Napsugár Street along with the Fekete family after Irén and László had fled the country. Up for settlement was also the matter of the fourteen hundred Hungarian forints mentioned earlier in connection with László's trial. The court ruled early the following year,

1959, that the abandoned property had not been donated but should be considered as part of community property, that is, joint ownership of the spouses, Irén and László. However, Etelka Gede's claim was rejected by the courts because of a late submittal. As a result, the property and money were to be split equally and pass to Marie Lengyel and the Hungarian state. The result, needless to say, was appealed by all parties and it would be several years before it was resolved.

Despite the legal wrangling taking place in Budapest, László, Irén and Marie settled into their new life. Much of it revolved around music and schooling. Irén enjoyed attending concerts as much as ever, a reminder of the life she had once led in Budapest. It was an opportunity to socialise with musicians and their partners and also catch up on local gossip and goings-on. László, though friendly, was not gregarious and kept to himself, busily making repairs to the apartment or to his car when the need arose. By now he was also giving music lessons to augment his income like he had done in Budapest. His job was demanding enough, though he enjoyed it immensely. He and his colleagues often found themselves the subject of reviews printed in the city newspapers such as *The Star* and *Sunday Express*. In one study of facial expressionism, László was pictured in *The Star* with lips pressed to his clarinet, along with flautist Francesco Maresca and tuba player Arthur Houghton also in action. One review from June 1959 mentioned that the orchestra would play the newly composed Tuba Concerto by Vaughan Williams in a forthcoming attraction. This was deeply satisfying as the orchestra was always keen to perform new compositions.

It must have been poignant when renowned Hungarian violinist Johanna Martzy toured South Africa in 1959. László and Irén were familiar with her work, though she had fled Hungary in 1944 and settled in Switzerland. She performed a live broadcast at the SABC studios in Johannesburg and included Vivaldi's Violin Sonata in D major, Bartók's Rumanian Folk Dances and Brahms's Violin Sonata No. 3 in D minor from her repertoire. Hearing the sound of Bartók again must have both thrilled and saddened László.

During 1959 László had accumulated enough money to consider building a home for himself and the family. He drew up plans to construct a house in a quiet residential suburb called Northcliff on a ridge of the same name. The ridge was the second highest peak in the city after Observatory Ridge and had unrivalled views. László considered it the most beautiful part of the city with its lush green foliage and red sandy soil. It was easy to see why he was attracted to the place. In many ways, it was history repeating itself: Budapest's Buda Hills transported to South Africa. The desire to live in the city yet apart still burned bright in him. At just over eighteen hundred metres the place was practically on a mountain top!

Unlike his house in Hungary, he did not build the new house himself and had to employ an architect in order to get planning permission. The design was a five-roomed bungalow comprising three bedrooms, a dining room and a split level living room. Both living and dining rooms looked out onto a terrace and beyond to a garden with spectacular views. A large kitchen and maid's room also featured in the plans. Though László never mentioned having a maid, it was common practice for white middle class South Africans to employ domestic servants, typically black. South African architects, in their designs, were mindful of racial legislation and the sensibilities regarding the two races sleeping at close quarters. Under the Group Areas Act 1950, it was illegal for black workers to live under the same roof as their white employers. The outside maid's room and toilet were hence part of the standard design in the suburbs. All this would have been distasteful to László, especially when he considered how much Zsófia – whom he had employed back home on Napsugár Street – had been like one of the family. Knowing László's frugality, however, they most likely did not engage a maid and Irén probably did all the cooking.

Construction on the house started in November and must have inspired László to put pen to paper at the time. Clearly, he was apologetic for not having written to his father for quite some time. The need to show his father back home in Debrecen that he was making progress in life had never deserted László. He was keen to let him know just how the modern the house would be: with hot and cold water, full amenities, and built in an American style. He even sketched the design with mathematical precision! The house was larger than the one on Napsugár Street and would cost 4,400 South African rand, which, he wrote, was equivalent to 440,000 Hungarian forints at the time.

Building a house was a clear sign that they were rebuilding their lives too. Nonetheless, for László this did not mean that their old life was gone forever and he was at pains to convey this to his father.

> This, however, does not mean that I shall never return to Hungary. I can sell my house at any time and, furthermore, there is news that the Russian troops might return to their homeland and all of you shall be free.

The city newspapers regularly reported on European affairs and László readily devoured any snippets of information about Hungary. From time to time, there were hopes of a thaw under the leadership of János Kádár, promoted to high office in the aftermath of the Uprising. László and Irén continued to live in hope. By now Marie was in the last year of her secondary school education and hoped to attend medical school in the following academic year. In a poignant note, László wrote she had promised that if they ever returned home to Hungary that she would take care of Papa Gede's medical needs and heal him. Sadly, that never came to pass.

In the summer of 1960 László received a letter bearing the sad news of his father's death on 13 July at the age of seventy. He had been hospitalised for some time suffering from various illnesses of old age. It was yet another blow to László, another deep loss keenly felt. Though oceans separated László and his friends and family, the distances were bridged by many a letter. He was a keen letter-writer himself but it was Antal Molnár, his stepmother's brother, who mainly kept him informed of all the news from home. Occasionally, László received some correspondence from his own family.

In the early 1960s, Kádár in Hungary had declared a general amnesty and set about curbing the brutal excesses of the secret police. It ushered in a more liberal cultural and economic agenda to improve the regime's image in the eyes of the people. Watching concerts on television was then the only source of entertainment for László's music-loving family and friends back home. Foreign conductors, singers and musicians were soon allowed to perform there and even tourism had picked up. The communist authorities wrote to László – as indeed to countless resettled overseas – inviting him to return to Hungary. Yet László could not bring himself to trust the communists – no matter how swift their conversion or conciliatory their tone.

At one time his youngest brother Zoltán was very anxious to join him in South Africa. For some reason László was unable to help his younger sibling, which no doubt must have caused the former great pain. There was always a close bond between László and his brothers. After their father's death, Zoltán and István Jnr decided to sell the family home – which by now was an extensive property on Hajnal Street. At the time István Jnr was living there with his own family. Their stepmother Borbála, in declining health herself, moved back to her family home shortly afterwards to be cared for by relatives. Some years before, Zoltán had built a new house on one side of their grandparents' spacious property on Szív Street and lived there with his family. In 1963, István Jnr and his family also moved into the old house. Reflecting on their father's ethos, the two brothers had honoured his wishes to take care of their families and now lived side by side.

Over the years László also kept in touch with Dr Lajtha. The composer had refused to collaborate in any way with the communist authorities, firmly rejecting their commissions. Instead sacred music became the focus of his work and helped him find meaning in life again. He also earned some money from collecting folk music and continued to compose music, though now deprived of an audience. After fourteen years, in 1961, he was granted a passport and allowed to perform abroad once more. Despite his career enjoying a brief resurgence, his struggles under communism took their toll and he died from a second heart attack in February 1963. It was another dent in László's armoury.

László took comfort in Northcliff and his home life helped restore his equilibrium. He was rightly proud of his new home and of what he had accomplished since his exile. The garden was his pride and joy and he planted many a shrub and tree, although with periodic droughts and water shortages in South Africa, I have no idea how he managed to keep it in such good condition. But knowing László he would have devised some ingenious method of irrigation. Around this time he also bought a German Shepherd, which he named Roy, and who brought much energy to their lives. László had a way with animals and treated them kindly – Roy was as good as family. Perhaps the fact that the breed is noted for its high intelligence and workability had appealed to László. Playing chess on the terrace under the warm sunshine and refreshing himself with Castle lager were other joys for László in Northcliff.

For the most part László was healthy, though he did become ill on one occasion and was hospitalised with a suspected kidney stone. Once the stone was located, he underwent surgery where it was successfully removed. For such an active soul as László recuperating in hospital was a severe trial indeed. He refused point blank to remain there, so very early one morning he somehow managed to flee the hospital wrapped in his dressing gown, climb into a taxi and head for home. Poor Irén nearly collapsed when she heard the key in the door and in walked László!

'Laci, Laci, what are you doing here?'

All László could do was smile triumphantly.

* * *

László and Irén may have felt at ease, happy and settled in their home in Northcliff but the winds of change were blowing in South Africa. A city of two halves, Johannesburg was sharply divided. It was equally home to great wealth and poverty, universities and illiteracy, villas and shantytowns. The first eruption of serious violence, at least for László and Irén, was when sixty-nine black people were gunned down by police in the Sharpeville Massacre on 21 March 1960. Soon László and Irén became aware of thousands of black people being forcibly relocated from Johannesburg suburbs to barren townships in the hinterland. The oppression and denial of human rights all seemed so familiar to László and Irén. South Africa declared itself a republic in 1961, but for its black citizens there was little or no democracy.

Travelling beyond Johannesburg gave László an opportunity to see the wide open spaces of Africa and how rural Africans lived. He used to say it did his heart great good. For patrons of the arts, music was certainly not just confined to Johannesburg. Indeed local cities like Cape Town and Durban also had their own symphony orchestras. The SABC orchestra visited these cities and Pretoria as well as rural towns and neighbouring countries, such as Mozambique, Southern Rhodesia and South West Africa. It was an added bonus that the shores of some of these cities were washed by the powerful Atlantic Ocean. The sea was always a joy to behold for someone like László coming from a landlocked country like Hungary.

The orchestras also brought the joy of music to both the cities and the townships. Throughout his travels, László delighted in seeing the young black children spellbound, beaming and eager when exposed to diverse classical music pieces and keen to learn about the various musical instruments. It filled him with hope for the future of these children.

There was great excitement among László and his fellow musicians in May 1962 when the ageing composer and conductor Igor Stravinsky came to South Africa at the invitation of the SABC. Stravinsky toured with the orchestra mainly in Johannesburg and Cape Town, often performing his own works. When the surprisingly agile Stravinsky himself was not conducting, the baton was held by American conductor Robert Craft, his close associate and aide. The visit was not without controversy, however. The United Nations was on the verge of imposing sanctions on South Africa for its apartheid legislation and a cultural boycott was in the offing.

Just before he left Paris for Johannesburg, Stravinsky telegrammed the SABC requesting that his concert tour be open to both white and non-white people. The SABC for its part insisted that the concerts would be held before segregated audiences in keeping with the laws of the country. Not to be outdone, Stravinsky insisted on performing separately in front of a black audience, despite the SABC making very little money available for the event. As it turned out, Stravinsky donated his fee to a black charity, keen to push his point.

That year in August saw Nelson Mandela arrested for inciting workers' strikes and leaving the country without permission – he had earlier been in Ethiopia and toured Africa and was also briefly in London to raise support for the banned African National Congress (ANC). László held Mandela in high regard and was struck by the courage of the man. He too could appreciate the difficulties Mandela now faced, incarcerated and awaiting trial in an oppressed state.

Meanwhile life went on; the city acquired a new landmark building in the shape of the huge concrete television tower in the suburb of Brixton, the Sentech Tower. Like many countries, people were embracing television as a sign of the future. The world was moving on and entertainment was constantly evolving. Even singers had their day. The duettists Anne Ziegler and Webster Booth found their music outdated in their native England in the late fifties and swinging sixties and had relocated to South Africa. Ziegler was a light opera singer, while Booth was a renowned tenor and oratorio soloist. The 1940s had been their heyday when on stage and screen they had entertained the masses, particularly during wartime. These sweethearts of song, as they were dubbed, went on concert tours in South Africa during 1964 and 1965 with the SABC orchestra under the baton of Edgar Cree and in which László played clarinet. Though they may have fallen out of fashion in Britain, Ziegler and Booth's voices were still as melodious as ever and beloved by audiences. Their signature song, 'We'll Gather Lilacs', would send people into raptures and earn standing ovations. It was a reminder of a bygone era of glamour and romance.

László never tired of playing the clarinet whether for classical or light entertainment. It was such a versatile instrument equally at home in classical, jazz or folk music. For him, it was a joy to practise in the lofty heights of Northcliff, playing for hours or listening to records. He believed the clarinet was the nearest instrument to the human voice and could literally speak to audiences. He marvelled at how composers, from operas to symphonies, could create such astonishing pieces for the instrument; for example, Brahms's Hungarian Dances No. 5 was such a joyful uplifting piece that it would stir the stoniest of hearts. The clarinet version of Rimsky-Korsakov's the 'Flight of the Bumblebee' was so startlingly close to nature, the bees could have swarmed into the very same room in which László played.

Whatever about László feeling at home in South Africa, Irén may not have felt the same. There was some correspondence between her and the Office of the United Nations High Commissioner for Refugees in Brussels during the summer of 1964. It would appear that she was trying to get official recognition as a refugee, which she did, receiving letters in Dutch and French confirming it. I believe that she had relatives in Belgium too, possibly in Grimbergen, and was considering moving there, going so far as to lodge money in a Belgian bank account. But, for whatever reason, it never came to pass.

Meanwhile back home in Budapest, László's property rights settlement was still dragging on. He clearly wanted his daughter Lívia's rights protected and in this respect László's father István, before his death, and Antal Molnár came to his aid. They had discussed pursuing the case further with Etelka and Lívia, then living on Bocksai Street. The appeal case finally came before the Hungarian courts in September 1965. It ruled that Etelka Gede had submitted a timely submission on behalf of her daughter Lívia Gede, contrary to earlier findings, and that her daughter had a legal right to the property. Etelka Fekete, Irén's sister, appealed the decision that it was community property, claiming that the earlier court had ignored the fact that part of the property legally belonged to Irén Gede. The court found there was insufficient evidence to prove their claim, so it rejected that appeal. The upshot was that half the property went to Lívia Gede and half to Marie Lengyel. Marie also received the Hungarian forints and Lívia the gold mentioned earlier. To be honest, in hindsight, László was not entirely happy with the outcome, on account of Lívia not receiving the entire property. Further complications set in when the state seized the Napsugár property and a communist party official took up residence. Only after repeated court cases pursued by Etelka Fekete did the property finally fall into the possession of Irén's family.

* * *

In February 1966 a letter arrived unexpectedly from the Irish broadcaster Radio Éireann based in Henry Street, Dublin. In time it would be a most fortuitous piece of communication. Penned by Kevin Roche, the head of light music, it informed László that the broadcaster was in search of musicians, mainly violinists and cellists, to fill vacancies in the Radio Éireann Symphony Orchestra and its Light Orchestra. The letter enquired as to whether any musicians in Johannesburg or in Pretoria might be interested in taking up a position.

László's name had come to their attention through his Hungarian friend Tibor Paul, principal conductor of the Radio Éireann Symphony Orchestra since 1961 and also director of music at the broadcaster. Tibor Paul was a man well remembered by László from his days in Budapest and they had moved in common circles. László's senior by six years, Tibor too had played the clarinet as well as piano before devoting his time to conducting. Full of charisma and a fiery temperament, the man's memory was reputedly so phenomenal that he rarely conducted from a score. It would appear that László also played under the conductor's baton at some point in Budapest.

Tibor was marked out for greatness early in his career, and there seemed no end to his achievements in his native city during the 1930s and 1940s; founding the Budapest Concert Orchestra, conducting his own orchestra and at the National Theatre, and becoming principal conductor for the Hungarian Broadcasting Commission. Yet like László the communist government would be Tibor's undoing. He fled Hungary in 1948 and settled briefly in Switzerland. He was quickly able to resume his career conducting for the Swiss Broadcasting Corporation and at the opera house in Berne. Like László, he too migrated to the New World in search of better opportunities and reached Australia in 1950. The two men kept in touch, however; kindred spirits across the oceans of the world.

In Australia, Tibor's talents did not go unrecognised for long and not least because his passion and drive were all-consuming; he conducted the New South Wales National Opera and was guest conductor with the Australian Broadcasting Commission (ABC), aside from various teaching and touring commitments. At one point László considered moving to Australia, but they had put down roots in South Africa and Marie was doing well at school. There was always the worry that there would be insufficient work for an immigrant musician in Australia. By this time Tibor and his family had become Australian citizens.

Tibor was ambitious and always trying to broaden his reach and enhance his career. The prospect of more engagements and regular work brought him to Europe and North America, and he visited Ireland several times beginning in November 1958. As guest conductor of the Radio Éireann Symphony Orchestra on that occasion, Tibor had thrilled audiences with a vibrant programme of Verdi, Richard Strauss, Blacher and, in particular, Beethoven's Seventh Symphony. Beethoven became the hallmark of his work in Ireland. Tibor eventually settled in Ireland in 1961 and took up the post of principal conductor with the Radio Éireann Symphony Orchestra and in the following year director of music for the broadcaster. Many would remember it as a golden age for classical music in Ireland.

Unable to supply native musicians in sufficient numbers to fill the orchestra, established in 1948, the broadcaster had looked to a ravaged Europe to attract talented musicians. In the aftermath of war, many were fleeing the destruction and collapsed economies of their homelands or, indeed like László, oppression. Famous conductors in those early days that landed on its shores were Jean Martinon – shortly after being released from a prisoner of war camp – Hans Schmidt-Isserstedt, Edmond Appia, Milan Horvat and Sir John Barbirolli. All would go on to have distinguished international careers.

Tibor sought to maintain the orchestra at symphony standard and in the 1960s had to look abroad again. Rather than being a direct offer of employment as such, the letter to László was in effect a request for help. It asked if László could supply the names of South African music academies or suitable newspapers or journals in which they could advertise the vacancies. Aside from knowing that Tibor was based in the country, Ireland had never been on László's radar before but he read the letter with great curiosity.

With characteristic goodwill, László supplied whatever information Kevin Roche required and sent good wishes to Tibor Paul as well. The Radio Éireann letter, however, was stored away and certainly not confined to the waste paper basket. It gave László serious food for thought as political unrest in South Africa grew and the ANC campaign began to disturb him greatly. Something happened that year that altered László and Irén's near idyllic life in Northcliff. In 1966, they moved from their residence in the northern suburb nearer to the city centre. I do not recall László ever mentioning why he left Northcliff, but correspondence shows there was a change in address. What I do remember him recalling was an event that had a horrifying effect on Irén.

Having come through a European war of domination, genocide and ethnic cleansing, László and Irén now had to witness with horror the apartheid system unfolding fully before their eyes. The political situation had begun to seriously unnerve Irén. Sanctions, censure or cultural boycotts on behalf of the international community seemed to have little effect on the ruling National Party. Whether they came from the UN, the Musicians' Union, British playwrights, Equity, British Screenwriters' Guild, or the American Committee on Africa, the South African government was still unswerving in its devotion to apartheid. Even in Ireland in 1964, the Irish Anti-Apartheid Movement promoted a declaration signed by twenty-eight Irish playwrights – including Beckett and O'Casey – preventing their work being performed in front of segregated audiences.

As Irén saw the ANC retaliating, she realised that living in South Africa as a white person was becoming ever more dangerous. Segregation was strictly in force and the SABC orchestra consisted of an all-white membership. Any orchestra that had tried to defy apartheid seemed to lose out. When in the early 1960s the Cape Town Municipal Orchestra held concerts in their City Hall open to multiracial audiences, at first with impunity but later the government clamped down heavily on the practice. In 1965, PW Botha, the then Minister of Community Development issued a permit for racially mixed audiences to attend orchestra concerts. It seemed like a breakthrough but was not. It meant that concert venues had to have separate seating, entrances, ticket offices and other facilities for whites and other races. The Cape Town City Council was then forced to renovate the City Hall at great expense, which eroded the budget of the orchestra.

Irén feared that orchestra members would become a target. When she heard a friend warn László to always carry a weapon in his car for protection, her insecurity soared. Crime in the city was rampant and their car was in fact stolen one day. Irén now longed to return to Europe. With human rights abuses so widespread, it was inevitable the ANC would step up its campaign of violence and internal resistance. By now Nelson Mandela and several ANC leaders were imprisoned for life on Robben Island. László's belief in humankind took another tumble.

Following an evening concert performance in the city, as Irén and László were driving back to their Northcliff home, a car in front of them triggered a tripwire. In the huge explosion that ensued, they witnessed fragments of body parts flying through the air. All this proved too much for Irén. Her nerves were completely shattered and nothing would satisfy her only to withdraw from South Africa.

'Laci, we must leave immediately. I want to leave and never return!'

László was now faced with a dilemma. There was no way that he could leave straightaway. He would have to arrange to sell their house and, obviously this time, wait until all the legalities had concluded. There was also the question of disrupting Marie's education. She was in the middle of her medical studies at the University of Witwatersrand and fully committed to becoming a doctor. None of these violent events seemed to have had any effect on her. Unlike her mother, Marie had no intention of going into exile and felt no fear living in her adopted country. László, keen to support his stepdaughter, knew that he would have to provide for Marie's education before he ever resigned from his job.

Shortly after this incident, in his concern for Irén, László looked to Europe for a way out. He visited the British Embassy and discussed with officials there the possibility of applying for a visa to live in the UK. Their advice was to relocate first to Ireland and subsequently apply for British residency and move across to England. László was resigned to the fact they would need to get their affairs in order and prepare to leave. It would only be a matter of time, whether it took a few months or much longer.

Whatever the circumstances, László began to gather up his life, for the third time, and prepared to start all over again in a new location. In the meantime they moved to 18 Soper Road to a two-storey apartment building called the Berkeley Court. Built around 1950, it stood among a series of high-rise apartment blocks in the suburb of Hillbrow. At the time, this inner city residential suburb was mainly inhabited by the white middle class and seemed to offer Irén some respite. Perhaps she felt less of a target living away from the affluent surroundings of Northcliff. I have no idea if they had to sell their dog Roy around this time or not – confining a German Shepherd to a city apartment would not have appealed to László.

With the Northcliff house on the market, László continued with work. In October that year, the SABC marked the occasion of Johannesburg's eightieth birthday by performing a popular concert in the City Hall on Rissik Street. This rather grand colonial-style building with clock tower housed an enormous pipe organ, entertaining audiences in its pre-orchestra days. The SABC was conducted by English conductor Edgar Cree and featured Anne Ziegler and Webster Booth. On this occasion they sang the old Irish folk song 'Love's Old Sweet Song' and 'The Holy City', among many other favourites. The ageing tenor reputedly was so unhappy with his performance that he told the conductor it was time he quit singing altogether!

László's final year with the symphony orchestra in 1968 proved as hectic as ever, with some special highlights. In February he along with his colleagues performed a series of concerts to mark the opening of the Rand Afrikaans University in Johannesburg. Later in June, there was a four-day concert tour in Mozambique, a Portuguese colony at the time, which he enjoyed immensely. They flew into the beautiful city of Lourenço Marques, as the capital city was then called, and revelled in the sight of its red acacia-lined avenues overlooking the blue expansive bay. The struggle for independence had started to take root in the country and indeed all of Africa seemed to be trying to cast aside the shackles of imperialism. László lamented that his days in Africa were drawing to a close. This was especially so when he could mix freely with black and white people in Mozambique and they could freely appreciate music.

Throughout those final months, László continued to offer lessons to those eager to improve their musical proficiency, to attend rehearsals and play the clarinet and occasional saxophone. On 17 November 1968, the music critic of the local *Sunday Express*, Ulmont Schneider, reviewed a concert in which László had played the saxophone.

> The concert ended with Mussorgsky's 'Pictures at an Exhibition' in the richly orchestrated version of Ravel. Woodwind, brass and percussion were there given ample opportunity to demonstrate their talents. The work was brilliantly played. How pleasant it was to hear the saxophone in a symphonic metier! An only too rare pleasure.

Clearly the performance and recognition brought pleasure to László too, though not mentioned by name. He kept the review among his possessions and scrawled his name beside the reference to the saxophone.

As time moved on, a decision had to be made. Irén could no longer tolerate the Damoclean sword hanging over her head. She grew more and more argumentative and pressed László to act. One morning in early 1969, with great reluctance, László wrote a letter of resignation to the SABC authorities in his fine hand. He placed the envelope on his desk and by the time he returned from work that evening Irén had already posted it. That final act deeply saddened László. It was no joy to uproot and move away from this beautiful land, a land he had fallen in love with and made his home.

Attempts to persuade Marie to come with them bore no fruit. She was set to graduate in 1969 and had decided to specialise in psychiatry in South Africa. She was not ready to leave and they would have to go on without her. As a young woman in her early twenties, she had certainly come of age and had a right to lead her own life. Though it broke Irén's heart to depart, for her own sanity she knew she could not stay. There was no resolution to apartheid in sight. The violence had become unbearable: the rioting, the protests, the arson, the strikes, the sabotage, the clampdown. For a second time, Irén would be forced to abandon her daughter.

László and Irén's dream of a new life was shattered only eleven years after arriving in this magnificent country. With heavy hearts, they flew out of Johannesburg and arrived at Heathrow Airport on Wednesday, 2 April 1969 to a sunny but biting cold London. Their life was ever bittersweet.

PART II

LÁSZLÓ AND EIBHLÍN

7.

IRELAND

Ah, my Belovéd, fill the cup that clears
To-day of past Regrets and future Fears–
To-morrow? Why, To-morrow I may be
Myself with Yesterday's Sev'n Thousand Years....

From Rubáiyát of Omar Khayyám
translated by Edward FitzGerald

László and Irén's stay in London was the briefest ever – several hours in Heathrow Airport in fact. Having cleared immigration and health controls without incident, they were allowed onwards to Dublin. László did find the time in Heathrow, however, to purchase a gold chain and gold German coin depicting a Kaiser that he would hold in his possession for the remainder of his life. The value of gold could never be underestimated where László was concerned! Late in the day, on 2 April 1969, they finally set foot in Dublin, tired but curious. If their arrival in Ireland was a unique event, so too was the lunar eclipse that happened that evening. But perhaps it was the weather that gave rise to more concern; heavy dark clouds and rain splashing against the cabin windows greeted them. And as they left the comfort of the aircraft, the frosty Irish air hit them like an Arctic blast. It was a sharp contrast to the sun-drenched lands of South Africa.

'What a cold, dull and wet land this is,' László remarked. 'Have we made a dreadful mistake?'

'I hope not,' Irén replied. 'There's no going back now.'

Prior to leaving South Africa, they had made arrangements to stay at Kilronan House, a Victorian guesthouse on Adelaide Road, not far from St Stephen's Green in central Dublin. This was to be their home for the next three months – at least until they made the move to England, as they saw it. They soon became good friends with the proprietress, who in time proved to be a godsend. The house, operating as a guesthouse since 1854, was full of old world charm from Waterford Crystal chandeliers in the hallway and lounge to period furniture and ornate ceiling roses and cornices. To someone like László, who appreciated good craftsmanship, it was a sight to behold. On the streets outside were new styles of architecture and design not quite encountered before. His curiosity made him scrutinise many a Dublin building, especially in the Georgian quarter of the city.

Given their nationality, the proprietress was curious about their lives. Hungary was not a country that many Irish people had been familiar with until hearing about the plight of its refugees in 1956 and its status as a predominantly Catholic country. There certainly were religious links down through the ages, such as the Irish Madonna of Győr. This story originated with Bishop Walter Lynch of Clonfert who had fled Cromwellian forces during the seventeenth century, taking with him a treasured painting of the Virgin Mary praying over a sleeping Infant Jesus. Wandering across Europe, Bishop Lynch was given refuge by the sympathetic Bishop János Pusky of Győr – a city in western Hungary that Irén and László had passed through on their train journey to the border. The painting hung for decades over a side altar in the cathedral and was venerated by Hungarians in thanksgiving for victories over the Turks.

Little did the faithful think that an extraordinary event would unfold on St Patrick's Day in 1697. As mass was being celebrated in the cathedral, the painting started to shed tears of blood for three hours. Among the congregation who witnessed the startling event were a Protestant minister and a Jewish rabbi, who testified to what they saw. A linen cloth was used to wipe the tears away and was duly examined later. The subsequent investigation could offer no physical explanation at all.

By a strange coincidence, however, the previous day back in Ireland the Irish parliament had passed a law – one of the infamous Penal Laws – banishing all bishops, priests and religious from Ireland. It was widely believed that Our Lady in Győr was weeping tears of blood for the people of Ireland and its clergy at this terrible turn of events. News of the miracle spread, especially after receiving apostolic approval, and the faithful flocked to the cathedral. It became a place of pilgrimage down through the centuries and still is today. That said, many an Irish person was wholly unaware of the story. More than likely László and Irén, as lapsed Calvinist and Baptist respectively, were not acquainted with the story either.

It was natural that László and Irén's conversations with the proprietress would turn to the fate of the Hungarian refugees in Ireland over a decade earlier. It was a sad sorry tale, as they came to learn. Ireland had at first volunteered to take in a thousand refugees, though only about five hundred took up the offer in the end. In Traiskirchen transit camp in Vienna – where László and Irén had been briefly housed – officials of the Department of External Affairs had carefully selected which refugees would best assimilate into Irish life in terms of race and religion. Ireland as an island nation, it must be said, was quite insular and traditional at the time, and economically depressed. There was also a perception that the refugees were Catholics driven out by the communists.

The refugees' first introduction to Ireland was a wild, windswept and misty land – not dissimilar to László and Irén's. They came with nothing but a few pieces of clothes and some a handful of Hungarian soil. However, the country lived up to its reputation for hospitality when hundreds of people turned up to welcome them at Shannon Airport on 25 November 1956 and they dined on a hearty meal of goulash. The refugees were then transported to Knockalisheen Camp, a disused army summer camp in the village of Meelick, County Clare, not far from Limerick city. The camp, under the auspices of the Irish Red Cross, consisted of seventy-two small wooden huts surrounded by barbed wire that afforded little protection from the cold and damp of the Irish climate.

The Red Cross did its utmost to provide every possible comfort to the refugees and attend to their needs with clothing and essential items.

In addition, each family was given fifteen shillings per week as pocket money. As with the South Africans in László and Irén's case, Irish people generously donated money and goods for the refugee appeal. Businesses donated everything from sewing machines to soap to penicillin. One local company, Imco Cleaners, even sponsored a programme of Hungarian music on Radio Éireann. That no doubt would have impressed László had he been among their number.

The intention of the camp was to be a transit camp, from where families could move on once the quarantine period of two weeks was over. Gradually some refugees acquired work and were lodged with Irish families, many of whom were Catholics. Children were certainly welcome to live with Irish families but on the condition they would be raised as Catholics – this must surely have smacked of religious intolerance to the cosmopolitan Hungarians. The camp set up classes to teach the children English; however, the plan to admit them to local schools fell victim to bureaucracy. The cuisine was not to everyone's taste either – common ingredients in Hungarian dishes like poppy seeds, red peppers, sour cabbage and sweet spinach were not available in Ireland, so the refugees resorted to picking wild sorrel in the nearby fields to flavour their food. The Irish food also gave many of them diarrhoea. You could say dining wasn't always a pleasant affair.

Over the following weeks, the refugees tried to occupy their time in the camp by creating handmade items, such as wooden toys and crafts, and many sought work locally. The occupations of the refugees ranged from housewives to miners and textile workers to lawyers and doctors. Nonetheless, with the Irish employment situation at a very low ebb there was not much work to be had and opportunities were scarce. Those with professions, for example, legal and medical, were luckily able to secure employment early on and leave the camp. Stuck behind high walls and away from the local community, the remaining refugees – under four hundred – found they had too much time on their hands. Some grew impatient and angry, while others succumbed to depression when inertia and boredom set in. The so-called transit camp before long became a semi-permanent home, where they could not come and go as they pleased.

The Irish Red Cross had been tasked by the government to place the refugees in jobs and in accommodation. However, they were simply unable to place families beyond the camp. The refugees' frustration at the camp conditions, uncertainty and lack of prospects soon peaked and a hunger strike ensued in March/April 1957. The Irish government was faced with the very public embarrassment of having been ill-equipped to deal with the refugee situation. It was then forced to act, entreating countries like Canada and the US to come to its aid. In the end it fell to established churches, such as the Catholic Church and the Unitarian Church, to help resettle the refugees abroad through their international contacts. Hundreds of refugees moved on to Canada, America, Australia or back to other European countries. Rather tragically, the Irish government even paid for some Hungarians to return home to Hungary. How depressing and worrisome that must have been for those refugees. The sixty or so refugees that remained in the camp were finally housed in urban centres in Cork, Limerick and Dublin, some finding work in Youghal Carpets and other factories. After two years in existence Knockalisheen closed its doors in 1958, putting an end to a doleful episode in Irish affairs.

Music featured in a farewell concert, as remembered in an article in the *Irish Examiner* in 17 May 2011:

> The majority of Hungarian refugees were flown to Canada in 1958 but, before they left, a farewell concert was held…. Many prominent Limerick and Ennis entertainers provided their services for free at the concert. Musicians played traditional Hungarian and Irish music and the highlight was when both national anthems were sung in four languages by the Hungarian children's choir. At the end there were moving scenes as many Irish and Hungarians parted for the last time.

Music could certainly help heal many a wound, as László and Irén knew only too well. It must be remembered, though, that Ireland of the 1950s was an impoverished place and haemorrhaged half a million of her own people to foreign lands, notably Britain and the USA. It was seen as the worst decade since the Great Famine and regarded by historians as a 'lost decade'.

Hearing that only a handful of Hungarians had decided to remain in Ireland must have been cold comfort to László. Nevertheless, whatever their reservations, László was determined their own future would be different – no matter how long they decided to remain in Ireland. Perhaps the one thing that Irén learned from the tale was that in Ireland being a Catholic was a useful way of fitting in. In the absence of an embassy, there was no Hungarian community as such in Dublin to guide László and Irén in settling in and acclimatising to Irish ways. Some other Hungarians had come to Ireland during or after the war – availing of its neutrality status – and often escaping Jewish persecution. Many years later I remember László summing up the situation.

'The only Hungarians in Ireland are watchmakers!'

Many a foreign musician found work in the Radio Éireann Symphony Orchestra. It was often those playing wind and brass instruments that were highly sought after, seeing that there was a dearth of such musicians in the country. The tradition of classical music in Ireland, such as it was, had largely been confined to the string section. Among the Germans, Italians, Czechs, French and Yugoslav musicians employed during the 1960s were some of László's compatriots too: violinist and conductor János Fürst, timpanist János Keszei, bassist Jószef Rácz, and trumpeters Jószef Csibi and Szabolcs Vedres. But the most famous Hungarian of all had been conductor Tibor Paul.

Indeed professional musicians from Hungary seemed to have been universally welcome throughout the globe. The Hungarian Uprising had practically drained the country of its professionals, its students, its athletes and, most emphatically, its artists – essentially its talent. But exiled musicians had fought tooth and nail to make a living and preserve their identity and skills. One group of exiles had even founded the Philharmonia Hungarica in Stuttgart that in time gained an international reputation.

No longer a young man at fifty-four years of age, László now had the difficult task of starting out once more on a new life, in a new land, with new people. The length of time he had been advised to remain in Ireland is unclear. It's unlikely he would have been offered a permanent post in the Radio Éireann Symphony Orchestra given his age. I do believe that he was perhaps guided in his decision by Tibor Paul, with whom he still corresponded. They understood each other very well, displayed mutual respect and had similar personalities – though László was a lot less forceful a character than Tibor. By the time László and Irén had arrived in Dublin in 1969, Tibor and his wife had returned to Australia for good. Ireland's loss was Sydney's gain, more specifically, the Elizabethan Theatre Trust Orchestra.

László became fully acquainted with the music scene and Tibor's legacy. Tibor's contract with Radio Teilifís Éireann (RTÉ), as the broadcaster was now known, had not been renewed under highly controversial circumstances and had been played out in public. Much of the problem stemmed from Tibor having had dual roles: both as principal conductor of the orchestra and director of music for the broadcaster. Often the roles raised conflicts of interest and required different temperaments, aside from being two full-time jobs. As far as I could gather, Tibor was your stereotypical sensitive, passionate artist, given to outbursts and furies and a perfectionist. Yet he had touches of genius and brilliance too – a real maestro. He moved mountains to raise the standing of the RTÉ Symphony Orchestra worldwide and made the 1960s an exciting time for classical music in Ireland.

Tibor was as much disliked as admired. With his movie star looks, tallness and sleek black hair, he had women swooning in the front rows, according to trumpeter Jószef Csibi. Tibor's manner – arrogant and temperamental – often did not endear him to his colleagues. He was territorial about his players too and hindered them engaging in freelance work, demanding their full commitment to the work of the orchestra. It was not uncommon for him to berate and rebuke them in front of their colleagues, much to their chagrin. His high-handedness resulted in many musicians, including his compatriots, leaving the orchestra, disgruntled and disenchanted. The most serious exodus occurred when the Ulster Orchestra was established in 1966 and Tibor was forced to urgently look elsewhere for replacements. Hence, the letter of appeal for musicians that László had received in South Africa.

One of the most desirable qualities in a conductor is that of preserving an esprit de corps. It seems Tibor did fall down on the score, to pardon the pun. It was perhaps inevitable that his controversial nature would force RTÉ to remove him from the post of director of music during 1966 and fail to renew his resident conductorship contract, or rather to offer him only guest conductorships. The shock was so great that it brought on a heart attack and Tibor was hospitalised; however, he thankfully made a good recovery. RTÉ's handling of the entire affair provoked public criticism and the matter was raised in Dáil Éireann!

For all his faults, Tibor Paul was responsible for ushering in a golden age of classical music in Ireland. His legacy was remarkable. From the moment he arrived he brought great energy and dynamism to his work. Guest conductors/composers and soloists from Stravinsky to Rostropovich and Segovia to Menuhin first stepped foot on Irish soil at his persistent invitations and wowed audiences. In fact, Stravinsky's visit in 1963 was so significant that he was granted an audience with the President of Ireland, Éamon de Valera, in Áras an Uachtaráin. Although Madame Stravinsky's tardy hair appointment meant she had to forego the pleasure!

Under Tibor's baton there were many firsts for the Radio Éireann Symphony Orchestra. It performed overseas at the Royal Festival Hall in London in late 1966, joining the lustrous Prague Symphony Orchestra, the BBC Symphony Orchestra, the English Chamber Orchestra and the Hallé Orchestra. How exciting that must have been for an Irish orchestra! Tibor's programme was drawn from favourites of his, Bartók, Brahms and Mahler, and was well received. Now Ireland could hold its own among world-renowned orchestras. Like László, Tibor had a particular appreciation of Beethoven, perhaps for the prominence the composer gave to wind instruments in his symphonies. The end of Tibor's tenure during 1967 was marked by the Beethoven cycle, his swansong concerts. It is said that Beethoven too pushed his players to the extreme and made intolerable demands on them. All in the service of great music!

Native composers, such as Brian Boydell, Seán Ó Riada and Seóirse Bodley, were not overlooked by Tibor. For example, he conducted the world premiere of Boydell's commemorative cantata 'A Terrible Beauty is Born' in the Gaiety Theatre on the fiftieth anniversary of the 1916 Easter Rising in 1966 to critical acclaim. Tibor's achievements were not all confined to Dublin either. The Limerick Choral Union was co-founded by him in 1964, where he led the first Irish performances of Mozart's Requiem (that included Bernadette Greevy as soloist), Beethoven's Missa Solemnis and Janáček's Glagolitic Mass.

Against this backdrop, László had to decide on the future direction of his career. It does seem likely that he met with the new director of music, Gerard Victory, and the new principal conductor, the Austrian-born Czech musician, Albert Rosen. Age was not on László's side, as I mentioned, and job security was a pressing concern. It was hard to believe that in the mid-1960s half of the orchestra players were foreigners. László knew that situation would not last indefinitely as the talents of native Irish musicians were nurtured and developed. He had witnessed something similar in South Africa. Perhaps too the pay and conditions in Dublin were not as generous as those in Johannesburg.

László had also expected the city to have more music venues and was surprised that it was without a dedicated concert hall or opera house. In fact, at the time there were many unsuitable venues in Dublin from an acoustics point of view. The rehearsal space for the orchestra and studio then was in the Saint Francis Xavier (SFX) Hall on Upper Sherrard Street in Dublin's north inner city. Many musicians found the place dreary and depressing, though large enough to hold several hundred people. Over the years, other venues were relied upon to host special symphonic concerts such as the Gaiety Theatre, the RDS Members' Hall, or even the Adelphi Cinema when Stravinsky had come to town. It would be another decade before the National Concert Hall on Earlsfort Terrace opened its doors to music lovers.

László realised there was no great concert-going tradition in Ireland, except for a minority. With little demand for orchestral music in the country, jobs were scarce. However, thanks to Tibor Paul, the country was viewed by international artists as less the musical backwater it once had been. From Tibor, László he knew that RTÉ had faced a dilemma when it came to broadcasting: trying to preserve Irish traditional values, especially folk music, and embracing modernisation by exposing Irish audiences to symphonic music. There was tension as taut as a violin string.

＊

All this uncertainty and lack of employment swirled around László's head. He finally decided against seeking employment as a professional musician or becoming involved in another large orchestra. Even so, it did not stop him from embarking upon a new venture some time later – chamber music. As far as I can remember, Tibor Paul had encouraged him to create a small musical ensemble, an octet or perhaps a quartet, and to play for pleasure. I am unsure of the exact composition of the ensemble, but I believe it featured at a minimum the clarinet, cello, piano and violin. Naturally, László played clarinet and the group possibly included some professional musicians.

The name of the ensemble is unknown to me as are the names of its musicians, with one exception. Dr Alex Tomkin was a young ophthalmologist at the Royal Eye and Ear Hospital on nearby Adelaide Road and a pioneer of contact lenses, who played the cello. László had been introduced to Alex by his father, Dr Harris Tomkin, a learned Jewish ophthalmologist who also co-founded Stratford College in Rathgar. When his eyesight began to trouble him, László had attended the Eye and Ear Hospital and Harris had treated him. In fact, other than requiring reading glasses, László's sight was excellent. With his keen eyesight and exceptionally quick reflexes, no insects were in fact safe. Indeed, he could catch a midget in mid-air, as I often saw him do.

A close friendship blossomed between László and Harris. One of the kindest doctors László had ever come across, the man spent sixty years giving exceptional care to the people of Dublin. By coincidence, the plight of refugees was an abiding concern of his, and he had been vice-chairman of the Jewish Refugee Aid Committee of Éire when it was established back in 1938. All that László had endured under Nazism and communism could certainly be comprehended by the benevolent doctor.

Harris's son Alex was certainly following in his father's footsteps, although had circumstances been different he would have pursued a musical career. As far as I can gather, the ensemble played weekly, while László also gave lessons to Alex to finesse his playing. The young doctor was a keen musician and quite accomplished having played cello with the London Medical Orchestra in his spare time. In 1972, Alex married Julia Hajnal from Hungary, so you could say the Hungarian influences were strong in that family. Alex practised the cello daily even after the birth of his three children, but he sadly died at the age of forty-seven in 1984. He had been involved in a number of quartets over the years, one of which included Tom McDaid and Louis Marcus, who both played violin.

Julia remembers László as being quite despondent over his music career in those early years in Ireland. He was disappointed and bitter at how his career had been destroyed by the communists, as I later came to understand. He was also experiencing dental problems at the time that may have forced him to abandon the clarinet for a spell. It's quite common indeed for those playing the clarinet or saxophone to put a lot of pressure on their lower lip to support the weight of the instrument and over time this can lead to teeth misalignment. In fact, any changes to teeth, lips, gums or jaw can affect the quality, tone, range and dynamics of the sound when playing. All his life László had been particular about dentistry, ensuring his teeth were even and promptly repaired – he had a mouth full of gold fillings to prove it!

The mechanical act of playing must have caused him some distress. Alex did everything in his power to encourage László to return to playing. He invited him to lunch at his home in Mount Merrion and slowly started to play the piano to whet his appetite. It seemed to have worked because the next time László came for lunch he brought his clarinet.

More than likely László's ensemble played at Harris's home, Clontra, an enchanting manor house in Shankill, overlooking Killiney Bay. It was built in an Italian Gothic style by Irish architects Thomas Newenham Deane and Benjamin Woodward in 1862. The upstairs drawing room was ideal for chamber music with its charming oriel window and high vaulted, frescoed ceilings and timbered beams. A dreamy romantic mood permeated the room thanks to the Pre-Raphaelite frescos of decorative artist John Hungerford Pollen depicting the Seven Ages of Woman as well as exotic birds and flowers. Most likely the soirées were frequented by Harris's family and circle of friends, all music devotees and some fine musicians themselves.

László very quickly realised that a long-term secure source of income had to be provided and one where music did not feature. The ensemble could never be a means of existence. László had to look in a completely different direction, yet in one way when he surveyed his skills it was not entirely foreign to him. So while one door was closing, another was opening. It was time for his engineering brain and skills as a craftsman to have their day. He had in mind to purchase a large property and convert it into small apartments or rather bedsits – a new word he came to learn in time. László planned to do most of the renovation work himself. There was much in his favour despite his age: an abundance of talent, energy, courage and determination.

In the 1960s the city was looking rather forlorn where its buildings were concerned. The rundown buildings were like decaying teeth across the cityscape and it was hard to credit that Dublin had once been the second city in the British Empire. The redbrick, the calp limestone and Portland stone of its once elegant buildings were now looking neglected and unloved. Many of the fine Georgian residences were no more than tenements in inner city slums. By the end of the 1960s over half of the Georgian buildings on St Stephen's Green had been demolished. In those days the value of conservation and protecting our heritage was not appreciated as it is today. There was a headlong rush to sweep away the old and put modern concrete office blocks in their stead – often motivated by greedy developers. However, László could appreciate the beauty of Georgian houses as homes; as he saw it they could be converted into proper apartments or flats with some hard work and dedication.

There was also a demand for flats given the times. Free secondary-school education had been introduced in Ireland in 1966, so there was an influx of students attending university in the 1970s. Choosing a suitable location was key, though. The proprietress of Kilronan House was of invaluable assistance to László and Irén in this respect, pointing out that Adelaide Road and its environs were particularly suitable. University College

Dublin was situated close by on Earlsfort Terrace and the Royal College of Surgeons and Trinity College were within walking distance for any student or potential tenant.

* * *

While László waited for a suitable investment property to present itself, he struck upon another idea to make a living. He was a born survivor after all, resourceful to his fingertips. Using money he had saved as capital, he bought a taxi licence as well as three cars and hired three drivers. One of the first things he had done after arriving in the city – as indeed in Vienna and Johannesburg – was to get a local driving licence. No doubt the proprietress of Kilronan had suggested there was a shortage of taxis in Dublin, and László had seized upon the notion with typical verve and gusto.

At the time there were about fourteen hundred taxis in the capital and demand was rising, thanks to an improved economy, population and tourism growth, and the creation of new suburbs. The idea then was not so madcap for a musician. After all, László was a good driver himself, never without a car, had the skills of a mechanic, and on one occasion back in Budapest had taken a defective car apart and restored it to good working order. Add to that his good business head and a keen sense of direction. I have no idea how he managed to get a licence in the days before deregulation when licence plates were tightly controlled. I believe it could cost around three thousand pounds to transfer a licence from one owner to another in those days.

Whatever obstacles László faced, he somehow managed to overcome them and luck was on his side. No matter the fare he took on, there were stories and tales galore. On one occasion an American priest came to Ireland looking for relatives of a deceased parishioner who had left behind quite a fortune. László ended up driving him the length and breadth of the country but all to no avail. No relatives were ever found to claim the inheritance and the priest duly returned to the USA. No-one would have ever believed the priest back home that he had been chauffeured around the country by a Hungarian musician! As for finding his way about, László knew Dublin inside out, even better than myself. A wonderful road map of Ireland was in his possession, indeed one of many, which I still use to this day, and he relied upon it greatly. He could drive anywhere and never once lost his way.

What his Dublin drivers made of László I do not know. I can't imagine he would have joined in in their banter and notorious pontificating and have reciprocated their laid-back attitude. That's not to say László had no sense of humour because he certainly could smile if something funny happened, but he was not given to gales of laughter and could never make a joke. In fact, laughter did not come easy to him at all and in our many years together I never heard him laugh once.

While running the taxi business he clapped eyes on his ideal investment property just across the street. Number 15 Adelaide Road had just come on the market. By now the plans to move to England seemed to be in abeyance. The building was Georgian in style, three-storey over basement and László made an immediate offer. True to his nature, if he wanted something he could not rest until it was his. Once the property was purchased László and Irén both moved in and occupied the ground floor. Of the previous occupants, I have no knowledge, other than those who lived there in the early twentieth century. In the 1900s, William Payne, a retired railway manager from County Wexford lived there with his wife Mary, English nieces Jane Massington and Margaret Guilmant along with their cook Jane Archer and housemaid Annie Hickey.

I remember László telling me how hard he and Irén worked converting the building into flats. It was the start of a new adventure for them, familiar with apartment buildings and what was required for city living. Irén made all the curtains and arranged the furnishings, while László, room by room, installed small kitchens, electric coin meters, heating system, and bathrooms at the end of each corridor. The cold experienced in the large draughty Georgian rooms reminded him of the chilly living conditions that greeted him in his early days in Budapest. For this reason, he lowered the ceilings for the warmth and comfort of tenants.

The tools and machinery needed for this work were purchased from McQuillans of Capel Street in Dublin. Having built up a workshop in each city where he lived – alas always having to leave tools behind

– László knew exactly what was required. This workshop included a vast array of equipment: saws and an enormous sawing machine, lathes, drills, hand tools, and so forth. Even the skill of plumbing was not beyond him, having learned the rudiments from his father. He became such a frequenter of McQuillans that he was soon firm friends with the proprietor and grateful for any advice he might offer. As ever, László created a well-stocked workshop for himself; this time at the rear of the building on Adelaide Road.

Following six months or so of sheer hard work, all the rooms in this building were in order and ready for occupancy. Some fourteen bedsits of different sizes had been created. With advertisements placed in the daily newspapers and also on the notice boards of nearby universities – 'Lettings available' – all were quickly snapped up. Sometimes the parents of young students would first come to inspect the premises and also to interview László. He greatly enjoyed this aspect of the business, as he met some very interesting people and also a few odd ones. It was an incredible achievement for a professional musician, but he was no ordinary man. He was multitalented and had an enormous capacity for work, which I was later to witness myself. His friends would remind me of this fact over and over again.

The house occupied all of László's time, even when the tenants moved in, and he loathed when anything fell into disrepair and if the house was nothing less than spotless. In fact, some of the antics of the tenants quite horrified him; he once had to scrape copious layers of grease off the floor after one tenant vacated the premises, while another bypassed the electricity meter and hooked himself directly up to László and Irén's own supply on the ground floor. László literally blew a gasket on finding out and promptly asked the tenant to leave. All grist to the mill for landlords. That said, he loved the house on Adelaide Road and was very proud of all that he had achieved.

After several months running the taxi business, László decided to sell it, as it was not working to his satisfaction. A row had developed between him and the drivers; perhaps they had taken exception to his very precise way of operating and, admittedly, he could get hot-headed at times.

Perhaps his frugality and workaholism – and expecting others to follow suit – might have played some part as well. Either way, the Adelaide Road house was now set up as his sole business and he and Irén could live off the rental income for the future.

* * *

As László settled into the role of landlord, he and Irén still kept in touch with family and friends abroad. The letters from Debrecen did not always bear good news. Sadly, poor health had dogged his brother István and he died in 1972 aged just fifty-three years. Tibor Paul was to die the following year in November 1973. Ironically, he had returned two days earlier from a trip to South Africa, where he had conducted orchestras both in Johannesburg and Pretoria. A second heart attack claimed his life, at the age of sixty-four. It was an untimely death and deeply lamented by László. While today the name of Tibor Paul may be largely forgotten in Ireland, his legacy lives on at the Royal Irish Academy of Music where the Tibor Paul Medal is now awarded to outstanding piano students.

Incidentally, helping students was something that always motivated László. While in Ireland, as he had in Budapest and Johannesburg, he gave music lessons to those who sought him out – especially the piano, violin, clarinet and saxophone. It provided a very modest income but was welcome all the same.

Writing letters to Budapest and Debrecen was always a touch hazardous for László, as it meant the Hungarian authorities could keep track of his and Irén's whereabouts. The authorities duly contacted him, and indeed countless other Hungarian refugees, inviting him once again to return to Hungary. They stated that László would not face persecution or prosecution back in his homeland and could enjoy a life of full freedom, or words to that effect. Yet László was not won over. Not only was it too late but great fear, suspicion and unease still existed at the very thought of the USSR. He could see no abatement of Soviet power at all. In neighbouring Czechoslovakia, for example, the joy at the new liberalism embodied in the Prague Spring of 1968 was only to be crushed by Soviet tanks rolling into the city six months later. It was a timely reminder and only reinforced

László's opinion. By now he realised and had convinced himself that he would never return to his native land.

* * *

László was now in effect a businessman. With that came all the joys of paying taxes and navigating the Irish taxation system. Pounds, shillings and pence were soon a thing of the past and decimalisation arrived. New taxes came in the wake of Ireland joining the European Economic Community (EEC) in November 1972; value added tax (VAT) was being charged on goods making such items as tools more expensive for László. He tried to work out his own taxes initially, but at some point decided to hand the task over to a professional. Trusting people did not come easy to him, so it must have been with some trepidation that he approached a firm of accountants on St Stephen's Green around 1974.

There he met with tax adviser Helen Murphy, who made a favourable impression on him. As he did on her. He was neatly dressed in a suit, waistcoat and tie and carried his trademark headwear, a grey Tyrolean hat. Everything about László pointed to a sense of order and perfection. He addressed her with great courtesy as was his wont and explained how his tax affairs were not complex with rental income being his only source of revenue. Once Helen had discussed all the arrangements and the charging structure with him, they shook hands; László went on his way and she went back to work. To her surprise, as she left the building that evening, László stood outside waiting for her. He was still as immaculately dressed as earlier in the day and quickly drew her aside.

'Can I help you, Mr Gede?' she asked. 'Is everything all right?'

Looking her full in the face, he came straight to the point.

'Mrs Murphy, I would like *you* to look after my taxes,' he began, 'as a private client.'

It transpired that László was not prepared to pay large fees to an accountancy firm and wanted a more personal, one-to-one relationship where his taxes were concerned. Having met Helen who impressed him, he was certain that he had found the right person. In his judgment she was someone of great integrity and honesty. His request took her aback, though, and she did not readily agree to it. She was quickly learning that László was a very determined man; once he set his mind on something, he did not give up easily. After a quick chat, she agreed to consider his offer and they exchanged phone numbers. A few days later, he rang her at home in Blackrock. Finally, she agreed to look after his taxes and to make sure everything was correct and above board. This was the start of a long business relationship.

For her part, Helen recalls that László was very intense and had a precision in the way he handled his affairs. A scrupulousness underlined all his business dealings; he retained receipts for everything down to the smallest nails and screws purchased and paid his bills with an astonishing promptness. His accounts, when handed over to Helen, would never have a figure wrong. Indeed Helen, in considering his abilities, often felt that he could easily manage his own tax affairs, but László had neither time nor effort to devote to them. In fact, László was exacting in all matters, be it music, taxes or the renovation of the Adelaide Road house. His taxes would be finalised and paid long before they fell due. Always on time for an appointment, it was unheard of that he would be unpunctual.

As time progressed they became good friends. It was clear to Helen that he did not trust people easily yet once you had earned his trust you were a friend for life. Living under communism had scarred him in that respect; even family members and friends were not above suspicion in that regime. Yet in a strange way it made László a good judge of character.

Over the years there were many topics of conversation between them: his love of music, how much he regarded and respected Tibor Paul, his travels, the horrors of communism and his hatred of it, having to climb over barbed wire when fleeing Hungary, and how their memories of South Africa had been soured by apartheid. Yet László, true to form, did not tell her about his imprisonment. Some things were just too personal, too painful to mention, and he was a master at pigeonholing his life. Though he rarely spoke about other people, he did give Helen the impression that Marie was his own daughter.

Marie had paid a visit to Ireland since her mother had settled in the country. At the time Marie was on her way from South Africa to Canada, where she was heading to start a new life as a psychiatrist. The joy for Irén at being reunited with her daughter was short-lived, however. Having spent some time with them in Dublin, Marie sadly fell out with László over her requests for money and László deeming her to be ungrateful. Even so, László could never be ungracious and later drove her all the way to Shannon Airport to catch her flight to Canada.

To Helen, László also appeared to be a rather lonely, melancholic and troubled man, deeply hurt by the communist regime. It had clearly taken a toll on him. She felt that he had experienced great sadness but great joy too during his lifetime. When they spoke of classical music – a shared interest – his eyes sparkled. His overwhelming understanding of the great composers, such as Beethoven and Bach, and his appreciation of music were envied by Helen. Wherever he went, people were always struck by László. To Helen he was a genius – a most extraordinary man, the most unusual and most interesting person she had met in her lifetime, and one never to be forgotten. There seemed no end to his intelligence and talents: businessman, craftsman, musician, music teacher, conductor and composer. The only pity was the music he had adapted in Budapest had never been recorded or had reached a wider audience.

* * *

Converting the house on Adelaide Road into small flats had proved a success and was providing a guaranteed rental income. The house was full of life, with students coming and going, though occasionally it grew quite noisy. It was only a matter of time before László and Irén would vacate their flat in favour of something more tranquil. It was inevitable too, knowing how much László found apartment life difficult. It was a pattern that wove its way through his life from Budapest to Johannesburg to Dublin. Detached houses in quiet suburbs were his mecca, where he could open a door and walk out into his garden, undisturbed by neighbours.

And so they set about finding a property to purchase for themselves. During the early 1970s a small housing estate called Cherrington Road was being built in Shankill, a small village close to the sea in south County Dublin. On one of their visits to Dr Tomkins's house Clontra, he and Irén had spotted the construction under way. László, having met the builder and examined the plans, decided to purchase one of these semi-detached houses, or rather a detached house in László's case. Both he and Irén at this stage were captivated by Ireland and had decided to stay. To them, the climate may not have been appealing but the people certainly were.

'In all my travels,' he recalled. 'I never came across a more friendly or kindly race of people.'

The Irish reputation for openness and friendliness and of being great communicators he could by all means avow.

The couple was no sooner installed in Cherrington, however, but László had more plans to extend it, building a balcony along the first floor and gable wall safeguarded by an ornate railing. Homes were always a work in progress!

A relocation to England, as originally intended, was completely out of the question by now; they were determined to make Ireland their home. Having carried 'stateless' passports since their escape from Hungary, they both now felt they should bring closure on the past. As long as they remained in Ireland, however, they would legally be considered as 'aliens'. Around this time they duly applied for Irish citizenship. This entailed producing proof that they had the means to support themselves and thus would not be a burden on the State, which of course they were able to do. Their applications were most likely sponsored by friends in Dublin, possibly Mr McQuillan. They luckily did not have to wait too long before being granted Irish citizenship.

Ireland at last had become their true home; they now felt that they could breathe easily, confining their 'stateless' and 'alien' labels to the past. One significant benefit of holding an Irish passport was that Irén could safely travel to Hungary and back on a holiday visa to visit her sister. This she did on several occasions and, though tinged with sadness as her parents were now dead, she relished seeing her sister Etelka and brother-in-law Béla and their married daughter Monika, encouraging them to reciprocate the visits. The same could not be said for László, however; his fear and distrust of communism overrode all others and he remained at home.

One Hungarian trumpeter, Jószef (Joe) Csibi, had rejoiced in gaining Irish citizenship. Having been recruited by Tibor Paul in Budapest to play for the Radio Éireann Symphony Orchestra, and receiving a visa from the communist authorities, he had arrived in Dublin in 1964. After eighteen months and a thoroughly enjoyable time in the city, he received a letter from embassy officials recalling him home by a certain date. He wrote to say that he could not possibly return as he had a concert pending and could not leave at such short notice. Sometime later another letter arrived reiterating the request. Again Joe responded saying he had a contract with the orchestra and had to honour his commitments. Finally, he was issued with a demand to report to a certain barracks in the city, bringing two changes of underwear, where he would be deported. Needless to say, Joe ignored it and stayed put!

Whatever his reservations about Hungary, it did not stop László from travelling abroad. He and Irén visited Italy, taking in the sights of Venice, Florence, Rome and Naples. Venice, in particular, struck a chord with him because it reminded him of Dublin, especially its ornate nineteenth-century Ha'penny Bridge. László spoke of this pedestrianised bridge as being rather Venetian in character, actually Dublin as a whole, with its canals and little streets and some of its architecture. The Liffey flowing beneath, with its ever-changing shades of green, sharply divided the city much like the Danube in Budapest. Dublin even had its own Grand Canal, though not as splendid as Venice's, which flowed not far from his house on Adelaide Road.

He and Irén also holidayed in Portugal, taking a welcome respite from the inclement Irish weather. The climate appealed to them so much they once toyed with the idea of relocating there, but obviously changed their minds. Trips were also possibly made to the shop of Henri Selmer Paris, the famous manufacturer of professional woodwind and brass instruments, especially saxophones, clarinets and trumpets, or its London branch on Charing Cross Road. Benny Goodman had been a patron of the Parisian shop from his early years, so what was good for the goose was certainly good for the gander. From Selmer's, László had purchased French Boehm clarinets and mouthpieces, and had fallen in love with Paris in the process.

The Boehm clarinets produced a slightly different but, some would say, delightful sound. From his earliest days in Debrecen and Budapest, László was used to the German/Viennese Oehler system – it had a hard reed and a narrow bore and fewer keys, giving a much deeper sound, almost like a cello, and less overtones than other systems. It is said that these clarinets gave perfect expression to German repertoires from Beethoven to Brahms. From listening to these composers and László's own views, I would tend to agree with that view.

The Boehm clarinet had a lighter, sharper sound, a more high-pitched tone, as I remember. I'm not sure exactly when László started buying clarinets from Selmer's. The trend of Boehm clarinets becoming the standard in modern orchestras had begun in the postwar period. I suspect that when László joined the State Opera House in 1945 he was already in transition, instrument-wise. Perhaps he had also realised the limitations of the German clarinets as a jazz musician when playing with Goldwin Gede before the war. Around 1952, the Selmer centred tone clarinet was launched, with its trademark large bore and endorsed by Benny Goodman himself. László purchased this full sounding clarinet with its deep woody tones at a cost of around seventy guineas each, possibly when he was in South Africa. It would last him for decades.

With every passing year in Ireland, László acclimatised to the Irish and grew to love its way of life. A far deeper understanding of Irish culture was born. Perhaps that is why he eschewed moving to Portugal for its sunny climes. There was a Hungarian perception that the Irish were rather simple people who just loved their country. There was no denying the patriotism of the Irish, which was something that László could appreciate. Irish patriots, from Daniel O'Connell to Arthur Griffith, had looked to Hungary for inspiration in their day. All held that Central European country in high esteem for its revolutionary thought and action.

László came to realise that Irish people had quite a different culture but equally valuable. High culture, the kind so prevalent throughout Old Europe – the appreciation of art and literature, classical music and architecture – in Ireland had been enjoyed by a minority. László and Irén regularly attended and enjoyed many of the concerts that Dublin had to offer at the time. Yet, as a fledgling democracy, Ireland was finding its feet and learning to appreciate other forms of expression. There was many a link between Ireland and Hungary. After all, one of the most celebrated figures in English literature, Leopold Bloom created by James Joyce, was the son of a fictionalised emigrant Hungarian Jew, Virág Rudolf, born in the town of Szombathely, the oldest recorded city in Hungary. Irish traditional music appealed to László too, feeling its importance much like Bartók had of Hungarian folk music and how it could influence classical music. Once on a drive to Shannon Airport he made a detour to Bunratty Castle, where he feasted on traditional airs and tunes – never to be forgotten.

* * *

The success of renovating the interior of the Adelaide Road house spurred László on. He was gifted at DIY and brought a craftsman's eye to every task. Furniture-making was within his powers too using the best of wood and the finest finishes. It was astonishing to see what he produced – dressers, cabinets, tables that would not have looked out of place in a bespoke furniture shop. By now he had converted his garage in Shankill into a massive workshop equipped with all the tools needed for a master craftsman – woodwork, metal lathes, welding equipment, and so on. He seemed to rise to the challenge each time. It still amazes me just what he turned his hand to: constructing enormous black wrought-iron gates for the owner of a garage in Cabinteely and repairing a crumbling stone balcony in Clontra. Because of its unique features, Clontra was a listed building so László had to be mindful of its preservation and the integrity of the house. Gerald Tomkins, another of Harris's sons, remembers László carving the stone balcony with great skill, careful that the loading and weighting were correct and that its pierced quatrefoil was restored.

One of the things László missed most in Ireland was his dog Roy. This pet had been such a positive fixture in their Northcliff house in South Africa, imbuing the place with energy and spirit. Now that László and Irén were living in Shankill with plenty of room to house a large German Shepherd, he promptly bought one and named him Roy too.

László just adored this pet. Through Roy he came in contact with Argyle & Bainbridge, a veterinary clinic that had just set up in Ballsbridge. Over the years he became friends with the vets, Malcolm Argyle and John Bainbridge, and their staff. With his active, ordered mind and a desire to help, László once designed and made a filing system for their establishment. I have learnt recently that this filing system is still in use today, called 'The Gede File'! It certainly was a throwback to the day László walked into the Jewish music store in Budapest and kindly offered to upgrade Mr Weisz's filing system.

László's creative spirit and imagination lent themselves not only to music but industrial design too. Many engineering and design projects filled his days and László felt at home in this milieu. After all, he had mixed with engineers and technicians when he had conducted the Ganz Works Orchestra back in Budapest as a young man. It comes as no surprise then that he worked with the Electricity Supply Board (ESB) on various projects during the 1970s. This most likely came about from his friendship with the McQuillans. He designed, or helped to design, various lifting equipment for the ESB, such as a type of lift or small crane whereby the worker could repair a streetlight safely. László also fitted out the ESB work vans with aluminium tool trays and shelves. There was also the matter of shopfronts, display cabinets and shelves built for businesses in Cabinteely, a suburb not too far from his home in Shankill.

You could say that László was a lateral thinker, who looked at a problem and used his imagination to fix it. Any kind of device that would help save a worker's health or hold or move heavy equipment or machinery was worth pursuing. There seemed no end to László's talents or his genius at reinvention.

8.

PARTING OF THE WAYS

What are the ways of this man's soul?
What course has he chosen, what goal,
wandering
where only madmen and demigods dare
or can soar?

From 'The Apostle' by Sándor Petőfi

IF their lives were now happy and blessed, then sadness was soon to engulf László and Irén once more. In early 1976, Irén began to feel unwell. On visiting her doctor and following many tests, bowel cancer was discovered. For the next few years she was in and out of Saint Vincent's Private Hospital, where she underwent surgery and various treatments. Sadly, all to no avail; the cancer continued to spread throughout her body. It was as a staff nurse employed at the hospital that I first encountered László and Irén. I had been working there for several years and had found my niche in nursing.

My nursing career had come about, firstly, because my godmother, Aunt Ida, whom I held in great affection, was a staff nurse herself, at what was then St Kevin's Hospital but later became St James's Hospital in Dublin. Ida possessed the same sunny disposition as her sister Sheila. I can remember as a child, Grandmother Maddison, my maternal grandmother, chatting to my mother over a morning coffee.

'Ida, late into dinner once again last night,' my grandmother tutted.

'She adores her patients,' replied my mother, nodding, 'and finds it difficult to leave anyone who is dying.'

My dear aunt was like so many young women, a devoted and caring staff nurse, and I always wished to emulate her. Secondly, at the age of twenty-three, I had been feeling unfulfilled with life until my sister's mother-in-law and close family friend, Patricia Egan, intervened. Just as László had been encouraged by his Uncle Bara, I too had my champions. It was Patricia, a woman of Scottish-Presbyterian descent with a great heart, who encouraged me to follow my dream and apply for nursing and see how I liked it.

But for Patricia's advice, I might never have met László and Irén. You can imagine, in a nursing career, that over the years I would have met countless patients and their families; it would be hard to single out any of them. Yet I can still vividly recall that first occasion when I met László. One afternoon in 1976, Irén had been admitted to a single room on the third floor of the hospital for treatment. With her routine observation checks due, I knocked on her door and entered to find László at her bedside – her husband and my future one. As I look back now, Irén was most particular in introducing him to me.

'László, László, here is Eibhlín,' she urged. 'You remember I told you about Eibhlín.'

My eyes rested upon a gentle yet strong countenance, embracing brilliant pale blue eyes that returned my gaze with deep gratitude. That encounter was tremendously powerful and its impact has not lessened with the passing years.

I can remember at that time just how caring a husband László was. Visiting daily, his kindness and dedication to his wife struck me rather forcefully and staff at the hospital often remarked upon it. Every afternoon he would arrive without fail bringing a fresh nightdress for her, neatly ironed and folded, along with other items that she might require. If there were any concerns about her care, he would come to the nurse's station to quietly discuss them with the staff, not leaving until he was satisfied. There was no haranguing of staff, mind you, just uxorious care and compassion. Nothing less than a private room would suffice for the woman he clearly adored.

As the months and years progressed and Irén was in and out of hospital, he never failed to care for his ailing wife. On one occasion he was greatly distressed by her condition and nothing would reassure him but to have the surgeon come from the operating theatre in the adjacent public hospital and hear him speak. Most days were spent sitting by her bedside keeping her company while she rested or read.

All her life Irén was fastidious and conscious of her appearance, ensuring her clothes were of the finest quality. Even as the disease took its toll and she became more debilitated, she continued to be well-presented. Her style was one of simple chic and understated elegance; unfussy clothes set off by high heels and handbags and tasteful jewellery; hair perfectly coiffed and her face flawlessly made up. With her body ravaged more and more by cancer, however, Irén became rather nervous and sad of soul. It became harder and harder for her to raise a smile. As nurses, we did our very best to make her feel cared for and special. Sometimes Irén would rally a little when we made a fuss of her; we did everything in our power to make her life a little brighter. On one occasion, when I was carrying out some nursing task, she suddenly burst into tears.

'I miss my daughter, my Marie,' she sobbed uncontrollably. 'If only I could see her again.'

I instinctively placed my arms around her and cradled her for a few moments until she calmed down. My colleagues and I had no idea or understanding of her life's journey, but did our best for her and, as with all our patients, made efforts to minimise her loneliness and isolation. In hindsight, I could understand why Irén was missing her daughter. Time was running out for Irén. By now her daughter Marie had flourished in the city of Hamilton, Ontario, where she had built a successful career as a psychiatrist, was married and had two children.

In the early 1980s Irén had written to Marie asking her to come and visit her as she was quiet ill. The cancer had now spread. In waiting for her daughter, however, Irén waited in vain. It was not possible for Marie to come given her heavy work commitments and the demands of a busy household. Marie was not long in her job as assistant clinical professor in the Department of Psychiatry at McMaster University at that time. Incredibly, Irén willed herself to regain some strength and made the long trip to Canada alone. It always astounds me how the human spirit has reserves far beyond our comprehension. After this visit, regardless of the drain on her energies, Irén appeared calmer and more at peace. Perhaps getting to see her grandchildren had been a boost too, spotting family resemblances and seeing another generation look to the future.

There had been much contact with Irén's relatives over the years. The thaw in East–West relations in Hungary during the mid-1960s meant that Irén's niece Monika was able to travel abroad in subsequent years. She and her husband Friedrich and children, among them Gyula, landed in Ireland during the 1970s and early 1980s. Trips abroad took months of planning and Hungarians were only allowed outside the Soviet Bloc once every three years. They had to get a visa for every country they landed in or travelled overland. That must have been an administrative nightmare for them, filling out endless forms and dealing with bureaucratic officials. That said, Hungary in comparison to other Eastern Bloc countries had a relatively high standard of living and had more relaxed travel restrictions. There was even a joke that Hungary was the best country to live in during the Cold War. These visits were always a great boost to Irén, all the more so when her visitors could see how successfully she had settled in Ireland.

Irén too had a cousin, Peter Czibula, who was married with a family and living in the city of Echternach in eastern Luxembourg. Peter along with his wife Patricia and children occasionally visited László and Irén in Dublin. László soon came to know this family quite well and a whole lot more in the years to come.

* * *

In April 1976, around the time I first met László, my own beloved mother died quite suddenly. Her health had never been robust and had declined over the years. Although heartbroken, I worked my way through my grief and hopefully did not display too much of my own sorrow in front of the patients. My mother had been such a life force and for a while I felt as if the life within me had gone too. It took all my strength to stave off a breakdown. My time off duty was taken up with caring for my ageing father in the family home on Dufferin Avenue, off the South Circular Road. During my mother's brief illness, the care and kindness shown to me and my family by the Irish Sisters of Charity, who ran the hospital, was exemplary.

To me, these women were remarkable for the dedication to their work and kindness to their employees. By employing sufficient staff, it enabled us to devote quality time to our patients and not strictly to nursing tasks ranging from drugs rounds to dressings. Having time to chat and listen was important as it allowed the sick to unburden themselves, especially of the awful fears that illness can bring.

Irén relished the opportunity to talk to me, as she had few visitors other than László. One day Irén turned to me and made a remark that rather surprised me.

'I have found a second daughter.'

I smiled, feeling the close bond that often exists between patient and nurse. I knew that it was a way for her to cope with her own illness.

'Would you mind if I looked upon you as my daughter?' she continued.

My gut instinct told me to be very careful and exercise caution. In the nursing profession, you deal with sick people when they are at their most vulnerable.

'Irén, I feel privileged that you should look upon me in that way.'

But I had to tread carefully as I continued to nurse her. Even afterwards when Irén and László would invite me to their home in Shankill, I never took up the invitation, never once visited. I felt nothing but concern for their vulnerability. It was a sentiment shared among my nursing colleagues at the hospital too. There was an *esprit de corps* among us on the third floor; we were supportive of each other, working closely together under the leadership of our floor manager, Mary O'Neill. An able supervisor, Mary ran a tight ship but would still accommodate us when we plied her with various requests, like changes to the duty roster. Sadly, Mary passed away in 2014.

Many of those colleagues of bygone days come to mind now, many of whom nursed Irén too: tall and stately Nancy Shannon and old-school Miss Twohig; golden-haired Rena Frawley with her china-doll complexion; Margo Andrews, fastidious about hygiene and forever cleaning; gracious Paula McGovern and her thoughtful sister Mary; neat and tidy Carmel Tighe, who kept all ward equipment in proper order; Ann Flanagan, forever fussy and busy making sure that all procedures were carried out correctly; ever-reliable Sally Brady, whose word was her bond; the rather reserved Mary Farrell; gentle and intelligent Catherine Mehigan; Geraldine Murphy, who reminded me of Princess Grace with her exquisite cinematic looks; faithful Marian O'Keeffe, a bright young nurse just out of training; tall and willowy Esme McCluskey; practical Joy Furney; and last but not least, unforgettable Margaret Thornton with her precious dog Ruby! Our floor secretary, Sheila O'Brien, ever-organised and efficient, was imbued with an enviable grace and serenity.

My bosom friends and colleagues were Kay Cooney, Máirín Leyne and Dolores McGauran. The company of such women inspired me on my constant learning curve in humanity. To observe Kay as she cared for her patients with such devotion and sensitivity was a great lesson in compassion, if not humility. Máirín, forever kind and motherly, had a tireless energy about her; no duty was ever too much trouble. Dolores had a positive disposition and kept any signs of negativity at bay. Her cheerful and jolly disposition helped patients and staff alike. In fact, all looked forward to her time on duty!

An opportunity to leave this environment presented itself in early 1981, but I was reluctant to go. One day, the acting matron on duty, Sister Cecilia, came to the third floor on her rounds. She was a nun who possessed a most tender and gracious manner, with a kind word for everybody. I happened to give her the ward report that evening and afterwards she asked me to walk with her as far as the lift. As we strolled along, Sister Cecilia informed me that the sisters in charge of their adjoining public hospital were thinking of offering me a post with them. My immediate reaction was to respectfully decline the offer. I was happy where I was and enjoyed working with my nursing colleagues in what was a family atmosphere.

László's brother István and his family in the late 1950s:
wife Éva, daughter Éva and son István

László's brother Zoltán with his wife Julianna and son László in the late 1950s

László (far left) playing the clarinet with the South African
Broadcasting Corporation Orchestra in the mid-1960s

László's Irish immigration certificate of registration in 1969

Eibhlín's great-great-grandfather, the
Reverend Alexander McCrae Maddison

The Maddison home at Doe Castle in County Donegal, painted by Elizabeth Maddison

The Masterson (Mac Máighistir) family on holiday in Gougane Barra in the 1950s:
John and Isabella with children (left to right) Eoin, Eibhlín and Áine, and dog Bob

Eibhlín's aunts: Sr Mary Paul (Aunt Vera, left) and Sr Mary Monica (Aunt Sheila) in Hastings, England, 1948

Eibhlín at home in Dufferin Avenue, Dublin, in 1976

John Masterson's scouting days in the 1930s (back row, fifth from left)

László's taxi plate from 1970

László's house on Adelaide Road, Dublin

László pictured outside his house on Cherrington Road, Shankill, in the 1980s

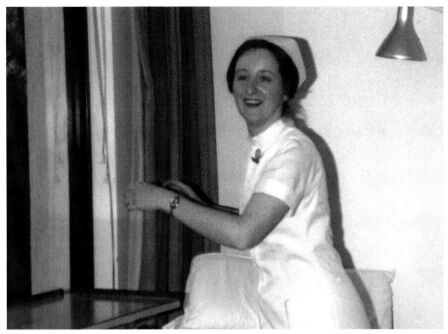

Eibhlín as a staff nurse at St Vincent's Private Hospital in the 1970s

László and Eibhlín's home in Springfield Park, Foxrock, in the early 1990s

The town hall in Echternach, Luxembourg, where Eibhlín
and László's marriage was registered in 1988

László parking outside the Chapel of Our Lady of Sorrows, Echternach,
where he and Eibhlín were married on 21 October 1988

For all the camaraderie among us, it was offset sometimes by the sheer sadness we encountered. During my early years working at the hospital, I nursed a beautiful young mother dying from cancer; she had three small children and an adoring husband who found it hard to hide his broken heart. One morning I was on duty as the life of this woman was ebbing away. As I observed her little children and husband tearful at her bedside, I was filled with a great anger that God could do such a thing – to deprive sweet, innocent little children of a loving mother. When the moment of death finally arrived the family was devastated. For quite some time afterwards I was very cross with God.

But I could not remain cross for very long. To be honest, for years I had struggled with the idea that I had a vocation, a calling, to be a nun. As far back as I can remember, I desired to live a life of prayer. In my late teens I had tested that calling and entered the Congregation of Notre Dame des Missions, a French order, whose mother house was then situated in Hastings in the south of England.

Their enormous sprawling building housed hundreds of nuns, or so it seemed to me at the time. I was impressed witnessing at first-hand these courageous young women preparing for a life on the missions. Although predominantly a teaching order, they covered a wide spectrum of professions and sent their sisters to far-flung corners of the globe: Africa, India, the Americas, Australia. These young women, filled with vitality and fun, and indeed many from Ireland, were the embodiment of self-sacrifice with a sincere desire to spread the gospel message. However, sadly for me it was not to be. After about six months my physical health declined, thus forcing me to leave. Yet I never quite relinquished the desire for a life of prayer.

Perhaps it was something that others too had noticed. Some months after Sister Cecilia had mentioned the post in the public hospital to me, she broached another subject.

'Had you ever thought of becoming a religious sister, Eibhlín?'

I was taken aback. It opened up memories of my time in the convent in Hastings and my unresolved feelings. Sister Cecilia herself was English-born and to judge by her accent from London. Of average height and a little rotund, she wore a grey modern habit with some of her hair peeking out from under her head veil. I imagined myself in her grey habit as a nursing nun but it didn't feel quite right.

'I'm afraid,' Sister Cecilia, that's impossible for me,' I explained. 'I'm caring for my elderly father.'

And there the matter rested. In hindsight there was no one better than Sister Cecilia to approach me and not feel offended by my refusal. Her saint's name alone was inspiring: patroness of musicians with a love for the music of the liturgy. However in 1983, sometime after my talk with Sister Cecilia, circumstances did change and I was no longer the sole carer of my father. With the best of intentions in my heart and those of my siblings, I felt free once more to embrace the religious life. The pull had now become unbearably strong and persistent. Years later I recall László's wise words, in his rich, slightly accented voice.

'Do not strive against nature, for nature will push you in the right direction.'

That is what it was like, some force pushing me into the monastery. My inclination this time was not towards the Irish Sisters of Charity, in a nursing capacity, but rather with a contemplative Carmelite order. Therefore, after much consultation and long interviews with a group of contemplative nuns and the Carmelite Fathers, I was granted permission to test my vocation once more. This time it would be within an enclosed Carmelite monastery – Saint Joseph's in Kilmacud, County Dublin. In the Carmelite order, these sisters are cloistered and completely cut off from the world, with no access to radio or television or daily newspapers. Thus removed from the world, talking was only permitted when necessary. This is what I believed I had been looking for, a contemplative life of solitude and prayer. My reasons for wishing this way of life were deep and inexplicable, difficult to comprehend, even to myself.

My decision to enter the monastery and leave my dear father admittedly caused me great pain. Even the thought of leaving my dog, a poodle named Púca, had caused nights of soul-searching. But I knew that my father and dog would be well cared for in the capable and secure hands of my family. With the decision made, soon it was time for me to say my goodbyes to hospital life and my nursing career. Friends and colleagues, though saddened to see me go, were supportive and understanding. Because of my imminent departure, my friend Kay asked me to take part in a small internal sweepstake that she was organising among hospital staff. The famous Irish Derby was about to take place that June at the Curragh Racecourse in County Kildare.

'Come on, Eibhlín, take a chance,' she urged with a laugh.

I did, much to my own amusement and that of my colleagues, as they knew how little interest I took in betting. I went and put my money on Shareef Dancer. For this reluctant punter, difficult as it may be to believe, the blessed horse romped home, first past the post, and I won quite a few pounds. Beginner's luck!

'Now go and buy a Government Prize Bond with this lucky money,' Kay insisted.

This I did. I had to get rid of the money anyhow, as I was divesting myself of all my worldly possessions in readiness for the monastery. There were also my clothes to dispose of and treasured items to give away as gifts. The Carmelite Order after all was dedicated to the poorest of the poor.

To a small number of patients, especially those I had grown attached to through recurring stays, I spoke of my plans. I would have counted Irén in that number had she not been so poorly. By now the cancer had spread to her liver and she was spending longer periods in hospital and failing fast. It had been seven years since her cancer diagnosis and our first meeting. Given that she considered me close to her, I had not the heart to tell her that I would no longer be around, perhaps when she felt she needed me most. But I did feel compelled to tell László so that he could break the news to Irén during one of her better days. Before I got the chance, however, he sensed something was afoot.

'What is happening to you? Is something wrong?'

'No, László, everything is fine but I'll be leaving my job soon.'

'But how can this be?'

'I'm going to become a nun.'

'A nun! Where are you going?' he asked. 'Where is this place?'

'I can't tell you.'

It was all I could say under the circumstances, especially with Irén unwell. That once plump lady was now gaunt and jaundiced but resigned to her fate. Her life in Ireland, though cut off from her daughter in Canada, had brought her peace. She had done her best to fit into Irish life, receiving the host when the Ministers of the Eucharist would wend their way through the Catholic-run hospital each day.

It was a difficult time for László. At this juncture, he had lost contact with his remaining sibling, Zoltán, and relatives in Hungary. Irén was his entire life and that was about to alter radically. His accountant Helen remembers him being visibly upset by his wife's illness, no doubt wondering how he would fare without her. As usual his way of coping was to throw himself into work.

The external bricks of the Georgian house on Adelaide Road were in need of repointing. He took to this task with gumption and erected scaffolding and acquired the necessary tools and equipment. He then plastered over the bricks, much to the dismay of the Irish Georgian Society, who lodged an official complaint with the then Dublin Corporation.

A planning official soon appeared on the scene and demanded that László undo all the work. In retrospect, you could not blame them; the Georgian Society only wanted to protect Ireland's architectural heritage after all. Acknowledging his mistake, László single-handedly removed the paintwork with a rotary hammer as well as brick bolster and masonry chisels over the Sunday of the June bank holiday weekend, spewing masonry dust everywhere. He then repointed the bricks, skilfully replacing the mortar all by himself. When something had to be done, it was best to do it straightaway and with lightning speed. It was also a brief respite from thinking about Irén.

*　*　*

Thursday, 30 June 1983 was the day I took my leave from the hospital. It was with mixed emotions I crossed the busy Merrion Road and made my way to Sandymount Strand nearby. Its fine views of Howth Head and surrounding hills across Dublin Bay were a perfect anodyne. The gentle lapping of waves had a most soothing effect upon my mind and in that tranquil setting I paused for a moment's thought. My friend Kay came to mind and the winning horse, making me smile.

The previous riot in my mind had calmed as I prepared to leave the security of my family home for my home-to-be in the monastery and all that that entailed. The scene of my childhood in the late 1940s and 1950s was Dufferin Avenue, not far from the South Circular Road. The area was a mixed community of Protestants, Jews and Catholics, where all the local children played together and religion was never discussed. It meant that our young minds were always open to different customs and traditions and not fazed by people who were not like us. Perhaps it was a reason why I was later attracted to an émigré like László. When our home was eventually sold to a very kind Muslim family decades later, it sort of seemed part of the natural order to us.

In a loving, close-knit family environment, my siblings, Áine and Eoin, and I were sheltered and protected from the storms of life. I truly only appreciated that fact as I embarked upon this new path. Some years ago I penned a simple verse called 'Apple Blossom', recalling those happy days, spanning three generations: a grandmother with three of her daughters, Isabella, Irene and Ida – all the I's – and Isabella's three children, Áine, Eoin and me.

> Sitting under apple blossom trees
> Isabella and Irene and Ida
> In gentle conversation with their mother,
> Ripples of laughter flowing through the leaves.
> Grandchildren Áine and Eoin and Eibhlín
> In background playing; at ease with
> Each other and in love with Nature.

With these happy thoughts uppermost in my mind, I realised I was about to close the door on a past life. Kay, Máirín and Dolores as well as Sheila, the floor secretary, accompanied me on my journey to the monastery late in the afternoon of 31 July. Moral support out in force! We all piled into Kay's car and headed for leafy Kilmacud Road Upper with the girls doing their best to be cheerful and in good spirits. Joining a religious order is always slightly tinged with sadness for Irish people; a life of self-sacrifice can be a lonely one indeed.

We drove up the driveway, seeing the two-storey, grey manor house quickly come into view with its double-height, rounded bay at both ends and a high pitched roof. Attached to the building on its left-hand side was a granite stone church. We all embraced and said our goodbyes outside the monastery porch. I fixed my gaze firmly on the building with a statue of Saint Joseph nestled in a curved window niche beside the porch. My home for the foreseeable future. As I crossed the threshold at six o'clock, the Angelus bell rang out from the old bell tower. I interpreted this as a welcome announcement!

9.

SEPARATION BY GRILLE

If I have all the eloquence of men or of angels, but speak without love, I am simply a gong booming or a cymbal clashing. If I have the gift of prophecy, understanding all the mysteries there are, and knowing everything, and if I have faith in all its fullness to move mountains, but without love, then I am nothing at all. If I give away all that I possess, piece by piece, and if I even let them take my body and burn it, but am without love, it will do me no good whatever. Love is always patient and kind; it is never jealous; love is never boastful or conceited; it is never rude or selfish; it does not take offence, it is not resentful. Love takes no pleasure in other people's sins but delights in the truth; it is always ready to excuse, to trust, to hope, and to endure whatever comes. Love does not come to an end ... in short, there are three things that last: faith, hope and love; and the greatest of these is love.

1 Corinthians 13: 1–13

M Y first introduction to the monastery, as the door snapped shut behind me, was the sight of the nuns, perhaps sixteen strong, waiting for me. They all came around me, embracing and greeting me warmly. This was followed by the welcome ceremony. The prioress, Mother Mary Francis, led a procession of about fifteen sisters bearing lit candles down along a dark corridor and into the chapel. In my postulant's brown pinafore dress and white shirt, I followed behind, anxious yet excited. The community assembled in the chapel for quiet prayer and reflection and the prioress held a crucifix for me to kiss, which I did. Afterwards I was led to the refectory where we all ate supper. It's so long ago now that I can scarcely recall the food.

The monastery building was a period residence known as Kilmacud Manor in former times. However, whatever vestiges of gaiety and comfort that had once existed in the house were well and truly gone by the time I arrived as a postulant. An atmosphere of stillness and silence now prevailed among the aroma of beeswax and boiled cabbage. From the very beginning, I found the daily routine of monastic life inspirational, loving the rhythm of each day and never tiring of it. Our communal prayer was broken into seven regular periods of fixed prayer, reciting what's known as the Divine Office. Our day also consisted of daily mass and meditation. This life of prayer uplifted my soul and I relished hearing my own voice blend in with the voices of the sisters.

We rose at half past five, washed and dressed and were at chapel at six o'clock to recite the Angelus and Divine Office. Mealtimes started with breakfast at eight o'clock, lunch at half past eleven, afternoon tea at three and supper at six. There were two periods set out for meditation: one in the morning and another in the late afternoon. Work was carried out between mealtimes and our daily routine of prayer. As it was a contemplative order where talking was forbidden, we did however have two recreational times allotted for talking: one session in the morning and another in the evening. However, you did not just sit around and talk, but had to keep yourself busy by knitting, sewing or painting. All sisters retired to bed around half past nine.

Despite the monastery employing a caretaker, who lived in the gate lodge together with his family, the sisters carried out most of the duties both domestic and outdoor. This included cooking, cleaning, dusting, polishing, washing, laundry and the making of altar breads.

Now the making of the altar breads was an experience in itself. It was carried out in a little bake house on the monastery grounds and took some getting used to. I remember being clad in an enormous plastic apron and having to stand in front of a large round electric hotplate. I would pour a ladle of specially prepared batter directly onto the hotplate and pull down a second large round hotplate on top of the batter, holding it firmly for a time. After a couple of Hail Marys, I would lift up the hotplate and add the bread to a container of already baked breads. By the end of the session you would be covered in batter, or at least I was!

There were also a fine lot of hens to be cared for – truly free range – and large henhouses that had to be cleaned out daily. I remember one afternoon when we were at prayer in the chapel, a tremendous commotion erupted outside and the sound of squawking and screeching hens filled the air. A couple of sisters left to investigate and after prayers the rest of us trooped out. A fox, it seems, had disturbed our feathered friends and ran off with one of them! Forming a horizontal line, inch by inch, we combed the grounds but in vain. As nothing was discovered, the calm was soon restored, but the fox had got the upper hand.

As a postulant and later on as a novice, I had daily studies of the Bible and Church doctrine under the direction of the novice mistress, Sister Mary John, a most devoted sister. So between work, study, prayer and recreation, our days were full. As with most monasteries and convents there was also an infirmary in the building. Here an elderly bedridden sister was cared for and, given my nursing background, this was an assignment I loved to carry out. Every three to six months all duties were reassigned, thus bringing some variety to the monotony of daily routine. It was all for good reason. If a sister given charge of the kitchen was not a good cook, the rest of us suffered no better than soldiers in the trenches for months. On special feast days, such as Christmas and Easter, the community was allowed to talk and a festive meal served. I used to regard these unique days as a children's party, being so simple yet intensely enjoyable. As contemplative nuns, no meat passed our lips, however. In the monastic way of thinking, if you truly loved the Creator, you could not possibly kill, let alone eat another living creature.

Each sister lived in a small room called a 'cell' that contained a wrought-iron bed, a small bedside table, an upright wooden chair, and a table with jug and basin, which was also used for writing or study. On the back of the door were two hooks on which to hang your clothing, such that you had. An enormous wooden cross hung on the wall and dominated the room and indeed our minds. Lighting came from a large window with wooden shutters and a single light bulb, minus its shade, hanging from the centre of the ceiling. What I found myself doing every so often was rearranging the furniture. Thankfully, the novice mistress, Sister Mary John, never objected. Another rather endearing memory remains with me. If a butterfly flew into the monastery, I could hear a whisper.

'Oh, we'll soon have another postulant in our midst!'

* * *

In the middle of August, Irén died. She had spent her final days in St Gabriel's Hospital, a small private nursing home in Cabinteely near her home. Her death proved too much for László and he was unable to cope with her loss. László was simply devastated, as Helen Murphy recalled. His close and trusted friend Jay McQuillan organised the funeral service and interment; Irén's body was cremated and her ashes buried in the people's plot in Glasnevin Cemetery, simply stating her name and date of death. No church service took place, in keeping with her wishes. Jay also assisted László in every way possible to manage this sad change in his life. Irén, in acknowledging her debt of gratitude to László, left him a farewell letter thanking him for his years of devoted care to herself and also for his goodness and generosity towards her daughter, especially for her education.

Irén then advised him strongly to fetch me from the monastery! It was only some weeks after I had entered the monastery. This he acted upon almost immediately and set about searching for me. On asking at the hospital, no one would divulge where the monastery was located. But, being László, he persisted and continued to return to the hospital in his efforts to find me. One day at the front desk, Andrea, the receptionist, felt sorry for him and quietly slipped an address into his hand, putting her index finger to her lips denoting silence. For this simple gesture, I bless dear Andrea for her kindness to this very day!

Again László wasted no time and one afternoon he pulled up outside the monastery. After ringing the front door, no-one appeared but the door opened automatically. Inside, he found himself standing in a tiny hallway looking at a black wrought-iron grille with a dark curtain behind it. From the darkness he heard a voice asking what he wanted.

'I wish to see Eibhlín Mac Máighistir.'

The voice instructed him to enter a parlour to his left. On entering this room, he was further confronted by yet another but much larger black wrought-iron grille with an equally dark curtain behind it. The room was sparsely furnished with a table and a couple of chairs not to mention a large crucifix on the wall. It must have looked rather forbidding to László, who by now had long parted company with God and faith. Such was his nervousness that he was unable to sit down and had to keep pacing the floor.

In the meantime, the porter nun had gone in search of Mother Francis, seeking permission for László to see me. Luckily for me, the prioress was a woman of great heart and conveyed her approval to the novice mistress, Sister Mary John, who in turn approached me in the middle of cleaning the brasses with a smile on her face. Then she gently whispered in my ear.

'You have a visitor waiting for you in the parlour.'

However, she did not say who it was and I was afraid to ask. Anxiously, I made my way along the dark corridor wondering who could possibly want to see me. On entering the little room, I discreetly peeked out before I drew back the dark curtain exposing the grille. My heart jolted when my gaze fell upon László. I thought I was dreaming. How could he be here in the monastery, in the parlour, before my very eyes? As I gazed in disbelief, it dawned on me that he looked rather downcast. Oh dear, it's Irén, I thought. László quickly approached the grille once the curtain had been pulled back.

'Eibhlín, it's you.'

'László, is everything all right?'

'Irén … she is dead,' he said quietly.

'I'm so sorry for you, László,' I began. 'Please accept my heartfelt condolences.'

He nodded. It was obvious in the course of our conversation that he was grief-stricken. I felt such sadness on hearing the news of her death and of course for him. Irén had experienced such sorrow in her life that László was now fully intent on carrying out her final wishes. He came straight to the point.

'I want you to leave this convent now.'

'I can't, László, this is where I belong.'

These were words that László refused to accept. As I look back upon the whole episode now and think of his reaction, it was rather startling. He took hold of the grille with both hands and shook it, demanding an explanation.

'How can you possibly live in such a place?'

'László, I want to be here. I've been called to be a nun.'

'Have you completely lost your senses?'

As his voice rose higher and higher, it began to distress me. Still he continued to analyse my decision.

'This style of life could not suit your type of personality under any circumstances.'

In my brown postulant pinafore and white shirt, I must have looked rather strange to him. I became very anxious and was sure that he would pull down the whole blessed barrier between us! Finally, he did calm down a little. Continuing to stand, we spoke long and hard about what had happened and what the future might hold. His sadness was also compounded by the death of his dog Roy, who had to be put down due to illness. Still László persisted in pacing the floor every so often, refusing to sit down. I tried to explain as best I could.

'László, it's impossible for me to leave. This is the life I've longed for, here within this monastery.'

'I don't believe you. How can you live here?'

'I'm in love with this way of living.'

But my words only agitated and confounded him even more. He truly could not understand why I would have chosen to bury myself away from the world.

'Come away with me at once.'

'I won't, László.'

We reasoned back and forth; I again giving my view of how I felt and he responding in disbelief. The fact that he was recently bereaved and grieving for Irén only reinforced in my mind that he was still vulnerable. He was in no state to form a new attachment so soon, no matter how much he held me in high regard. Finally, he conceded defeat.

'All right, but promise me something…'

'What is it?'

'If you ever leave here, you will do me the courtesy of writing to let me know.'

'Of course I will. I promise.'

I made the promise, thinking little of its possibility at the time. There was no denying I had some feelings for László, but I had tucked them well away out of sight. As I tearfully watched him withdraw and slowly walk out through the parlour door, a part of my own heart encircled his and wished him well. The enormity of the situation then seized me and I sought refuge in the cloistered garden, shedding bitter tears. Later one of the nuns, Sister Immaculata, whispered to me that she had spotted László leaving in great haste. Such was his distress that he had reversed his van into the granite walls of the monastery. That news only made me feel worse.

By now László was done with Ireland. Irén's cousin Peter and his family had visited him after her death, and suggested he move to Luxembourg where he could be near them. He promptly left the country a short time later. I have no idea who was left in charge of managing the house on Adelaide Road or his home in Shankill. All the light had gone from his life and he was still distraught. So at the age of sixty-eight he was once more starting a new life; yet once his grief abated he would embrace it wholeheartedly. His resilience and reserves of strength knew no bounds.

* * *

László's visit had taken me by surprise, yet I knew I had made the right decision at the time. To everything there is a season and a time to every purpose under heaven. For László it was a time to mourn and a time to heal; for me it was a time to plant and a time to reap. The seeds of my devotion to God may have been sown a very long time before but I had to nurture and prepare for a life in service to him. In the days and months that followed it was a joy and privilege for me to live among the sisters and observe these self-effacing, good women.

As the year progressed I felt more and more in tune with the community of sisters. Strangely enough, though, life did its best to uproot me from the monastery. My father's monthly visits kept me in touch with the outside world – in Ireland there were phone tapping scandals, economic woes, and the political leaders in Ireland, Britain and Northern Ireland had started down the long and winding road of peace talks. On one occasion, a nationwide referendum was being held on whether there should be a constitutional ban on abortion or not. One of the nuns phoned my sister Áine, asking her if she would like to take me with our father to the polling station to cast my vote, thinking it would be nice for us to be together as a family.

And I could hardly credit it when my Prize Bond number came up some months after I had entered the monastery. Miracle of miracles, I won the sum of fifty thousand pounds in the draw. It was a king's ransom at that time; lightning had struck for the second time. Either that or it was temptation thrown at my feet!

It was comical in hindsight. Unsure as to what I should do with the ticket, I had brought it with me into the monastery and had even registered my change of address. When the notification letter arrived at the monastery, disbelief was etched upon the nuns' faces. So much for dispatching all your worldly goods! I could hardly post back my winning ticket, terrified it would go astray, so nothing would satisfy me but to have the ticket couriered to the Prize Bond office. God bless the nuns for agreeing to it. I'm sure they were relieved when I put the money into a bank account and made out a trust fund for my family and a friend.

Having finished the postulant training in June 1984, I was allowed to go forward and become a novice. It was a memorable day for me, not least because my bare head now received a white veil. I had been given permission to choose the readings for the ceremony and thought of Saint Paul in Corinthians 13 and his wise words on love and its true meaning.

Without love, then I am nothing at all …. If I give away all that I possess, piece by piece, and if I even let them take my body and burn it, but am without love, it will do me no good whatever …. Love does not come to an end … in short, there are three things that last: faith, hope and love; and the greatest of these is love.

Aunt Vera, who was a favourite of mine, had come to mind as well. A religious sister herself, she had taken the name Paul of Tarsus, that is, Sister Mary Paul, so the reading was partly a tribute to her. The name I took that day was Siúr Treasa le Muire Spiorad Naomh, or Sister Mary Teresa of the Holy Spirit in English.

Mother Mary Francis gently guided me through the ceremony, her smiling face a beacon of support. All was going well until about halfway through the ceremony. Suddenly, there was knocking as loud as thunder on the bolted chapel door that would not cease but boomed on and on, echoing into every corner like gigantic waves crashing upon a rocky shore. The sisters heeding their strict discipline ignored it all and the ceremony continued as if nothing was happening. I had at first thought that this persistent knocking was a cry for help from someone somewhere. For a brief second or two, I thought it might even have been László. But it was not. In fact, I was to learn later that it was my cousin Peadar Dempsey, my father's nephew, knocking at the door, anxious to support me and witness an occasion of great joy for me.

* * *

The solitude of monastery life left much time for reflection and often my thoughts turned to growing up in Dufferin Avenue. I tried to visualise our redbrick two-storey terraced house and those on the myriad streets that fed into the South Circular Road like tributaries. Donore Presbyterian Church, which in time would become a mosque, stood at the top of the street and nearby the sprawling Griffith Barracks.

A small railed-off garden of flowers and grass lay to the front of our house, while a long garden ended in a double garage and laneway at the back. To me as a child this garden seemed a wonderland of trees, apple and lilac, with shrubs and bushes in a glorious profusion of colours, not to mention the fragrant fruit bushes. My mother, Isabella Maddison, took great pride in her garden and it seemed to flower all summer long. My father, John Joseph Masterson (Seán Mac Máighistir), worked hard as an electrician with the Irish railway company, Córas Iompair Éireann (CIÉ), entrusting the care of the household to my mother, though in poor health herself. Thankfully, she had domestic help in those early years in the form of the middle-aged Mrs Timmons, whom we called Timmy, and a young girl called Mary, whom we named Smiley.

My mother had to open our home to paying guests, as she called them, in order to supplement my father's income. At first they were mainly tourists from England, Scotland and Wales but later she took in country girls working for the Civil Service. There was always good karma in the house and we enjoyed the coming and going of the guests, especially the girls dressed in their finery when attending local dances. My mother went to great lengths to make the girls feel at home, converting our dining room into their own living area and our conservatory into their own kitchen. By the time we reached our mid-teens, the paying-guest period had come to an end and the house reverted to a family home again.

Religion featured strongly in our household. In the family room at the lower return of the house, my mother had constructed a little altar to the Blessed Virgin Mary, where a tiny electric blue light permanently glowed. In the same room high up over the range ran a long narrow shelf, in the centre of which stood a statue of the Sacred Heart. Here too a red electric light quietly shone. Each night after dinner, around seven o'clock, my family would form a circle and kneel to recite the rosary in Irish. If a friend called in, they were invited to join in or wait in the front living-room until prayers were finished. My siblings and I were each given a special country to pray for: my sister Áine was asked to keep Russia in her prayers, my brother Eoin instructed to remember China, while I was given Hungary and told to think about its people.

This started an affinity and lifelong attraction for all things Hungarian. I went on to read about its fascinating history and looked up geography books and atlases to discover its lands and read about its culture and people. It's no wonder then that a bond existed between me and László.

My parents were clever insofar as by encouraging us to pray for these countries, it helped open our minds. Making us inquisitive about countries and their inhabitants helped us learn, quite a lot as it turned out. Books were always our delight. My mother took pleasure in reading to us at bedtime and loved having us around her as she read. A favourite book, which belonged to my paternal grandmother, Margaret Kelly-Masterson, was *Little Women* by Louisa May Alcott. So reading was our passport to exciting worlds, although our neighbourhood was exotic enough.

The streets around the South Circular Road, specifically Portobello, were known as Little Jerusalem because so many Jewish people had settled in the area over the centuries. At one point there had been no less than six synagogues in the area. I recall on Friday afternoons my parents prompted us to help out in our local synagogue, Greenville Hall, in readiness for the start of the Sabbath. The synagogue was large, dating from the 1920s, and had an impressive portico of grey Ionic columns and a pointed pediment. There in that building we would polish and dust and carry out odd jobs along with the caretaker's children. When a wedding took place, we were often allowed to enjoy the reception and made a fuss of, much to our delight.

On Jewish feast days, such as Pesach and Yom Kippur, Áine and Eoin would call into many Jewish homes in the locality and light the fire or stove, turn on gas or electricity, or carry out any work prohibited by Jewish observance. The families used to call Áine and Eoin their *Shabbat goy*, the name reserved for a non-Jew who carries out such tasks. An insight into another fascinating culture.

During the 1940s Ireland was far away from the theatre of war. Under its policy of neutrality, the country was somewhat spared the horrors of the Second World War, unlike László who experienced it at full force. Yet still my neighbourhood was given a taste of German hostility in the early hours of 3 January 1941, some years before I was born. A German air raid along the South Circular Road, in particular Donore Terrace, badly damaged Greenville Hall synagogue, destroyed three houses and damaged over fifty. The National Boxing Stadium, Greenmount and Boyne Linen Company, the Hospice for the Dying, Donore Presbyterian

Church, Wills tobacco factory, Saint Catherine's Rectory, and the White Swan Laundry all fell victim to the Luftwaffe's supposed navigation error as well. Thankfully, there were no fatalities but twenty people were injured nonetheless, some trapped in their homes and had to be extricated by the fire brigade. Coincidentally, the previous night a bomb was also dropped in Terenure, a Dublin suburb to where many Jewish families had relocated over the years.

There was many a happy day in Dufferin Avenue too when excitement reached fever pitch and all the communities pitched together. One such occasion was when Princess Grace and her husband Prince Rainier of Monaco visited Dublin in June 1961 on a state visit. Princess Grace was the epitome of glamour and sophistication for us, made all the more special by her Irish roots. Her cavalcade was due to pass along the South Circular Road on its way to the President's residence, Áras an Uachtaráin, in the Phoenix Park one day. Surprisingly for the month of June the weather was inclement and we had to endure squally showers as we stood waiting on the pavement intent on giving her a warm Irish welcome. The rector of Donore Presbyterian Church took pity on a few of us and crossed the road to invite us in to view all from the rectory windows! This we did and had a bird's eye view and were dry into the bargain.

* * *

Monastery life continued with the monthly visits of my father and occasionally my siblings, who were now caring for him. Many an hour was spent reflecting on my family and what I had relinquished on coming into the monastery. My mother had loved all her children, but especially Áine, her firstborn, with her raven black hair, sallow skin and beautiful almond-shaped brown eyes. In truth, I was rather in awe of her. She was striking, even at the age of eleven, when she caught the attention of Irish artist Seán Keating, famous for his paintings of the Irish War of Independence and of the ESB hydroelectric scheme at Ardnacrusha on the River Shannon. A noted portrait painter too, he wished to paint Áine and had asked permission from Grandmother Maddison, accompanying her on that day's outing. The permission was denied him, however, when my parents got to hear of it. We shall never know what the outcome of this proposed work of art would have been! In later life Áine did work as a part-time model, so Keating was certainly not alone in his appreciation.

Áine, by now running a busy household and rearing three children, sometimes visited me in the monastery. Her husband, Gregory Egan, was an architect and old family friend, whom she had married in 1966. It gave me considerable joy to be godmother to their older child, Karin-Isabella. My brother Eoin along with his family also called into the monastery from time to time. From his cradle days, Eoin was a strong healthy fellow and could do no wrong in my mother's eyes. The prized and precious son, so revered by Irish mothers. Following a training in business management, he was now running his own company and worked extremely hard, his motto being: 'work till you drop, sitting in an armchair is not good news'. He had married a talented teacher from the Philippines, Josephine, and had three children.

It was always good to see my siblings and catch up with news of their lives. One afternoon as I was cleaning the brasses in the monastery, Áine even brought my little dog Púca to see me, under cover of course. In the parlour was a wooden swivel hatch at the grille used to deliver items such as cakes or various presents to the nuns. That day was probably unique in what it delivered. Áine placed Púca on the turntable and within seconds she was in my arms. I placed her upon my knee and hugged her tight; by now she was yelping with joy! How I loved that darling dog. But I was reluctant to rub her as my hands still held the aroma of paraffin. The visit had boosted my spirits no end.

As the months progressed, I began to notice a change in my father's concentration, a vagueness of thought, a slight distraction in his manner. There was also the fact that he could no longer hold a conversation in Irish. We had developed a custom, since my mother's death, of devoting one day a week to speaking Irish. So from dawn to dusk, of whatever day we picked that week, we could discuss any topic under the sun in our native tongue. I could see it had become a strain for him to speak in Irish, which he had learnt as an adult. Naturally, his deterioration was a cause for concern and I sometimes wondered should I leave the monastery. But I knew that he was in good hands surrounded by my family and felt all would be well.

Whatever about my father, change had come my way too. Living as I was in the monastery with such stoic women, whom I looked upon as little saints, I soon began to realise that a cloistered life was not for the faint-hearted. Its rigid regime of prayer, work and recreation, with little or no flexibility, began to gnaw away at me. It dawned on me that my own personality, my individuality, was melting away, leaving minimal room for personal growth. Was that what religious life was all about? Denying your individuality and giving yourself entirely over to the will of God? Certainly an enclosed life gave a wonderful sense of security, for those whose personality could cope with self-stagnation, as I saw it. I feared that without proper nourishment of soul it could turn into self-absorption, which is not what I wanted. I was also reacting to what I was being asked to follow – the narrowness of the Church line. As time went by this seeming narrowness became too much to understand, to grasp. I began to feel I was being slowly suffocated.

Looking back, I was in a tiny boat on a vast ocean, rowing madly with all my strength in one direction wishing to remain in the monastery, while waters raged violently about me, tossing the boat hither and thither, with gale force winds driving me back from whence I came. Eventually, I submitted to this rage and allowed the power of nature to carry me where it wished. My spirit yearned to be free. At heart I was a restless spirit beyond anchorage. And so the greatest discovery of all came when I realised that it is not important what religious belief we aspire to; it does not matter our station in life, be it married or single; or our sexual orientation; it is of no consequence where we dwell, be it in isolated desert or overcrowded metropolis. What truly matters is the love and compassion we hold in our hearts towards our fellow human beings – that for me is the crucial truth.

Though love and compassion are Christian values, the place to express them adequately, I felt, was not in the monastery. And so my religious fervour started to abate. The wise words of Aunt Vera would often come back to me.

'The real saints in this world are mothers,' she said. 'You don't need to be inside a monastery.'

As summer turned to autumn my own physical health declined; I found it difficult to eat and began to lose weight. The decision to stay or leave weighed heavily on me and ill-health began to dog me like it had my mother. I had been her last child, born with fair curly hair and blue eyes and resembled her most in appearance. From an early age she had been delicate and in her twenties had developed asthma. Unlike nowadays, there was very little treatment for asthma in her day. I remember whenever an asthmatic attack occurred, she would sit very straight in a chair and quietly try to control her breathing, anxious not to distress us observing her gasp for air. Her heroism made me admire how she coped with such difficulties. I had had my own difficulties with life but they had never held me back. Three months after my birth a tragic accident left me partially blind – a fall from a height onto a hard red-tiled floor – and despite undergoing eye surgery nothing could be done.

I wondered how my mother would advise me on the situation I now found myself in were she alive. Some indication from heaven, perhaps. She had been so proud of me when I had entered the Notre Dame des Missions convent in Hastings in my late teens, thinking I was following in the footsteps of her sisters Vera and the very sunny Sheila, who took the name of Sister Mary Monica. In those days because of the prominent status of religion in the country, it was quite common for Catholic families to despatch daughters to the convent and sons to the priesthood, especially if you were not in line to inherit the family farm or business and if you lived in rural Ireland.

The Maddisons were no different. From Ireland to Perth, Australia, my Aunt Sheila had become a pioneering nun, bringing her talents as a music teacher well beyond the cloistered walls of the convent. She had taken a house in the community, living the gospel message, and was joined by another nun Sister Mary Xavier, who was a most talented musician too. Truly, women before their time!

What hopes, if any, my mother had of me doing suchlike had been brought to the grave with her. Leaving the convent at the age of twenty had not upset her and indeed she and the rest of my family could not have been more supportive. My mother had marshalled my brother and sister to take me to the cinema; and so we found ourselves in the Corinthian Cinema on Eden Quay, watching *Seven Brides for Seven Brothers*, the musical staring Howard Keel and Jane Powell. How we laughed – it was the perfect antidote and a welcome distraction from reality. The Corinthian had been a popular spot with us, for it was where *Sissi* was screened and other films about the Empress Elisabeth of Austria. During all my mishaps in life my siblings were there for me.

The sole exception, where support was concerned, was Grandmother Maddison; she had been very stern towards me, thinking I had let down the family and concerned my reputation would be tainted. She was a product of an Ireland that was ultra-conservative, narrow-minded and inward-looking at the time. People who were cowed by a dominant Church that ruled by the head and not by the heart. In hindsight, though misguided, she was probably just trying to protect me.

When I think of my mother I strangely think of László too. Not alone for her sharp intellect but her love of music which was equally deep-seated and which ran in her family. In the late 1940s when a fledgling choir calling themselves Our Lady's Choral Society occasionally gathered for a practice session at her family home, it was my mother who accompanied them on the piano, which she played as beautifully as her sisters. There in my grandparent's drawing room in a tall Georgian building on South Circular Road near Harrington Street, I would stand beside my mother at the piano as her sister Irene, in rich mezzo-soprano voice, blended with her fellow choir members. The choir used to practise in two halves owing to its size, but luckily the enormous drawing room could accommodate them, or so it always seemed to me. I well recall during these sessions that many houses in the vicinity opened their hall doors and windows allowing the voices to waft in through their homes. Indeed some residents could be seen standing at their front steps enthralled!

Our Lady's Choral Society went from strength to strength and in April 1967 gave a performance of Handel's *Messiah* in St Patrick's Hall, Dublin Castle accompanied by the RTÉ Symphony Orchestra under the baton of Tibor Paul, no less. The oratorio was broadcast live on RTÉ television and marked the 225th anniversary of the first performance of the *Messiah* in Dublin.

Yes, music ran in my family veins for sure. One touching memory will always stay with me. When my brother Eoin earned his first ever salary, he visited a music shop and purchased a record for our mother, Puccini's *Madama Butterfly*, as I recall. I was present when he handed it to her, watching her face light up with joy. She was quite overcome so it's a memory I hold dear.

* * *

My unhappiness in the monastery grew deeper and my health deteriorated to the point where I needed to be hospitalised. That September 1984, I ended up spending a few days in Saint Vincent's Hospital, near my treasured friends and former colleagues. They visited me and tried to rally my spirits as best they could. The rest and hydration did me a power of good, but the respite was too short for my morale. Nothing could be done other than return to the monastery. On the Friday that I was discharged, Kay appeared.

'I'll drive you back to the monastery,' she offered.

By now my father was residing in Dundrum in an apartment that had been purchased with my Prize Bond money. Knowing that my father was now living alone, Kay made a suggestion.

'Let's take a detour, Eibh,' she said, 'and see how your father is coping.'

'Absolutely not, Kay, it's forbidden to visit your home.'

However, Kay was nothing if not persuasive.

'Shure, we'll just take a quick look at where he's living, no harm in that!'

And so a detour was made. Before long we had arrived in Dundrum and were impressed by the apartment complex, brand new and surrounded by trees and a garden. In fact, it was an idyllic place for him, seeing that he had a great love of nature. My childhood memories are seasoned with trips to the Dublin Hills after mass each Sunday, from spring to autumn, weather permitting. Haversack on his back, my father and the rest of us, including our dog Bob, would walk up to Kilmashogue, one of the lower hills in the

Dublin Mountains, and spend a glorious day there. My parents would rest or become engrossed in a game of chess, well-worn from frequent use, while we ran about exploring and later feasted on a scrumptious picnic. To me, my father was a shining light of all that is good in the world.

My brother-in-law Gregory had familiarised my father with his new abode, which eased my mind no end. Seeing that my father was the only resident installed in the complex at the time, we went inside and took a quick look around! The apartment was well-appointed and nicely furnished, much to my relief. Yet despite my siblings' best efforts, the place was upside down and untidy, and very obvious to me that my father was unable to manage alone. In that short visit I attempted to tidy things somewhat but on a personal level it was all too much. A decision quickly formed in my mind.

Back in the monastery I explained to the nuns that I had visited my father on the way home from hospital. They were aghast. I had broken a fundamental rule. In contemplative life, you must never ever visit your home; even on request it is absolutely forbidden. Now with my deteriorating health plus the worries over my father, it was plain to them that life in the monastery did not suit my personality, or my current frame of mind. And so the sisters and I reached a mutual understanding. It was time for me to leave – the very next day!

That night I had a fearful panic attack. It was so severe I thought I would die. As all my possessions had been given away prior to entering the monastery, I was at a loss what to do. I had only the convent habit to my name.

'Who shall I contact, Eibhlín?' asked Sister Mary John, the novice mistress, the next morning.

'Can you ring my friend Máirín, please?' I began, 'and ask her if I may borrow a dress and jacket to go home?'

Sister Mary John nodded.

'I'll ask her if she can come and collect you today.'

When Sister Mary John rang Máirín's house, she learned that she was on duty at the hospital that day. So it was her husband, a colonel in the Irish Army, who came to the monastery in the late afternoon, armed with his wife's clothes. I was soon dressed and ready to go. As six o'clock in the evening approached, the Angelus bell rang out from the monastery bell tower, calling to me its blessing and its farewell. The now rather mournful sisters lifted their voices in plainchant. *Salve, Regina, Mater misericordiæ, vita, dulcedo, et spes nostra, salve. Ad te clamamus exsules filii Hevæ, ad te suspiramus, gementes et flentes in hac lacrimarum valle.*

And as their sweet strains wafted through the old building, I with equal emotion stepped over the threshold and back to reality. The Angelus bell had signalled my arrival and now my departure. What lay in store I could not tell, no matter how brave a face I tried to put on the situation. László's words came back to haunt me. *This style of life could not suit your type of personality under any circumstances.* I was beginning to think that he knew me far more than I ever could. After all, I was supposed to be an adult, a grown woman of forty.

Though László had rejected religion, it was not that simple for me. A mixture of failure and confusion now pervaded my thoughts. Part of me felt that I was going against my nature. If there is such a thing as a religious gene, then it had coursed the veins of my family for generations – both Catholic and Protestant. Many family members on my mother's side had been Church of England clergymen. Yes, the Maddison men had been vicars and military men ruled by their heads more often than not. My great-great-grandfather Alexander McCrae Maddison, however, seemed to have broken the mould. Following a period in India, as captain in the 50th Regiment of Madras Native Infantry, he studied theology at a German university and became a rector. From there he arrived in North Donegal in 1857 to minister to the local people.

His refusal to return to England some time later at the behest of his father, the Reverend John George Maddison, and take up a ministry in a selected parish led to his downfall or salvation, whichever way you look at it. His father duly disinherited him for insubordination. John George clearly took his position in society very seriously and the lineage of the Maddisons. The family could trace their bloodline back to King Edward III, and John George's cousin, the Reverend Arthur Roland Maddison, had been Priest Vicar and Prebendary of Lincoln Cathedral.

I liked to think that Alexander had experienced Celtic spirituality and had embraced it to his very core. The kind of spirituality that is driven more by the heart and soul than by the head. He struck me as a rather romantic figure, which made me admire and love him all the more. He had taken out a lease on the remote Doe Castle in Sheephaven Bay, near Cresslough, County Donegal, from where Owen Roe O'Neill had once led the Ulster Army of the Irish Confederate forces in 1642 during the Wars of the Three Kingdoms. And it was to here that Alexander brought his bride Elizabeth. And so in that sixteenth-century tower house magically suspended at the tip of a peninsula and surrounded by water, he and Elizabeth started a family and forsook England. He would later take up a post as rector in Agivey, County Derry and endear himself to his congregation.

I was close to him spiritually and always kept a picture of him by my bedside. Plain in appearance, he possessed quite a long face and nose and had the palest of blue eyes. His light brown hair was slightly curly and a chin curtain beard in the style of Abraham Lincoln dominated his features. A softness, however, a childlike innocence, suffused his face, while his eyes were touched by a deep serenity. Perhaps because I had inherited some of his nature I found the regime of monastery life so rigid and unyielding and eventually my heart rebelled. Turning my back on the monastery was my way of regaining Celtic spirituality, or so I liked to think.

10.

TWO GOLD RINGS

'Tis the time of year when the dogwood gleams,
Quivering white through the green bird-bowers;
The bridal time, when the wooing beams
The young earth's bosom adorn with flowers.

From 'Dream Garden' by Hans Zinsser

THAT first night I stayed with Máirín and her family. Their untold kindnesses touched me, trying their best to soothe my broken heart and shattered dreams. The evening was spent crying hot, rueful tears. Máirín drove over to my father's apartment and gently broke the news to him, explaining that she would bring me around the following day. The minutes seemed to tick by agonisingly slow as I waited for her return. Finally, I heard her car pull up outside.

'How did he react?' I asked no sooner had she come in the door.

She smiled and hugged me tight.

'His face just lit up and he was delighted!'

Though relieved, I still could not stop sobbing. Máirín drew me a hot bath and put me to bed. Exhausted from crying, I slept all night long. The next morning Máirín brought me to Sunday mass before driving me to Dundrum.

My father and I embraced tightly. The warmth of his embrace set me thinking that everything would be all right again in time. In hindsight, the setback was something I held in common with László – broken dreams and hopes, unfulfilled plans, and having to start all over again. I had nothing to my name, not even a stitch of clothes. However, any clothing I did require was soon provided by Ann Flanagan, another close nursing colleague. She arrived one day in September with a bag of items ranging from skirts, dresses and blouses to assorted scarfs, gloves and jackets.

'Eibhlín, please don't be offended,' she said. 'Use these until you get stronger and can cope with shopping again.'

In the days that followed, stillness reigned in the house, more so since poor old Púca had died some weeks before. All around me life was going on: things came into being, had their day and passed on. In this natural order I was trying to find a foothold, to find my way. My brother visited as soon as he heard of my homecoming, giving me a big bear hug – the delight plainly visible on his face. By now he and Áine did not know what to make of me. In fact, it would have been impossible for them since I hardly knew myself. I was *trí na chéile*, as we say in Irish – all mixed up – but at least my family were close at hand.

My mental health had taking a battering and it would take time to heal. All I could do was try and keep busy by putting a shape on the apartment and making it more comfortable for both my father and myself. Áine donated a fold-up bed to use until such time as a carpenter could put my Grandmother Maddison's antique bed together. It did feel a bit ironic eventually lying in her bed – *I've made my bed and I can lie in it* – but bygones are bygones. She only had my best interests at heart.

The apartment became my new mission and allowed me to focus on something other than thoughts of the monastery. I began to rearrange the furniture – a perennial occupation – and had more wall units added to the kitchen and built-in wardrobes fitted in the bedrooms. It helped in so many ways, though not quite in building up an appetite. During those early days the sight of food would make me rather ill and it was hard to keep anything down. The most I could manage was tea and toast, which gave rise to some concern on my father's part.

'Most people live to eat, but you, Eibh, do not eat sufficiently to live.'

He was right, yet in my heart I thought I was making progress, albeit at a snail's pace. He often quoted lines from a poem called 'The Quitter' by Robert W. Service that seemed to pinpoint my condition so well.

'It's dead easy to die; it's the keeping-on-living that's hard.'

My father was terrific at poetry and engendered in me a love for it too. With him constantly reciting lines from 'The Quitter' and other encouraging poems, I started to grow stronger. Determination that had lain dormant for many months slowly returned as did my old feisty spirit. My appetite improved and I soon progressed to porridge and to Irish stew, and slowly became conscious of my appearance.

Friendship was my rock of stability. All of my friends, I later realised, had played a part in what you could call my rehabilitation through their acts of kindness. And, of course, my father. Strictly speaking, though I was caring for him, in truth it was the reverse. He was the one who helped restore my health, mind and body to its former state. Being in his company was the perfect balm for me at this time. At the start of this memoir, I said there was none the equal of László, with the exception of my father. It was true. All of the fine qualities that László possessed, my father had in equal abundance, minus his musical talent, of course.

The image of my father out cycling to work in the early morning had frequently filled my mind in the monastery. He was a handsome man, with a long face and nose inherited from his Kelly relatives, brown eyes and dark curly hair that greyed in his fifties. Though he was of average height, his stature was enormous to me. He had worked as a railway electrician with CIÉ, in the Inchicore Works a couple of kilometres from our home, for most of his life, bar his apprenticeship at the Guinness Brewery and a brief spell at the ESB. Coincidentally, my maternal grandfather, Roland Guy Maddison, also worked as an electrician for CIÉ at the Inchicore Works, having served his time as an apprentice in the Belfast shipyard of Harland and Wolff. Inchicore was the main engineering works for the state railway company. Like László, my father too was an extremely hard-working individual, who toiled all the God-given hours and could never rest. I liked to think there was some kind of cosmic symmetry in the fact that both our fathers had worked for railways companies.

My father's time at CIÉ was marked by great transformation. The fledgling company had come into being in the same month and year as my birth, January 1945, joining together the Great Southern Railways Company and the Dublin United Transport Company. The times were surely a-changing. In Britain, nationalisation of the railways took place in 1948 and Ireland followed suit in 1950. At that time the steam locomotive was in decline; the Irish fleet was ageing and clapped-out and the high labour costs made it uneconomical. Ireland soon followed the lead of America and Britain in introducing diesel-electric locomotives, unlike the rest of Europe which chose to embrace electrification. Coincidentally in Hungary around 1945, the first of the electric engines had been introduced, owning to the railway system having been bombed to pieces during the war. This meant modernisation for László and his fellow citizens. The new railway cars and engines were constructed at the Ganz Works in Budapest, where László would have conducted its orchestra members at the time.

Ireland took the bold step of changing its entire stock over to diesel traction straightaway. After all, modernisation of a different shade was in the air and with no reserves of coal the country could not rely upon its steam engines. And so by April 1950, the first diesel locomotive in its green livery was whistling through the Irish countryside.

The Inchicore Works had a training school where apprentices from fitters to electricians came to learn their trade, and which allowed for further skilling once qualified. The changeover meant that my father was sent to study the intricacies of the new engines and their systems, most likely to Birmingham and Manchester, where British railway locomotive builders were mainly located, but also to other engineering works possibly at Crewe and Derby. These training visits were organised through the British Railways Workshops.

It was an exciting time for my father, and not least for us. My childhood was punctuated by these training visits. I remember him at home with what he called his 'blueprints' spread out across the dining room table. Inch by inch he absorbed every detail of the electrical systems of the new trains. Sometimes standing next to him, I looked on in amazement at what seemed to me a chaotic maze of never-ending horizontal and vertical lines running hither and thither into circles, angles and squares.

The anticipation we experienced as children, awaiting our father's return at the end of each trip, was exhilarating. He never forgot to bring presents, and I especially loved the illustrated books of magical fairy worlds with toadstools, fairies and butterflies in vibrant blues and pinks. As we grew older, nature books displaying the fine detail of flora and fauna fired our imaginations. It helped that my father was an avid reader too. In this respect, the Inchicore Works played a part. The philanthropic-minded Sir John Aspinall, who became the chief engineer in 1882, ensured the employees benefitted from a reading room, dining hall and dispensary, to name just a few of his additions. Daily newspapers and books could be read by all workers, while outdoor amenities such as a pond, garden, fountain, bandstand and ball alley on the grounds could boost morale and a sense of well-being. Like many a Victorian manufacturer, Sir John certainly had an enlightened and benevolent attitude to employment.

By the end of the 1950s, my father witnessed a further one hundred diesel locomotives entering service, many built in Britain and shipped over to Ireland. Inchicore Works was now operating at the height of its powers, building and maintaining the rolling stock. The works siren was a sound everyone in the locality was familiar with and could be heard for miles around. It would sound at eight in the morning, at lunchtime and at five o'clock to signal the end of the working day.

As a teenager much of my time was spent studying in front of the big sash window in my bedroom, overlooking the back garden. Sometimes I observed my father returning from a hard day's work; often working overtime and arriving home around eight o'clock in the evening. Having secured his bicycle in the garage, he would walk down the pathway towards the house with exhaustion etched upon his face. I would knock on the window and wave down to him, his face breaking into a broad smile as he returned the wave. I always studied hard to please him, wishing him to know how much he was appreciated and loved.

A man of few words, my father had a most positive mind and a good sense of humour. He was devoid of ego and quite simply lived for his family.

There was always a willingness to see the good in others and make a positive contribution to society – I suppose lessons learned from his boy scout days, which he passed on to others in adulthood as scout leader and later scout master. His gentle and calm demeanour permeated the household, creating a strong sense of security for us. I was never aware of a cross word spoken between my parents; there was no smacking of children or physical punishments for us, only discipline maintained in a kind and verbal manner.

* * *

Within a few months of leaving the monastery, I could stand on my own two feet once more. Life was moving on. Indeed Áine and her family had relocated to Boston around this time, so change was in the air. The purchase of a car saw me driving again and helped restore my lost confidence. Often I would prepare a food basket and take my father and a newly acquired King Charles spaniel out for the day. I named him Patch, thinking it an appropriate name, as we were all stitching up the unravelled threads of life again. This company of three would drive up into the nearby Dublin Hills and gaze down upon the splendour of Dublin Bay as we enjoyed our picnic.

By then I had no regrets. I had given the monastery my best shot but it had not worked out. I could still live my life, do my best to make the world a better place but in my own way. Something, as László had pointed out, more in keeping with my nature and character.

During all this time László was never too far from my thoughts. So in January 1985, I took my courage in both hands and duly penned him a letter informing him that I had left the monastery. Seeing that I was unaware he had moved to Luxembourg, I posted the letter to his Shankill address. No written reply or telephone call followed, which left me thinking he had moved on, metaphorically speaking. There was no describing my joy, however, when he landed on my doorstep shortly afterwards, having driven all the way from Luxembourg! I was in a state of shock, in fact.

'László, is it really you?' I gasped. 'I can't believe you're here.'

He smiled and took my hand, shaking it gently. Despite his seventy years, he scarcely looked fifty. The years had been kind to him and his good looks had not deserted him. Luckily for him, there were few traces of baldness or a paunch that beset many an older man, only dark hair flecked with grey.

Within seconds, I had ushered him indoors and introduced him to my father. His visit had taken me unawares, but I quickly gathered up my scattered wits to make some show of hospitality. I prepared tea and refreshments as the men chatted, no doubt each curious about the other. László revealed that he had moved to Echternach in Luxembourg, near the German border, where Irén's nephew, Peter, lived with his family. There was a marked contrast since I last saw him. He looked relaxed and content and seemed to have borne his bereavement bravely. Afterwards, he and I went for a drive in the Dublin Mountains, passing up through Ballinteer and Glencullen towards the Devil's Elbow happy to be in each other's company. We stopped the car at one stage and strolled around, looking down across Dublin Bay and the ships at sea. Despite the bleak winter, the air was crisp and clear and a magnificent panorama unfolded before us. I had to pinch myself it was happening at all.

László stayed for the duration of the visit in his house in Shankill; thankfully, it had not been sold. In the following days we went out for dinner a few times, once to Killiney Castle Hotel, and also for walks in Marlay Park in Rathfarnham. It was very easy to converse with László as we strolled through the grounds, getting on exceptionally well. After Irén's death, and I suppose my rejection, he had sought solace in music, as he did during every major upheaval in his life. He had reconnected with the music world but this time it was folk music that held sway. I liked to think that Ireland had played some part in the direction he had taken. From his days in Ireland he had come to appreciate Irish traditional music, recognising the significance and range of the various instruments from fiddle, tin whistle, flute, harp, uilleann pipes, to button accordion, concertina and bodhrán. All types of music were of interest to him, and I imagine the influences of Bartók and Kodály and their regard for Hungarian folk music was not too far off either. Folk, as the music of the people, was just one branch of a very large music tree for him.

László had become a member of a European folk festival committee, which I believe was headquartered in Luxembourg. I'm not sure of its official name. Either way, it involved him being a member of a judging panel at various folk music competitions and visiting festivals throughout Europe. In fact, there was so much travelling involved that he bought a BMW so he could drive with some comfort – which was highly unusual for the thrifty László. There had been something of a folk revival in the 1950s and festivals began springing up all over Europe, not least Ireland. However, a trip to Ireland did not feature in László's newfound role.

As a teenager, in May 1959, I remember about sixty folk dancers from France, Denmark, India, the Netherlands, Switzerland and Ireland had performed at the National Stadium, off the South Circular Road, close to my family home. They later toured the nearby Wills tobacco factory and gave a spirited performance in the factory garden, especially a French Peiroutoun by dancers from Bordeaux. The range and variety of all their costumes had made for a dazzling display of colour.

Though László travelled throughout Europe, Hungary was still out of bounds for him. There was always the chance of meeting fellow Hungarian musicians at these festivals, however. The trips were touched by nostalgia hearing the familiar sounds of his early youth performed in front of him. The work of judging performances was immensely stimulating to him, often coming across children with indescribable talents. Many an hour slipped by as he regaled me with tales of these festivals.

László stayed in Dublin for a few days, just long enough to rekindle our friendship. To my surprise, he asked for a favour, seeing that he was living abroad.

'Would you keep an eye on my house on Adelaide Road?' he asked, 'and collect the rent money from the students living there?'

I hesitated. Perhaps now that friendship and trust were established, he felt he could rely on me like I were a family member. Obviously, whatever arrangements he had currently in place were not to his satisfaction. The request, believe it or not, was one I felt I could not honour.

'I'm sorry, László, I can't.'

Saying no was hard for me because I was still building up my lost confidence. The prospect of having to deal with tenants, possibly disruptive, and sort out their issues, I guess, overwhelmed me.

'No need to worry, Eibhlín,' László said reassuringly. 'I'll find a solution.'

This he did along with promising to return to Dublin in three months' time. Within the week he had returned to Luxembourg, but if words were unspoken at the sadness we felt at parting our mutual understanding needed none.

* * *

Seeing László again boosted my self-esteem and I convinced myself that it was time to return to my nursing career. And in the words of the Hungarian poet Endre Ady, 'steeped in the humours of old creeds, my torn and tortured self I gather up', and so I sought work. This time I set my sights on caring for the elderly, given that I had amassed some experience in this area! I took up duties in various nursing homes and hospitals for the aged around Dublin. The work could be challenging at times, but it was balanced by staff who adroitly made those in their care comfortable and content. There was one colleague whose kindness and deep-rooted spirituality impressed me profoundly: Kathy Watts. Our friendship blossomed and she became a confidante I treasure to this day. She in turn introduced me to Mary Monahan, deeply spiritual as well, who became a wonderful friend.

My father's health then deteriorated to the point where I had to curtail the amount of hours I worked. I then nursed part-time in Cedar House Nursing Home, run by the Sacred Heart Order at Mount Anville. It was a small nursing home, newly built, that provided care for their own religious. Luckily, it was located in Goatstown, quite near our home in Dundrum. For me, it was a sanctuary of peace and tranquillity and gave you the feeling of being in a special place. Had I been convalescing there, I would have been restored to health in double-quick time.

At the nursing home I frequently met its director, Mother Vera Power, who was genuinely full of charm and joy. From early morning until late at night she greeted each and every staff member either coming on or going off duty. Moreover, she understood the position with regard to my father.

'Our staff have a life outside these walls,' she said, 'and we as a congregation must be mindful of this.'

When I would come off duty around ten in the evening, I would find her at prayer in the little chapel located near the entrance door. Out of genuine concern, she always came out to wish me a safe journey home. As I say, she was an inspiration to all who had the privilege of meeting her.

* * *

László, true to his word, visited Dublin three months later and at three-monthly intervals or so after that. It gave our friendship a chance to mature and for us to get to know one other further. And, indeed, my father got to judge the measure of the man as well. It was reassuring that he considered László a fine man, a lovely man, and liked him a great deal. It cannot have been easy for my father seeing that he was a very private person and not much of a conversationalist. What's more he was in the early stages of dementia, which seemed to come in waves or spasms before he reverted to normal again.

The more I learned of László, the more I found we had much in common. Not just that both our fathers had worked for railway companies but that music was a common bond. Whereas my mother's family had been steeped in classical music, my father's had roots in traditional music.

His family, Mac Máighistir or Masterson in English, originally hailed from Newry, County Down, but had left the area in the 1800s and made their way to Dublin. His maternal grandfather, Nicholas Kelly, a Kildare man from the village of Ballymore Eustace, had married one Bridget Geoghegan. Nicholas was a tailor by trade and also a well-known traditional fiddle player and storyteller, or *seanchaí* in Irish, in the locality. His daughter Margaret, who became my grandmother, played the concertina and sometimes accompanied her father at local sessions. Sadly, my father was not musically gifted and lamented his lack of talent to me.

'My mother played an instrument, my grandfather played an instrument, my cousins play instruments, but I don't have a note in my head.'

Nonetheless, my father still could appreciate music and would welcome László's views and opinions on the subject. Like many children, my sister and I studied piano, though neither of us proved a great talent either. After I had left the convent in Hastings in my early twenties, my siblings clubbed their money together and purchased a guitar for me. Music lessons in Walton's school on North Frederick Street followed, where I did manage to strum a few cords for a short period. The guitar eventually found its way to a cousin in America.

The duration of László's visits varied quite a bit – often ranging from one week to a month. Sometimes he was taken up with his financial affairs and at one point put his house in Shankill on the market. He wanted to be rid of the property and its memories, preferring to keep a flat for himself in the Adelaide Road house. It was there in Adelaide Road that he would occasionally play the clarinet for me, pieces such as the Adagio from Mozart's Clarinet Concerto, its atmospheric sounds filling the building and allowing me to wallow in the mood of the moment. The magic he could conjure up with those notes made it my favourite instrument, followed by the cello.

Regardless of the length of his visits, once he was gone, László left a tide of emotions in his wake – sadness, longing, excitement. It was a bittersweet. As the months went on, I wished the intervals were shorter and the visits much longer. The times when he spent an entire month in the country were bliss indeed. The fact that he lived alone sometimes concerned me too; that he might be absentminded or too engrossed in this work to notice what he was doing. After all, he had poisoned himself accidentally on one occasion. I am not sure of the exact details, but it seems he added some washing-up liquid to whatever he was cooking and collapsed after eating the meal. Thankfully, he was able to ring Peter, who lived up the road, and summoned medical help.

Or else I would worry for his safety catching ferries and driving hundreds of kilometres across Luxembourg, Belgium, France, England and Wales before arriving in Dublin port. I can well remember on one occasion in March 1987, when his imminent visit coincided with the Zeebrugge ferry disaster in Belgium. The MS *Herald of Free Enterprise*, heading for Dover, had capsized minutes after leaving the port of Zeebrugge, killing about two hundred passengers and crew. The ship's bow door had been left open on leaving the port and the sea had flooded her decks almost immediately. When my father and I heard the tragic news over the radio and the extent of the fatalities and injuries, we were distraught. I convinced myself that László was aboard.

Worried to distraction, I ran to my car, jumped in and drove to the Phoenix Park, where the Garda Síochána Headquarters were located. There I spoke to two female detectives, who, observing my distress, sat me down and gave me a cup of tea. I explained my concerns. They tried to reassure me, and said they would get in touch with Interpol. There was nothing for me to do but return home and stay by the phone. The police work paid off and several hours later they rang to say that László was safe. He had travelled via Calais instead and was at that very moment nearing Whitchurch, not far from the Welsh border. At this news, my father placed his arms around me.

'All in well, Eibh,' he said, 'all is well.'

Yes, indeed it was. Later I sent the two detectives a bouquet of flowers and thank-you card for their compassion and kindness. When László eventually arrived in Dublin and I greeted him with a big hug, he was visibly touched by my concern. It was a sign, by his reckoning, of my feelings for him and his hopes rose that I might consider marriage one day. In fact, the question of marriage surfaced again and again during his visits. There was no question that I had fallen in love with László. He was unique in my eyes and capable of surprising me day after day – all the facets of his personality, his life story, his talents and achievements. Unlike the company of other men, I felt comfortable in his presence and the conversation flowed. He could put me at ease, which was no mean feat. But marriage was a big step, even if I had known him for eleven years. László tended to make up his mind rather quickly, whereas building trust and security were prerequisites for me. And they took time.

Where marriage was concerned, László also knew that I was in a difficult position as my father suffering from vascular dementia needed someone to care for him in his own home. And I was loath to abandon him for a new life in Luxembourg. During those visits, László observed just how much care my father required – with preparing food, dressing and mobility – and displayed nothing but patience and kindness towards us. It was plain to see that it weighed on his mind.

'Eibhlín, please listen to what I say, just listen,' he said one day. 'You know that your father is not well and needs you to help him. I will help you care for your father. It is not possible for you to care for him on your own.'

'All right, László, I'll think about it.'

Despite his offer, I was at a loss as to how he could in fact help. And so I dithered and declined. Perhaps, by this stage, László felt obliged to wind down his business affairs in Dublin. That year he sold the house on Adelaide Road – it can't have been easy trying to collect rents when you lived abroad in a pre-digital age. It was a great sadness to me, seeing that he had put so much work into renovating and maintaining the house. But László was a pragmatist, after all, and knew it was time to let it go.

And so the months ticked by; 1987 ran into 1988 and while his visits filled me with bliss, his absences brought me low. In September of that year I had a change of heart and I finally agreed to visit him in Luxembourg. To assuage my worries, I arranged for a kind and efficient housekeeper, Agnes, to care for my father while I was away. This lady, whom I guess was in her late sixties, proved to be an absolute godsend and we soon became fast friends.

* * *

Luxembourg, believe it or not, was not such a foreign place to me. I had been there once before in my early twenties along with a group of twenty-five others, touring Europe in a convoy of two Land Rovers. The trip was thrilling for us eager youngsters not least because we also travelled through parts of the then USSR still in the grip of communism! A forbidding place but highly exciting all the same. It was the 1960s after all and we were embracing life to the full. My only regret was that Hungary was not on our itinerary.

On this occasion, two decades later in the month of September, I flew from Dublin to the airport in Luxembourg City alone on my European adventure. From the minute I stepped from the aircraft, I fell in love with its exquisite landscape all over again.

A smiling László was there to greet me at the airport. I embraced him quickly, knowing how undemonstrative a person he was in public. In glorious sunshine we drove leisurely out of the city and headed in the direction of the Ardennes. The landscape always reminded me of an enchanted garden, with its flowing streams, captivating hills and valleys, and abundant wildlife. In the coming months and years I would get to know it thoroughly. Most of the little villages and hamlets along the way displayed colourful hanging baskets laden with nasturtiums, geraniums and a host of other flowers.

'László, look at all those flowers!' I exclaimed.

As soon as we reached the next village, László hopped out of the car and disappeared. Moments later he emerged from a florist shop, opened the passenger door and duly presented me with a large bouquet of flowers. I sat dumbstruck in the car, revelling in the romance.

On we went, heading northeastwards until we reached the small city of Echternach, on whose outskirts László's house was located. It was a real beauty spot and practically on the German border. In fact, it is the oldest city in Luxembourg still encircled by stout medieval walls and towers. The journey from the airport had taken about two hours and now I stood in front of his home lying close to dense forest. The stone house was detached, one-storey over basement, which stretched the full length of the house. The high pitched roof made it quintessentially European for me, a common sight in mountainous regions. True to form, László had purchased the building in a terrible condition and had totally renovated it himself with some local help. The first thing he did was to give me the guided tour. I could feel his delight as he pointed out some of his handiwork.

'Look, here are the steps I made!'

All I could see were beautiful steps as polished and pristine as marble leading up to the front porch.

'Over there, see this wood panelling in the hall, I did that.'

The front door made of thick glass gave the hall a dazzling glow during daylight hours. The lounge-cum-dining room was enormous, taking in the full width of the building, with large windows at either end, adding to the brightness. The house seemed bewitched by radiant light. In one part of the basement was his trademark workshop with machines, drills and hand tools for woodwork and metalwork. I could see that renovating the building had been his antidote to grief and unhappiness. As long as László had music and work he could overcome any adversity or setback. I marvelled at how he could pick up the pieces of his life with such composure over and over again.

Echternach was a city steeped in music and organised an annual festival each year since 1975 during the months of May and June. However, László had relinquished his role as a member of the folk committee and no longer adjudicated at festivals. From our conversations, I gather that politics had played too close a role in the world of music, both folk and classical. Some gifted children were not being promoted as much as they should, which did upset him. Indeed, he always felt it would be better to allow innate talent to rise to the top rather than through the machinations of others. But I suppose that's human nature. Perhaps he was reminiscing too about those bygone years when Dr Lajtha had suffered at the hands of the communists.

Being reunited with László brought me unimaginable joy. The week we spent living under the same roof was a boon and a blessing; listening to the music of Brahms and Mozart; taking strolls beside a nearby lake; and driving to scenic viewpoints where we would picnic and László would play his beloved clarinet. Before the first evening had drawn to a close, I had agreed to his marriage proposal. Such was his joy that he had to phone Harris and Susan Tomkin back in Dublin and announce the news. His patience and persistence had finally paid off after four years! And an engagement ring on my finger when I returned to Dublin was proof of that.

* * *

Part of my reluctance to readily engage in a relationship with László, and indeed men in general, was rooted in a distressing childhood experience that had stolen my innocence. At the age of nine, unknown to my parents, I had a brush with child abuse. A young Catholic priest, who was a member of a religious congregation in Dublin, had ingratiated himself into our family circle and was the cause of my great sadness.

The first incident took place in the family home on Dufferin Avenue, the priest having found some pretext or other to be alone with me. Thus emboldened, he sought permission to take me and my siblings on a holiday to his family home at a seaside location on the west coast of Ireland. This, he said, was a way of thanking my parents for their kindness to him. Naturally, my parents were delighted, and so the three of us were bundled off on a supposedly happy summer holiday. The next incident occurred on a beach dotted with gigantic sand dunes, or so it seemed to me at the age of nine. While Áine and Eoin were swimming in the sea one day, the priest cornered me in one of those sand dunes. I remember being transfixed with fear and unable to move at the time. I could not even cry out. All I could do was pray to Our Lady to come to my aid. After what seemed like a lifetime of terror, I suddenly heard a voice beyond the dunes.

'Eibh, where, where are you? Eibhlín, Eibhlín, where are you?'

I recognised my sister's voice but still could not alert her. With that, the priest scarpered as quickly as he could. And then I saw Áine's shadow looking down into the large sandy dune. Having spotted me, she ran down to me and took my hand.

'Are you all right?'

I nodded but said nothing. Then we walked to the water's edge and played together before being joined by Eoin and eventually by the so-called reverend father! Áine at that time was just twelve years of age, but endowed with wisdom beyond her years and a protective spirit. Nonetheless, the cunning priest had still been able to assault me during that holiday. It was decades later as mature women that I broached the subject with her. I asked what possessed her to come looking for me when she was enjoying her swim.

'An uneasy feeling came over me and I felt an urge to find you.'

I never spoke of the incident to my mother on our return home; however, with her sharp intellect she must have sensed my fear and dislike of the priest. For after that holiday the abuse came to a sudden end and I was never left alone with him again. Of course, the underlying shadow of fear and terror that it caused was always there and never left me. I became a nervous young girl and something of a homebird, finding it difficult to be separated from my parents. Many years later I penned a verse about that first encounter, called 'Nine Years Old'.

> Mother is not at home,
> Little girl alone
> Save one.
> Figure of blackness
> Upon staircase,
> White roman collar to neck.
> Follows her down to parlour
> Brings her to himself,
> Darkness.

Thankfully, in recent years, the exposure and discussion of Church abuse scandals have helped me to understand more fully this humiliation and exploitation. My way of coping for many years was to partially block the experience from my mind and leave it dormant in my subconscious.

* * *

László was an untold source of healing for me. His gentle nature helped to melt away my fears of intimacy and in his company I felt secure and loved. He took to calling me Pixie, which I liked a great deal. Perhaps it was my short stature and spirited, girlish nature that appealed to him. Once I had made up my mind, I wanted to marry him straightaway. After all, neither of us was getting any younger. We set the date for the following month, 21 October, and I quickly returned to Dublin to make preparations with lightning speed. The news of our engagement was greeted with pleasure by my father, who genuinely was fond of László and trusted him implicitly, despite the disparity in our ages.

Getting married in Luxembourg was no easy matter, however, as there was mighty bureaucracy hurdles to surmount – both Church and State – regardless of age. At least László was a legal resident of the municipality so it was possible for our marriage to take place. By law both of us had to undergo blood tests – to outrule tuberculosis and blood ties – and X-rays and doctor visits in order to receive a health certificate. We also had to sign reams of forms and send a report to the Luxembourg authorities stating any relevant information with regard to our forthcoming marriage. The Catholic Church, in contrast, was not quite as difficult, requiring us to sign some forms and send documentation from Ireland stating my marital status and religion and supplying birth and baptismal certificates. László, having been raised a Calvinist, was of course of no concern; mixed marriages took place in Luxembourg all the time. Despite having no interest in organised religion, László was steeped in spirituality all the same with his deep love of music and of the natural beauty surrounding him.

The marriage would be a low-key affair but it still demanded the purchase of a wedding dress. Not having a good eye for fashion, I called upon my faithful friend Kay once again for advice. She came to my aid and we visited two well-known department stores on Dublin's Grafton Street at the time: Switzers and Brown Thomas. Kay with her usual flair for couture picked out a most elegant dress at Brown Thomas. It was a light shade of purple just below the knee in length with long sleeves and a mandarin collar. It felt wonderful to wear, with Kay insisting on my turning this way and that way, making sure it fitted correctly. So once Kay was satisfied the purchase was made.

Not long before I set off for Luxembourg, Máirín arrived at the apartment in Dundrum with a wedding present. When I opened it, I discovered a beautiful watercolour of Donegal. It was a peaceful scene of a fisherman sitting in his boat awaiting a catch, set against a leaden sky and mist-coated mountains. More remarkably, it depicted Sheephaven Bay, the place associated with my mother's family, the Maddisons. Máirín had purchased the painting, totally unaware of the significance. Nonetheless, I liked to imagine that this gift was a sign of a blessing from Alexander McCrae Maddison.

Ten days or so before the wedding, László had posted the marriage banns in the city hall. The civil registration of our marriage took place in the town hall on the morning of 21 October 1988 followed by a champagne reception. The registration was conducted in English for my benefit but from the French-speaking staff we got the impression they were highly amused at our union. Given our ages of forty-three and seventy-three, they joked about us being in receipt of pensions, which I must admit was somewhat embarrassing. The staff after all had no knowledge of either of our life stories and it gave neither of us any pleasure to be figures of fun.

That afternoon we were married in a little chapel-of-ease in the parish of Echternach. The Chapel of Our Lady of Sorrows was very tiny indeed, about five seats deep but had a calm atmosphere all the same. A baroque altarpiece dominated the plain interior with a very old and faded statue of Our Lady looking down on us. Only László and I along with the priest and church clerk were present, neither of us wishing a fuss to be made.

Great care had been taken by László to purchase two gold rings and have them engraved with our initials. During the service as we exchanged the wedding rings, ever the romantic, he quietly whispered to me.

'Please Pixie, always have my initials face towards your heart.'

After the ceremony we walked back along the riverbank to what was popularly called the Cathedral – a seventh-century Benedictine abbey entrusted to Saint Willibrord, the patron saint of Luxembourg. He was an English monk born in Northumbria in 658 AD who had a strong connection with Ireland, which pleased me very much. At the age of twenty or so, he travelled to Carlow to study in monastic schools established earlier by that great Irish missionary in mainland Europe, Saint Columbanus, as he wished to live a more perfect life among the monks. One of these sites in Carlow was Rathmelsh, where Willibrord transcribed psalms, bibles and prayer books in the scriptorium and was eventually ordained. From Carlow, he led a mission to Frisia in the present-day Netherlands to spread Christianity along with several other monks.

The abbey's basilica was badly damaged during the Battle of the Bulge towards the end of the Second World War and following reconstruction a stained-glass window was installed depicting Saint Willibrord at Rathmelsh. The basilica, even today, is a sacred and serene space. I felt privileged that our marriage was blessed by this great saint.

We then returned to László's car and drove just across the border to Trier in Germany, an old Roman city on the banks of the Moselle. It had many ecclesiastical links down through the ages and was renowned for the protection of its precious relic, the Holy Tunic, the garment that was reputedly worn by Christ when he died. It was also a charming city with many Roman monuments and medieval churches to see. László had booked dinner at a hotel restaurant, whose name I cannot recall, but I do remember the chef coming all the way up from his kitchen enquiring if we found the meal to our satisfaction. Mine was Wiener schnitzel, a perennial favourite, with roast potatoes and swedes, followed by a sumptuous cream gateau. With a towel tossed over his shoulder, the chef clearly must have got wind of our marriage, as he congratulated us heartily.

The first evening of our honeymoon was spent listening to Wagner. The dramatic strains of 'The Ride of the Valkyries' reverberated through the room and made my heart skip a beat. The choice of Wagner was no accident. His great opera to passionate love, *Tristan und Isolde*, was also a favourite. Beneath László's idiosyncrasies lurked the soul of a romantic, seeking to make our honeymoon special and memorable. He had prepared delicious morsels for us to eat – canapés, nuts, biscuits and little cakes – delicately laid out on a tray. Like the German author Hoffmann, whom he admired, László believed that romantic opera was the only genuine opera because music belonged in the realm of romanticism. And like the eponymous poet Hoffman in the opera *The Tales of Hoffman,* composed by Offenbach, László had three past loves, but the muse of poetry, or rather music in László, had her in his grip. The sentiment appealed to László and was a work that he turned to again and again in his much-read *Opera Guide.*

Every minute of my time with László I cherished; it was simply wonderful travelling around the countryside in his company for a few weeks. I would have loved for it to go on and on! However, the reality of life soon tapped us on the shoulder. My father became my uppermost concern again. Difficult as it was, László and I had to part and resume our routine of visits back and forth from Luxembourg to Ireland.

I journeyed home to continue caring for my father and return to my part-time nursing position with the Sacred Heart Sisters. All I could do was store up those warm feelings that László evoked of being special and being protected for the long days and weeks ahead. My fuel for the winter months.

11.

DEVOTION AND DUTY

The beauty of this world hath made me sad,
This beauty that will pass;
… Will pass and change, will die and be no more,
Things bright and green, things young and happy;
And I have gone upon my way
Sorrowful.

From 'The Wayfarer' by Patrick H. Pearse

IN mid-December that year, 1988, László returned from Luxembourg to visit us for Christmas. Since our marriage it became obvious that being apart was proving tougher than expected, and I worried that he would feel lonely and neglected in Echternach. I was torn between him and my father, though László never once complained or voiced an objection. Because I loved my father dearly – still dressing neatly in his tailored herringbone tweed suits – I looked upon his care as a privilege and not a chore. My situation was not unique. When emigration ravaged Ireland in the 1940s and 1950s and indeed the early 1980s generations of Irish husbands worked abroad with aged parents minded back at home by wives and sisters. In those years, the word carer was not part of the nation's vocabulary, unlike today. Most people willingly cared for their own elders themselves, being stoic and tough and getting on with the business of living.

Eibhlín's father John and Aunt Kathleen in Foxrock;
the fire surround was crafted by László

László and friend Jay McQuillan (right)
in the early 1990s

László in the garden of the house in Drinklange, Luxembourg, in 1997

László and friends near Troisvierges, 1999

László enjoys a game of chess overlooking Vianden Castle, Luxembourg, in 2002

László on picnic near Trier, Germany, in 2002

Eibhlín and László at home in Drinklange in 2005

Maurice McMahon (left) with László on the terrace of the Drinklange house in 2005

László Gede interred in the Garden of Remembrance at Glasnevin Cemetery, Dublin, in 2006

Eibhlín at the grave of László's
parents, István and Zsuzsánna Gede,
in Debrecen, Hungary, in 2006

Eibhlín and Yvonne McMahon (right) revisiting
the Gede grave in Debrecen in 2009

László's house on Napsugár Street, Budapest, in 2006

Meeting László's relatives in Budapest in 2009: (back row) nephew
László Gede and niece Éva Gede Tóthné; (front row, left to right)
László Gede's wife Éva, Eibhlín's friend Kathy Watts and Eibhlín

Eibhlín and Éva Gede Tóthné (left) beside the newly erected Gede headstone in 2012

That December László arrived with news that he had purchased a house in Foxrock in the Dublin suburbs. A family home for all of us was in order, he declared – a house, rather than an apartment. From Luxembourg, he had negotiated the deal so that when he arrived he had gone straight to the solicitor, picked up the keys and moved into the partially furnished property, albeit in need of some modernisation. To say I was surprised was an understatement but delighted all the same. The property was a detached, double-fronted bungalow with a high-pitched roof located at the end of a cul-de-sac in Springfield Park. It consisted of four bedrooms with two en suite, a family bathroom, a large bright lounge/dining room and a good-sized kitchen installed with an Aga cooker. In addition, there was a laundry room, a garden at the front and rear, and a garage.

A blue Volkswagen van was another new addition in his life; transporting furniture and various equipment back and forth from Ireland would become a regular feature of his life. The plain truth was that László needed constant challenges, projects, to motivate and give him a thirst for life. Everyone needs a reason to get up in the morning and this was certainly his in those years – renovating houses to enhance and show them in their best possible light. It was his addiction. Given the number of times he moved, frequently buying and selling property, there was a rather nomadic aspect to him too, the restless spirit so often associated with creative people. Sometimes it was linked to his desire to better himself, to provide for the future, to live away from the hustle and bustle, or other times through force of circumstance like war and misfortune, or indeed marriage. It was not a case that he had no roots, but rather he could uproot and transplant himself at a moment's notice and start afresh. Moving house is traumatic for most people at the best of times, I know it is for me, but with László he had a resilience and strength that endured well into old age.

The Christmas festivities that year were celebrated in Dundrum and what a most memorable time we had. Two close relatives joined us at dinner: my mother's sister, Aunt Vera, and her cousin, Aunt Kathleen, as we called her. I picked both of them up in my car, Kathleen from her home in Monkstown and Vera from the Notre Dame des Missions convent in Churchtown, where she was residing whilst home from Kenya. Aunt Vera,

183

being a reserved and sensitive soul, had much in common with László. A piano teacher by profession, she had taught in many notable Notre Dame des Missions schools in Britain before moving on to Africa. There was no shortage of conversation between her and László – Schubert, Bach, Brahms and Beethoven being great favourites of both. And Aunt Vera had a great love of Irish traditional music as well. The sounds of Beethoven's Spring Sonata and the Pastoral Symphony accompanied our time-honoured Christmas dinner with all the trimmings.

'László, tell me, is it very difficult to conduct,' asked Aunt Vera. 'I'd love to know.'

László liked nothing better than discussing the intricacies of conducting, so he happily obliged. Before we could eat another mouthful of turkey, he had jumped to his feet at the dinner table.

'One, two, three,' he cried, waving his hand in the air and beating out the time.

This demonstration of conducting received a round of applause from a very receptive audience. And while László conducted the music, we were transported to some grand opera house in our heads. Sadly, Aunt Vera was suffering with terminal cancer during that period but in good spirits nonetheless, buoyed up by the music and company. For her, we played Tchaikovsky's Humoresque in G Major, the piano jaunty one minute, meditative the next.

My mother had a close relationship with Aunt Kathleen; in truth they were more like sisters than cousins, which was replicated in their offspring. Aunt Kathleen appreciated art very much, and in older life when she lived alone invariably spent her Sunday afternoons browsing through the National Gallery on Merrion Square. Many an hour was spent lost in admiration of the Dutch masters and Italian Renaissance artists, notably Raphael and Leonardo da Vinci. A marvellous conversationalist, even well into her seventies, Kathleen could speak knowledgeably about such artists and retain nuggets gleaned from the various art lectures she attended. My taste in comparison was more modern and I revelled in the works of Van Gogh, in particular his *Sunflowers*. László too appreciated art and had purchased a number of paintings.

However, where the visual arts were concerned, they had to be personally evocative for László. In particular, there were four paintings I remember. He had commissioned two large oil paintings of Paris and Budapest from an Irish artist called Frances Bunch Moran, possibly during the 1970s. The first was called *A Parisian Scene* and depicted the iconic Cathedral of Notre Dame, while the second showed the façade of the State Opera House in Budapest – the pinnacle of László's music career. The choice of Paris was forever linked to his joy of buying Selmer clarinets and mouthpieces in that city. In his possession also was a Tyrol scene painted by an artist whose name was Wolf. I imagine László must have purchased this painting on a visit to the area. Similarly, an oil painting of a Portuguese fishing scene by an artist named Coll must have caught László's eyes when holidaying in that country. Its pale blue skies were dotted with seagulls, small fishing boats with orangey-blue sails and sea shacks against a backdrop of sloping white houses with red roofs. The place must have struck a deep chord within him that he wished to have it captured in oil.

Yes, that Christmas the conversation was dominated very much by the arts! It pleased me that László had become acquainted with these women, so dear to me, who in turn became kindred spirits of his. My taciturn father even contributed to the conversation, regaling us with stories of his love of nature and of the great outdoors, a joy fostered in his scouting days and the troop gatherings at Powerscourt Estate in Enniskerry, County Wicklow. Opportunities to meet the founder Lord Baden-Powell sometimes had presented themselves at these gatherings, leaving an image of the great man indelibly fixed in his memory.

'What was Baden-Powell like?' László asked.

'He always struck me as a man with an innate sense of goodness,' my father replied. 'I felt nothing but respect and admiration for him.'

My father had wholeheartedly enjoyed his years with scouting friends Jack Brigs, Jim O'Connell and Charlie Egan, so much so that Jim was the best man at his wedding. Jim and my father in time went on to become scout master and assistant scout master in Ireland, and along with the troop attended jamboree meetings in Britain and mainland Europe

– they even met a Hungarian troupe one year. These were great social gatherings, enabling the youth to interact with each other and experience different cultures.

The thoroughly enjoyable day soon came to an end and I delivered Aunt Vera safely home, while László dropped Aunt Kathleen off in Monkstown on his way to Foxrock.

Over the next few months, László worked steadily and thoroughly on the house, despite his advancing years, bringing all his skills in engineering, carpentry and general DIY to bear. This was all done in between trips to and from the Continent and discharging his duties there. He divided the house into two units: the main portion for ourselves and a smaller, separate apartment for my father, which was part of an existing extension. The heating and electrical systems were upgraded and added greatly to our comfort and security. For me, the most striking features carved by his own hand were a dark mahogany fire surround in the lounge and hall panelling made from light oak transported by László in his Volkswagen van from Belgium. He had also used the same wood in his house in Echternach. When all was finished, the house looked remarkable – bright and airy. By Easter 1989 we were all installed in our new home.

During the purchase of the house and all the legalities satisfied, László had made contact with the previous owner Mrs McDonald. She had built an extension to the property, which served as the base for my father's apartment. A friendship with her developed and László would consult her on various issues from time to time, such as planning permissions. She also furnished him with a complete history of the dwelling, including the fact that the first owner had been an English lady known as Miss Primrose, who had named the house Windward. The name with a kind of musical connotation – woodwind – somehow seemed appropriate.

Though László could be accused of parsimony, he was also one for making grand gestures when the occasion demanded. Our marriage was one such event. He wanted to give me a wedding present of a handcrafted dining room set, something splendid in mahogany or teak. When it came to furniture nothing but bespoke would suffice for László. To this end, he brought me to Higginbotham's, a firm of Dublin furniture makers whose factory was located in Fairview on the northside of the city. They were also friends of László's, long acquainted with fellow craftsmen in the city.

Once at the factory, we strolled about and observed various craftsmen at work.

'Is that what you would like, Pixie?' he asked, pointing to this and that type of furniture in the making.

The choice was hard but in the end I set my heart on an ornate mahogany dining table with brass claw feet along with four chairs and two carver chairs as well as a cabinet and side table. The dining set took up residence in our home in Foxrock and even my father was impressed. The other wedding present from László was a crystal chandelier purchased in Blackrock, County Dublin. To me, this symbolised a very romantic László – after all, chandeliers had adorned many an opera house in Europe and, though an extravagance, were almost magical as they sparkled and glittered in the light.

* * *

The new arrangement in Foxrock worked to everyone's satisfaction. Now at last, care, companionship and privacy were guaranteed and convenient for all. Sometimes I thought of my own marriage as one of convenience. Not in the conventional sense of the phrase, that is, for purely strategic gain. After all, László and I loved each other dearly but life experiences and ageing had made us vulnerable. Together, we could care for each other and offer mutual protection against the travails of life. Being together made us stronger. It also slightly terrified László that he could lose me. This had come to the fore even before our marriage when I had decided to visit my Aunt Vera in Kenya. It was also an opportunity for me to see Africa, a continent brimming with excitement if not danger. After six weeks there, I received an urgent letter from László.

'Would you ever get out of that country?' he wrote. 'You'll catch some kind of disease!'

However, I soon came to realise that László had a restless spirit, like me, and constantly had to be engaged in new projects. And the more daunting and challenging, the better. His obsession was buying houses, renovating them and selling them on. The house in Echternach had fallen out of favour and so during 1989 he disposed of it and a large house in the hamlet of Leithum fell victim to his passions. Leithum was in northern Luxembourg high up in the southern reaches of the Ardennes famous for its hilly ground and wide leafy forests. In fact, it was so close to the Belgian border you could have skipped across. The hamlet was pristine and set in rolling, carpeted countryside but terribly remote. It was hard to believe the peaceful spot had once experienced German aggression and was the last place in the Ardennes liberated by the US Army on 1 February 1945. The Ardennes had earlier entered the theatre of war in the gruelling Battle of the Bulge, where, aside from vast military losses, three thousand Belgian and Luxembourg civilians were killed.

László's house had previously been owned by a master carpenter from the Belgian Royal Palace and had all the hallmarks of a miniature palace. László set about renovating it with gusto and bought two antique armchairs from the owner upholstered in red velvet with ornate arms and legs, which he displayed in a special room off the hall. The only downside was that the house came with no garden to speak off and no surrounding land.

László and I started to build a life cemented by common interests. When he realised that I shared my father's appreciation and love of poetry, he quickly introduced me to the works of two well-known Hungarian poets, Sándor Petőfi and Endre Ady. Petőfi, born in 1823, captured the Hungarian romantic spirit and is considered Hungary's national poet. As a nationalist, he wrote with passion and fervour about his beloved country and reputedly inspired the Hungarian Revolution of 1848. At the age of twenty-six, his life came to an end on the battlefield, like many a romantic hero, and today is still beloved by the Hungarian people.

The revolutionary Ady was born in 1877, and as a young man studied law at the Reformed College in László's birthplace of Debrecen. Highly introspective and a keen observer of the world around him, his work is replete with haunting descriptions of war. In 1916, during the First World War, he wrote that 'man who has power over the world is destroying it', and witnessed his country descend into chaos. I could understand why László in his own exile turned to these poets over and over again. As I read from their works, I realised that László must truly have loved his country and felt a terrible loss at not being able to return. I, for one, cannot imagine a life worth living if denied entry to Ireland, the land of my people.

However, the year 1989 was another turning point in his country. László had always taken a keen interest in world affairs and kept abreast of changes. His eyes were on Gorbachev when he came to power in the Soviet Union in 1985 and slowly started to introduce the reform policies of *glasnost* (openness) and *perestroika* (restructuring). A sea change was in the air, but László doubted if there could ever be a human face to socialism. Events in Poland and the strikes organised by Solidarity in 1988 looked promising, but still László was not entirely convinced. Life in Hungary had become difficult again with rising inflation, massive foreign debt and widespread poverty, forcing János Kádár to retire after thirty years plus as communist leader. During 1989, revolts starting in Poland had spread from one Eastern European capital to another. Refugees streamed out of East Germany to Austria via Hungary, reminding László of his own escape decades earlier. The collapse was spectacular and communist governments all fell like dominoes. By October, the Hungarian communists introduced legislation for free elections and a presidential election. The news was pure rhapsody to László.

'At last, at last,' he exclaimed, 'the chains of oppression holding down the human spirit are gone.'

Even so, he was reluctant to return to Hungary. There had been little or no news of his brother Zoltán, the only other surviving family member, and their relatives. In László's mind, Hungary was frozen in time and he was averse to disturb it.

* * *

My father was more than happy in his new habitat in Foxrock. The move did not interfere with Eoin's visits, and he continued his routine of looking in on him every Sunday afternoon, sometimes accompanied by his wife Josephine and one or other of their children, Neil-John, Denise or Ciarán. All of them sincerely loved their grandfather and

189

he reciprocated the feeling. It was a pleasure to observe my father and brother engrossed in conversation; both men possessed a quick wit that sparked off a spirited banter, as in days of old. Eoin's Sunday visits were a good way to stimulate my father's brain and get it to respond to conversation. Although he continued to suffer from vascular dementia, it mostly manifested itself as a mild cognitive impairment, where his memory and orientation were affected somewhat.

With time on my hands I was eager to improve the garden, as László had little time to devote to it with his mind firmly focused on the house in Leithum. On one occasion, I got the idea to surprise him. As soon as László had sailed out of Dún Laoghaire harbour bound for mainland Europe, the workmen sailed into our driveway. A front tarmacadam was laid and the back garden redesigned. I ordered a ceramic plaque decorated with squirrels and woodlands bearing the house name Windward and fixed it to the gatepost for good effect. His reaction on his return was certainly one of surprise – not at the transformation of our garden but at the expense I had incurred!

'Pixie, it's just as well I have a strong heart!' he declared.

László, well into old age, was as frugal as ever and wouldn't spend tuppence, as we say. My spending all that money was seen as an extravagance – almost like a disease. Our personalities would sometimes collide on issues like that. Yet it was something that I just accepted, knowing that I could never change his ways.

The apartment that László had created for my father, albeit smaller, resembled the one he had just vacated, or so my father thought. It was curious but László almost instinctively knew what would keep my father calm and content. Being able to look out upon trees, birds and the garden flush with life was better than any tonic. It reminded him of his boy scout days and the troop gatherings in County Wicklow. All his life he had been a man at ease with nature and loved nothing more than walking the hills or enjoying a picnic in the wilds.

My father, well into his eighties by now, could follow the political situation to some extent in the country, thus fulfilling his love of politics, and he also continued to solve the crossword puzzle in his daily newspaper.

All this helped to keep his mind stimulated and active. Politics was a passion that I shared with my father, and László to a lesser extent. My father had experienced politics at first hand as a boy when Ireland was under British rule and had witnessed the birth of the Irish state in 1922. In my youth, I had been very idealistic and nationalistic, driven by an enormous love for my country. Much of my 'greenness' had been fostered by my education through the Irish language.

However, László tempered my patriotic views and opened my eyes up to the threat of republican violence and the dangers of extremism. He had good reason after all. Since the 1970s, László had followed Irish current affairs on television and in the newspapers so could comment intelligently on the situation. He could see how Ireland of the 1970s and 1980s was dominated by the Troubles in Northern Ireland, when sectarian violence broke out among loyalists and republicans. The Irish Republican Army (IRA) then was very different to the one that had existed at the foundation of the Irish state, the Old IRA, as we called it. Back in 1917, the original IRA, known as Óglaigh na hÉireann, had formed when Irish Volunteers refused to enlist in the British Army during the First World War and had subsequently fought in a just War of Independence. However, there had been so many splinter groups in the succeeding decades, many of whom engaged in criminality, that it was now a far cry from its original ideals. László could only see the havoc it wreaked with its bombing campaigns and lives lost and destroyed. On the day that the republican hunger striker Bobby Sands died in the Maze Prison in Northern Ireland in May 1981, I pulled down all the blinds in the house as a mark of respect. I was so outraged that I was tempted to sign up to Sinn Féin, the political wing of the organisation.

'Pixie, nationalism is very dangerous,' László remarked one day many years later. 'And radical nationalism is a playground for the unenlightened.'

My father too had tried to curb my youthful radical views, fearful they might be put into action one day. As a young lad, he had joined the nationalist youth organisation Na Fianna Éireann, which was a kind of boy scouting movement run along military lines. Boys, between the ages of eight and eighteen, took an oath on joining: 'I promise to work for independence of Ireland, never to join England's armed forces, and to obey my superior officers.' My father would have been about eight in 1917. He along with the other boys would have learned skills such as drilling, first aid, map reading, scouting, signalling, musketry and field sketching. There was also a cultural element in so far as the Irish language and the history and legends of Ireland were taught. My father never spoke much about his activities with Fianna Éireann, although he kept his badge from the organisation, which I still have today. He would have been a member during the War of Independence and the Civil War, with many of the boys carrying messages to and from rebel leaders.

Some of my father's cousins, the Dempseys, of whom he was most fond, were staunch nationalists, and I imagine they encouraged him to join. His first cousin, Gerald Dempsey, was a member of the proscribed Irish Republican Brotherhood (IRB) and was on the run during the War of Independence, while his brother Joe was a member of the British Army who later fought overseas during the Second World War. Another brother, Bertie, was killed in action during the Gallipoli Campaign, aged just twenty-three years. Our family had military men on every side of the divide!

Death seemed all around in those years. Like László, my father had endured great personal tragedies but never displayed his sadness. By the age of twenty-three in 1932, he was orphaned, having buried his entire family: mother, father and three siblings. His younger brothers, Brendan and Gregory, along with his grandmother, fell foul of the 1918 influenza pandemic; his mother died from cancer of the womb in 1920; his darling sister Philomena died from tuberculosis aged just seventeen; and a heart weakened by alcohol claimed the life of his father in 1932.

The political party Fianna Fáil, which had formed in 1926, became my father's second family. As he matured into a young man, he joined the party, giving of his time and work voluntarily. He helped to build up the political organisation at grassroots level and sometimes enlisted the help of me and my siblings. We worked with him in filling envelopes and going from door to door with party literature, attending meetings and helping out during election campaigns. To us, it all seemed rather exciting at the time.

My father had a quiet pacifism, much like László's father returning from the First World War. His dislike of extremism and aggression was ever-present when I was growing up. On one occasion, there was a strike in CIÉ, which was nothing short of catastrophic for our family. The dispute, over pay rates, began on 16 December 1950 and ended, for most workers, through the intervention of the Archbishop of Dublin, John Charles McQuaid, on 28 January 1951. However, the Electrical Trades Union (ETU), of which my father was a member, were not satisfied with the result and called their members out on strike once more. This second strike lasted eighteen long months and was confined to electricians only, bringing unimaginable suffering to their families. Meanwhile, CIÉ had engaged outside electricians to keep the trains running during the protracted strike.

During those bitter months, my parents had to endure the hardship of paying the mortgage, mouths to feed, two children prepared for First Holy Communion and another for Confirmation, as well as two Christmases without an income. The paying guests seemed most difficult to find during these endlessly long months. My mother set up a kind of soup kitchen in the family room of our home. I well remember seeing a cauldron of hot soup permanently perched on the range, with ETU strikers trooping in and out when relieved of picket duty at Harcourt Street and Heuston Stations.

Through all the upheaval, our family witnessed extraordinary kindness, generosity and graciousness from relatives. Bridget Dempsey saw to it that food was always on our table. Her husband, Uncle Gerald, then deceased, had opened a grocery shop that thrived; my mother's sister Irene, then living in New York, sent money home to help. Being a skilful tailor, May Dempsey presented a suit and beautifully tailored overcoat for Eoin to wear on his First Holy Communion day. A Scottish Presbyterian friend of Grandmother Maddison, whom we called Aunt Nan, made a gorgeous taffeta dress of turquoise blue for Áine's Confirmation and also one for me.

Christmas of 1952 was a tough one, though. Áine, only ten years of age, suddenly came upon my mother in tears not long before the festive season began. My mother sat her down and took both her hands in hers.

'Áine, dear, Santa is not able to come this year,' she revealed. 'Please do not divulge this to Eoin and Eibhlín.'

That Christmas, however, saw my sister receive a pair of bright orange slippers with black squares that she can still vividly recall. My mother's brother and sister had come to our rescue! Aunt Ida supplied a doll and other small items for me, while Uncle Tom purchased a cowboy outfit for Eoin.

Finally, at the end of his tether, my father contacted his Augustinian friend and confidant, Father Aloysius, at John's Lane Church as well as Andy Clarkin, the then Lord Mayor of Dublin and a Fianna Fáil senator. Putting their heads together, it was decided to form a petition to return to work and to get as many strikers as possible to sign it. My father was first to sign his name in an effort to encourage the others and many followed suit. The intervention was made out of sheer desperation but to the displeasure of the union. The strike ended almost immediately to the great relief of the workers. However, an ETU official later asked my father would he be willing to join the union committee or board, having recognised his integrity in leading people. My father's response to this invitation was a measure of the man.

'It's not in my nature to lead people,' he replied. 'I'm not capable of it.'

He was always moderate and careful in his ways, advising us to avoid aggression and never to embark on negativity and to stay in the middle ground. That advice still rings in my ears today. And, although I do not always succeed, I try to live my life with these concepts in mind. In fact, those words could have been delivered by László himself. Some politicians did leave their mark on László. I remember him recalling that Alan Dukes, Minister for Finance during the mid-1980s, had a great intellect and put revitalising the economy above party politics. Martin McGuinness, who was Sinn Féin's chief negotiator in the Northern Ireland Peace Process, also had a great brain, as he saw it.

Old regimes and old orders seemed to be falling around the world. In 1990, apartheid in South Africa dramatically collapsed and Nelson Mandela was freed in February that year. Images of Mandela flashed around the world and we watched on television as he left Victor Vester

Prison, outside Cape Town, holding the hand of his wife Winnie. Twenty-seven years spent in prison was hard to credit, even to László, who had once endured incarceration for several months.

'Now there's a man of great courage,' László remarked.

It brought satisfaction to László that the country which had sheltered him and Irén, that had educated his stepdaughter, could now finally rid itself of its inhumane and brutal policy of apartheid. The stain on the country's soul could finally be washed clean.

Words could never adequately sum up my feelings of gratitude to László, in enabling me to care for my father. To me, my husband was a very special person and an inspiration in human kindness. Not every partner would have been as understanding and tolerant as he was.

* * *

Now that László was settling back into Irish life and had taken up residence, he renewed previous acquaintances. One was with Helen, his former tax adviser. She had not forgotten him, since he was someone who invariably left a lasting impression on people. However, trying to locate Helen took some time. Unbeknownst to László, she had moved to Monkstown in County Dublin in the late 1980s. He arrived at her old house in Blackrock, only to be told she had changed residence. His pleas for knowledge of her new whereabouts fell on deaf ears at first, but he persisted.

'I'm not leaving until you give me her address and phone number.'

The new owners relinquished the information, suspecting that László was not a man to be trifled with. That evening Helen's phone rang, and to her astonishment and delight László was on the other end. She wondered why he wanted to contact her.

'Mrs Murphy, I want you to meet my new wife.'

The next day he called down and introduced me to Helen and her husband John. Helen, who struck me as very pleasant and efficient, had noticed a very obvious change in László and was pleased to see him looking so happy. It was, she felt, as though he had a new lease of life.

László also made contact with Dr Harris Tomkin and his wife Susan. Thereafter, we would visit them at their house, Clontra, for tea every fortnight. The visits were always a pleasure because of their enjoyable company and the sheer uniqueness of their house. There were so many enchanting features from the trellised veranda to the grand stone staircase that led up to a central wood-panelled hall. The house contained a *piano nobile* common in Italian villas, whereby the bedrooms were downstairs and reception rooms upstairs to avail of the splendid views of the gardens.

Under the magnificent frescos on the vaulted ceilings of the dining room, László would talk about his life in Luxembourg and music in general. Susan would prepare tea with scones and sponge cake on Royal Albert Old Country Roses fine bone china. A few short years later, when her husband died, Susan wished me to have the entire tea set to remind me of the lovely teas we had. And, whenever I use it, I remember those precious days with affection. Those visits to Clontra were indeed a step back in time and a welcome retreat from the cares of the world.

László still took an interest in musicians, in particular Irish ones, and thought John O'Conor was a most gifted pianist; in fact, as far as László was concerned, he was another Liszt! O'Conor's interpretation of Beethoven was also masterly and beyond compare. László, in general, considered Ireland to be a very talented and rich country, music-wise. He looked upon flautist James Galway as a genius, and would become absorbed in his playing whenever listening to a recording. Ireland was also blessed in having so many notable opera singers in the past, such as Margaret Burke Sheridan, Veronica Dunne and Bernadette Greevy. To be honest, I did not truly appreciate the richness or intense beauty of the human singing voice until I met László. Yes, of course I loved music and choral work, but he explained to me that the human voice was the best instrument of all. It could thrill and soar to heights that musical instruments could never reach. Its range was almost spellbinding. After that conversation, I looked anew at opera singers and formed a deep appreciation of them.

László's passion for renovating houses had not deserted him and so in 1992 he swapped the house in Leithum for one in Troisvierges, a little town about twelve kilometres from the border. There was a tinge of sadness that Leithum was quitted, as the house had been beautifully restored and was something very special. Part of me would have loved to bundle up the catalogue of houses that László had renovated over the years, all unique in their own right. However, from a social viewpoint, Troisvierges was bustling in comparison and well served by transport links. In fact, the place boasted the very first railway station in the northern part of the country. While László could throw himself wholeheartedly into work and eschew company, I could not. To my delight, Troisvierges had one main street, which at that time had three small grocery shops, two bakeries, two butchers, a boutique, hairdresser, undertaker-cum-pottery shop, a dental surgery, optician and doctor's surgery. It was practically a metropolis after the remoteness of Leithum.

The new house, centrally located, was quite spacious and even had a walk-in wardrobe for me. But the best part was our new neighbours, Nicolas and Maria Lamy-Pleger. Maria was an elderly lady, fair-haired and fair-skinned, and of medium height. In time I would learn that she was most careful about her appearance and always dressed beautifully. For his part, Nicolas was tall and elegant and forever smiling; in fact, he seemed to live in a bubble of positive energy. Every year I would see them when I came to visit from Ireland. Luckily, they both spoke English.

* * *

In the last years of my father's life, I continued to nurse part-time while László still divided his time between Luxembourg and Ireland. Caring for my father and confined to the house for long periods also set me thinking about furthering my nursing skills. I had in mind to pursue a diploma in hospital management at the Faculty of Nursing at the Royal College of Surgeons in Ireland (RCSI). My mind was ready and eager to grapple with new experiences, even in my late forties.

First, I sought the advice of my former tutor, Annette Donnellan, at the hospital where I had completed my training in 1971. This was St Laurence's Hospital on North Brunswick Street in Dublin's north inner city, which consisted of the Richmond, Hardwicke and Whitworth Hospitals. These hospitals were steeped in history and part of the fabric of Dublin City. They were known collectively as the House of Industry Hospitals after an Act of Parliament in 1772 sought to improve the relief of the poor and destitute in Ireland by setting up such institutions. A mere mention of that name in the twenty-first century is enough to strike fear into your heart. However, it was far from the case when I arrived in the hospital.

My memory of Annette was that she was a rock of sense and had coached each and every student as though we were her own children. Upskilling, as they say nowadays, was something every nurse was aware of from the start of their career. After qualifying as a staff nurse, I had applied to the Royal Victoria Eye and Ear Hospital on Adelaide Road for a diploma in ophthalmic nursing, where coincidentally Dr Alex Tomkin was one of the lecturers. Little did I think I would meet his family over a decade later. After receiving my diploma there, I went on to study children's nursing at Our Lady's Hospital for Sick Children in Crumlin, but didn't remain there for long. Children's nursing was not for me. From there I took up duty at St Vincent's Private Hospital, where I was to spend nine very happy years.

With Annette's encouragement in the early 1990s, I applied for the RCSI course and went on to enjoy the challenge. My new venture also received the backing of László, keen to see me happy and fulfilled. The fifty or so students participating in the course were much younger than I was, but that did not hamper the experience at all. It was an eye-opener to observe their enthusiasm, zest and thirst for knowledge. Whenever my father was particularly unwell and I missed a lecture, without fail my fellow students would supply me with whatever notes and clarification I needed.

There was a varied programme of subjects, such as leadership, organisation and delegation, and dealing with conflict – topics new to me in theory but old as the hills in practice. We also touched upon initiating and managing change, motivation, and teaching skills. There was no shortage of opportunities to discuss issues with my fellow students and pool our knowledge and experiences. In hindsight, it was a most detailed course that I found exhilarating and challenging, making me realise that further education is healthy and essential for nurses. Sadly for me, I was unable to take the RCSI examinations as my father was too ill at the time.

My father rallied somewhat, enough for me to consider visiting László in Luxembourg that August. It had become customary for me to spend a month there each year. Agnes, who by now had become a trusted housekeeper and friend, would care for my father in my absence. It was a relief to know that he was in good hands and that I could return each time to a spotless and tranquil house. In 1994, I made preparations to leave as usual for my holiday and join László.

However, prior to leaving, my father's condition deteriorated and he was admitted to St Columcille's Hospital in Loughlinstown for a few weeks. His dementia was beginning to take its toll at this stage. He grew distressingly confused about where he was and the people around him. Thankfully, Saint John of God Hospital was situated nearby and had a more modern and well-equipped unit for those suffering with this illness. Together with our family doctor we arranged for him to be cared for there, while I visited László. Its dedicated nursing staff took over and relieved me of the pressure I was under. It was reassuring to leave my father in such a caring, protected and secure environment. Little did I realise that it was to be the last.

In Troisvierges, my joy at being reunited with László was dinted by worries about my father. Basking in the warm Luxembourg sunshine and rewinding was off my radar now. Much as László tried to comfort and help me relax, nothing would ease my mind until I returned home and saw my father again. Once back in the country, I immediately drove to the hospital and brought him home. His condition had worsened further and he hardly knew me or anyone else for that matter. There was little to distract his attention now, not even his pipe tobacco nor our dog Patch. In fact, the elderly Patch had died not long before, worn out by diabetes.

During those early days of September 1994, Eoin would come out early in the morning and again late in the evening to help me nurse and settle my father. Every hour of the day was spent tending to my father. On informing Áine that our father's time had come, she immediately travelled back to Dublin from Boston and within hours was at his bedside.

The following day Áine, Eoin and I nursed him together. Later in the evening at around nine o'clock he gently and peacefully slipped away from this world.

At eight-five years, my father had lived a full life, and it was not easy letting him go. At the graveside as family and friends paid their respects, many spoke of his peaceful and gentle ways and also of his integrity, honesty and goodness. His suffering was at an end and with that came solace for us. However, from that day on, dearest László had my full and undivided love and attention.

PART III

LIVE AND LET LIVE

12.

LIFE IN LUXEMBOURG

A journey can become a sacred thing.
Make sure before you go,
To take the time
To bless your going forth,
To free your heart from ballast.

From 'For the Traveller' by John O'Donohue

I T was February 1995 and four months after my father's death when I moved to Luxembourg to be with László permanently. It brought a welcome end to us dividing our time between two countries and our unconventional set-up. Finally, we would be reunited under the one roof. Strange as it may seem, leaving Ireland did not worry me. It was not hard bidding farewell to the unsettled Irish weather after all; downpours and flooding, high winds and dull skies had marked the months since my father's funeral. Also, at this juncture my nursing career had come to an end, but I eagerly embraced the promise of new challenges and adventures abroad. Saying farewell to Aunt Kathleen was not easy, admittedly, as she was like a second mother to me and I loved her dearly. However, Luxembourg beckoned like a bright beacon on the horizon.

Arrangements were made to rent out the house in Foxrock and the apartment in Dundrum for the foreseeable future. So once again László packed up his blue Volkswagen van and trailer with our belongings.

There was no way I wanted to part with my poetry books and twenty-five volumes of *Encyclopaedia Britannica*. There was also the matter of the chandelier wedding present. Our neighbours, Maurice and Yvonne McMahon, made our final days memorable and gave us a good send-off. Yvonne's mother had been the previous owner of our house, Windward, thus Maurice and his wife had become good friends of ours.

With our departure imminent, my excitement and exhilaration grew. Yvonne had invited us to dinner a couple of days beforehand and that evening became a joy to remember. The four of us sat at a large dining table with their four beautiful children and tucked into a freshly caught salmon. Such laughter and good humour softened the sadness that farewells brought to me. As for László, he rarely showed emotion. Maurice, an obliging Kerry man, assisted László in loading up the van and no matter how many times László rearranged furniture and other items, Maurice took it all in his stride with great patience! Maurice, a brilliant history teacher, was one of the few people in whom László confided as he gained a foothold in old age. László had left a lasting impression on him too. My husband's shrewd, academic mind mixed with a Protestant or rather Calvinist ethic – frugal, hard-working, honest – were hard not to notice.

So, as a further chapter in our lives came to an end, another was about to begin!

* * *

In the early morning mists, I waved goodbye to Windward as the Volkswagen van and trailer slowly moved out of the driveway. We headed for Dún Laoghaire ferry terminal and crossed the Irish Sea to Holyhead. Luckily, the crossing was calm and uneventful. As we drove into Wales, László smiled with that serene kind of look I miss to this day.

'I have a surprise for you,' he announced, beckoning to the road ahead.

Instead of taking the most direct route on the A55, we headed towards the breathtaking Welsh hills in Snowdonia National Park on the more historic A5. Meandering streams, quaint little bridges, stone cottages and an abundance of sheep greeted us along the way. A light dusting of snow covered the land in places, but László managed to manoeuvre the van and trailer perfectly through the slippery roads. He seemed so finely in tune with his vehicle and could handle it adroitly like it were a clarinet or saxophone. Travelling along those ancient spellbinding roads, we were transported back in time to when stagecoaches and mail coaches ploughed their way between London and Holyhead often to catch the mailboat to Ireland.

Hours later we were scurrying down the motorway towards Dover and that evening crossed the English Channel to Ostend in Belgium. László preferred to bypass France altogether, believing the French to be rather aggressive, whereas the Belgians were more retiring. Because of the trailer in tow, László had to drive slower than normal anyway and keep an eagle eye on the road. From Ostend, we continued our journey on into the night through Belgium and Luxembourg. A fine winter landscape seemed to grace all of Europe with remnants of snow everywhere. But after a few hours I settled into a deep slumber, while László drove on.

By the time we reached Luxembourg, we had been on the roads and high seas for over twenty-four hours. The powers of concentration that László possessed when driving never ceased to amaze me, if not frighten me at times. They were truly phenomenal, pressing on and on as he did no matter what journey we made. From the time he left Ireland on that occasion, he never once took his hands from the wheel for a break, with the exception of the two ferry crossings and a short break in Dover, when he had no choice but to rest. It was no small feat for a man who had put his youth long behind him. At eighty years of age, he just fixed his eyes on the road and continued driving with our furniture in tow, while I broke the monotony by chatting or snacking.

It was perhaps a measure of just how restless and obsessive László was that he constantly changed houses. In the previous month, he had sold the house in Troisvierges and purchased another in the nearby hamlet of Drinklange – another new challenge for him. Even so, it felt like a new beginning for both of us, wiping the slate clean and starting anew. Though the house was situated in the heart of the undulating countryside, at least Troisvierges was not too far away.

László's choice of Drinklange and Troisvierges – and indeed Leithum – was curious, but revealed much of his mentality. The area was within a kilometre of three borders: Germany, Luxembourg and Belgium. To him, it offered security, plain and simple. Straddling three borders meant he could escape quickly, if political circumstances ever changed and he was forced to flee. A perennial distrust of the Germans lurked in his heart but it did not stop him from visiting Germany frequently. That we lived in peacetime and there was no unrest or conflict in these regions meant nothing to László. He had lived during atrocities, deprivation, conflict, human rights violations and it was hardwired into his brain; he was taking no chances. As he grew older, these things weighed even more on his mind, perhaps becoming irrational fears. At least the beauty of the Ardennes was a balm on a soul as tortured as his.

It was early afternoon when we entered Troisvierges and straightaway made for our friends' home, Nicolas and Maria Lamy-Pleger, to collect our house keys. On arrival, there was no hiding Maria's delight as she waved from the hall door, while her husband Nicolas ran down the steps to greet us, laughing as he spied the loaded van and trailer. Our neighbours led the way to our new home in Drinklange, while we followed in convoy, and at last our manoeuvres were finally over.

Snowflakes were falling as we entered the driveway but we were soon indoors, installed in the warm cosy interiors. Kind-hearted Maria busied herself making a pot of tea and produced a plate of delicate sandwiches made earlier. As we sipped and nibbled, I took stock of my new surroundings. From first setting eyes on the house, I had fallen head-over-heels in love with it. The building was in a Swiss chalet style with a gabled, high-pitched roof and wide eaves, and the hall door was flanked by large windows on either side. All the windows had wooden louvered shutters painted in pale green and cream in keeping with the surrounding countryside. László's car had been safely stowed away in the garage before he left for Ireland. He had described the house to me beforehand, but now it seemed almost like a fairy tale stretching before my very eyes.

By now, László was on the verge of collapse. So, Nicolas and I ushered him to bed, where he fell into a deep exhausted sleep. Nicolas and I then began to empty the van and trailer of its contents and after several hours unpacking we left everything in order in the basement. The snow had now arrived in earnest but at least we could retreat indoors for the rest of the day.

A delectable aroma filled the air as we climbed the stairs to the kitchen. Earlier in her own home, Maria had prepared chicken and pasta with peas, carrots and broccoli in a delicious sauce, which she now removed from the oven. By that stage, László had felt rested and restored enough to join us for the meal. It was a relief to me, worried as I was that he had overdone it.

Our new life got off to a good start, sitting around the kitchen table and exchanging news about the trip and village gossip with our friends. Luckily for me, Nicolas and Maria preferred to speak in English and, of course, their native Luxembourgish.

'László, how could you drive all this way so quickly, at eighty years of age?' Maria asked.

'Oh, I'm used to it,' he replied. 'It's my way.'

To be honest, I could barely concentrate on the conversation. I was filled with such deep exhilaration it was like the very stars in the firmament had entered the room and were dancing about in merriment. Our new home was far beyond my expectations. The purchase of the house had come about through Maria and Nicolas. A cousin of Nicolas's, an elderly woman, had lived in the house previously but had died suddenly in her hallway trying to summon help after receiving a fatal bee-sting. Once all the legalities had been settled and László learned of the vacant property, Maria and Nicolas had helped negotiate the purchase on his behalf.

As evening grew into night, Maria and Nicolas took their leave, biding us goodbye in Luxembourgish.

'*Äddi, äddi*, dear friends, until tomorrow.'

They then drove quietly off in the newly laid path of snow. To have one friend is richness but to have them at home and abroad is indeed a treasure.

In the days that followed I unpacked in earnest and began to put a shape on our new home. When it came to home furnishings and décor, László had a simple, rather functional outlook, whereas I now liked to be surrounded by items precious to me. These were trappings that said as much about my personality and taste as my upbringing. Indeed, my mother would have taken great pride in her home with such things as family portraits, fine bone china and a piano to create a comfortable atmosphere. My Aunt Kathleen was just the same. From Ireland, I had brought Irish linens, Czech crystal, framed photos, family paintings, two bookcases and the many books acquired on family history, poetry and, of course, the *Encyclopaedia Britannica*.

Prior to living in Foxrock, László did not have any framed photos of his own. I had remedied that on one of his many trips to Luxembourg, and he was thrilled when I duly presented the result on his return. These photos took pride of place in our dining room in Drinklange; one wall was devoted to my relatives and another to his. A framed scroll of my mother's family tree and a portrait of a distant relative, Sarah Maddison, did catch his eye. Sarah was dressed in an eighteenth-century blue velvet riding habit that spoke of a bygone privileged age. I'm sure László too must have felt his own family were well consigned to the past. By now there was very little contact with his relatives in Hungary and he rarely spoke of them. There had been a falling-out with Irén's cousin Peter Czibula, who was living in Echternach with his family. Over what, I do not know. A distance of over sixty kilometres now separated us and our paths never crossed in the ten years that I spent in Luxembourg.

Several items belonging to László were also transported from Ireland, including silverware and furniture such as his handmade cabinets. Among the silverware were trays and teapots and a coffee set acquired over many years, no doubt when Irén was alive. For László, the handmade furniture he made was sufficient decoration in our home because he was not one for gilding the lily. You could say they were works of art. He was a genius with his hands, as Maurice once remarked. The care and skill he later put into making a polished burr walnut bedside locker for me was better than the costliest diamond ring. Even today when I roll my eyes over its beautiful edges and surfaces, it takes my breath away.

With László busying himself in the house, I was eager to get out and about. Luckily, the train station in Troisvierges was no distance away, and before long I was making weekly visits to Luxembourg City. It satisfied my desire to embrace the world and learn new things. The city is best known for its opulent cathedral, Notre Dame, which holds the casket of the Grand Duchess Charlotte in its crypt, lying behind ornate golden gates. Her son, Jean, was the reigning Grand Duke during my early years in Luxembourg. I soon got my bearings in the city and started strolling around its spotless streets. The city was divided into two distinct parts: the lower district, known as the Grund, sinks beneath the city and straddles the River Alzette; the upper part is a partially walled fortress, known as Gibraltar of the North.

In this hub and hive of activity, I passed by the fairy-tale Grand Ducal Palace where the Duke and his family officially reside. As I came to learn, the Luxembourg people are very proud of their royal family, particularly the Grand Duchess Charlotte, who was a symbol of hope during the Nazi Occupation. The city boasted charming squares, public buildings, restaurants, shopping centres, hotels and cafés. In fact, the cafés overlooking the Grund and the Alzette were frequented by me in particular. After visiting the shops, I liked to sit and ponder there, often losing myself in thought, or simply watching life go by. Three vast parks also weaved their way through the city, and I often walked from park to park just to absorb the sights and smells of the trees, flowerbeds, shrubs, fountains, ponds and green open spaces.

The biggest challenge for me was deciding which language to learn so I could converse with the locals. It was less of a problem for László, competent in French, German, English and, of course, Hungarian. Naturally, he managed far better than I did! Luxembourgish, similar to German and Dutch, was recognised as the national language, while French and German were both used in all official business. When László asked which language I intended to study, I opted for German. I reckoned that being a Saxon language it would be less difficult for me as an

English speaker. That and its guttural sound and grammatical likeness to the Irish language would prove an advantage, or so I thought. There was also the reason that I liked all things German.

Not long after my arrival, a young neighbour offered to help me improve my German. Harriet was a tender soul who was married with three young children. Once a week I would visit her at home for an hour or two and we would chat and laugh over a cup of tea as I struggled to string out a sentence. I never mastered the language, admittedly, but spoke enough in time to make myself understood. Of course, necessity is undoubtedly a great motivator!

* * *

Living in mainland Europe filled me with a desire to see new places. After all, this had been one of the attractions of moving to Luxembourg in the first place. And László was more than happy to drive me around and take an occasional break from his labours. Sometimes we would take a picnic and visit various locations in Luxembourg, such as the fairy-tale Vianden Castle, and the surrounding countries. Generally, they were days out as László never wished to stay overnight – cost never ceased to be a consideration. Instead we would set up our picnic table and chairs and eat *al fresco* and play chess. In Germany, we visited Aachen, Cologne and Düsseldorf amongst many other places. To me, these cities were magnificent, despite their bold heavy architecture and what looked like centuries of soot clinging to the towering steeples of Cologne Cathedral. Everywhere in Germany, I was mesmerised by the order and the feeling of everything in its correct place.

Belgium, on the other hand, seemed rather like a poor sister of Germany. There was no denying that the country had a lot to offer, but its wealth seemed unfairly divided to me. I came across many a rundown, impoverished area in the years László and I travelled there. It did contrast too with the high standard of living enjoyed by the people of Luxembourg, one of the richest countries in the world. Visiting the Netherlands, especially Amsterdam, was an absolute joy, however. It was a mecca for tourists – its bright narrow canal houses with pointed gables, its myriad meandering canals and bridges, and what seems like hundreds of bicycles – all very romantic!

One place in Luxembourg that we enjoyed visiting was Clervaux, or Clef as the local people called it. This was a picturesque little town snuggling in a pine-forested valley a short distance from Drinklange. The approach road spiralled downwards with breathtaking views of the medieval chateau, Benedictine abbey, forests – and even local cemetery – before reaching the town centre, where the River Clerve flowed. The same river, in fact, flowed through Troisvierges but was known as the Woltz upstream of Clervaux. Picnicking beside the river was magical for me and László, who was as much a nature lover as I was.

I could see that László felt at home in Europe. He was European to the core and had an abiding love for its musical and cultural heritage not to mention its food and customs. Wiener schnitzel, the national dish of Austria, was his idea of culinary heaven. There was German blood in his veins and the more Germanic-speaking the country, the better. Whether you consider them clichéd stereotypes or not, I could see many Germanic traits in him: efficient, disciplined, hardworking, organised, punctual, traditional, and lacking a sense of humour.

While the Luxembourg natives look upon themselves as being more akin to the French, to me they were Germanic in their ways. Most were extremely courteous and good-natured. Everything about them trumpeted cleanliness, order and discipline – admirable traits to me but of absolute necessity to László. Travelling around Western Europe during the late 1980s and early 1990s had opened László's eyes to how countries could live in harmony. The European Union had given him great hope.

'You know, Pixie, the European Union is important for peace,' he remarked one day. 'Conflict between countries can rupture overnight and quickly spiral out of control.'

'Indeed it can, László.'

'The lives of ordinary people can be completely destroyed. But at least the European Union is there to prevent it now.'

Living in Europe, only fifty short years after the end of the Second World War, somehow brought history alive to me. To many Europeans, the horrors of war were part of their psyche, for which there could be no easy forgiveness. For Nicolas, the memory of German armoured cars advancing through the Ardennes in 1940 and invading his country was still very much alive in his mind; he along with his fellow countrymen had been conscripted into the German military, leaving him with the scars of war. There were others who were prepared to let bygones be bygones. In Drinklange, our house and land bordered a large farm and it was satisfying for me being able to converse in German with the gentle farmer in his sixties. Occasionally, we would discuss what was happening in the world, especially the awful ethnic conflicts raging in the former Yugoslavia during the 1990s. The horrors in Srebrenica, Sarajevo, Vukovar and later Kosovo were brought to our attention each night by the world's press. Ethnic cleansing was a word that entered our lexicon but there was nothing new about it. I vividly remember this farmer's words of wisdom when we spoke of the Balkan turmoil.

'*Leben und leben lassen.*'

Yes, live and let live was a lesson for us all. László's fear and distrust of Russia, however, never abated. The Soviet Union may have been consigned to the past but, knowing the Russian spirit as he did, its leaders would want to regain lost territories and power. So László was staying put, straddling the borders of three countries. Mentally, he was prepared for flight at a moment's notice should political upheaval of any kind be visited upon him. Old habits die hard.

* * *

László's career as a musician may have been long over but there was no let-up in the manual work he engaged in. Retirement was not a word in his vocabulary, even in his eighties. The basement of the house served as his workshop and he was most proud of its well-stocked shelves. As a skilled craftsman he was in his element sawing, planing, welding, plumbing; the sound of a lathe or saw became music to his ears. He was never idle and could turn his hand to anything and was forever upgrading our home.

When we moved in, the house was heated by electric storage heaters, which proved rather expensive and unsatisfactory. László would not rest until he had installed an oil-fired central heating system. This he did with the help of a young local engineer. Day after day they worked steadily together for several weeks until the house was complete. At László's advanced years, this was a physical feat in itself! The result proved a great success and in the long cold winters we had a cosy warm house and much-reduced heating bills.

With one major task finished, he embarked upon another. As the house had no balcony or second garage, he decided that both were essential. He constructed, again with some local help, a garage attached to the back of the house and over this fashioned a terrace. This terrace could be accessed via the first or ground floor and was a novel addition to the house. László painstakingly covered the terrace surface with a bright red tile and crafted an iron railing to surround it. It provided us with a perfect suntrap, dining area, viewing point and place of relaxation. From springtime through autumn we lived on this terrace overlooking the fields and farmlands of the Ardennes. We began to recognise the seasons with what played out across the fields below us: new-born calves being brought to the fields and watching with joy as they frolicked about and grew in confidence; the planting of wheat, oats and barley and their harvesting several months later.

Our split-level house took some getting used to. If I wished to access the back garden, I had to descend a flight of stairs through the basement and then out into the garden. The garden was one of the high points of our life. Encompassing a small acreage, it was roughly divided into three sections and contained many bushes, trees and flowers when we first arrived. One part comprised vegetables and flowers. There were also two enormous strawberry beds along with bushes bearing various fruits: blackberry, loganberry, gooseberry, raspberry, blackcurrant, redcurrant, and white currant. László and I planted a huge vegetable plot of carrots, peas, runner beans, potatoes, lettuce, tomatoes, and cabbage. These vegetables almost made us self-sufficient. László took to the operation with military precision, using a spool of twine and running lines down and across to guide us in our planting. The cultivation of these plants fell more to me than to him. It was no drudgery tending to the plants, as I loved handling the earth and the smell of the soil, winter or summer.

I was also fortunate in that another neighbour, Annette, had remarkable green fingers and would sometimes come and give me tips about our vegetable plots. A young Luxembourgish couple, Annette and her husband Antoin owned property across the street from us. Their house was large and spacious with an extensive garden. Practically all year round, I looked out from our front windows upon a glorious perfusion of flowers and shrubs. The couple lived there with their four children, a boy and three girls, and were peaceful and reserved people. A sort of tranquillity seemed to infuse their house.

Autumn time saw both László and me very busy picking the fruit. Sometimes Nicolas and Maria would join us, and what we had we always shared. From the fruit I made what seemed like tons and tons of jam and preserves, all carried out under László's instruction. There was no shortage of preserving jars and huge pots either, having inherited quite a lot from the previous owner. There were also endless tarts and pies made from the fruit by me. Yes, you could say we were as self-sufficient as monks in a monastery.

Another part of the garden was more forest-like with a shrubbery and more fruit bushes; while the third section was mostly lawn bordered by yet more trees. I also planted a line of cypress trees, perhaps twenty to thirty, along part of the perimeter fence. However, the *pièce de résistance* that I planted was a weeping willow tree – a sign of endurance and strength – unaware that it was one of the symbols of the Calvinist faith. It stood for good luck and a church flourishing in the face of adversity. My willow quickly took root and became a favourite of mine.

Neither did I know at the time that Calvinism was the religion my husband had previously subscribed to! It only came to light after his death. To be honest, the subject of religion had not come up before we married. It was immaterial to me what faith he professed or none. I knew he was not a Catholic but thought perhaps that he was a lapsed Jew. I even went so far as to tell that to my friends. Many of his musician friends in Budapest and acquaintances in Dublin were Jewish and I could see that he had a great affinity, indeed a great love, for the people. Sometimes he likened the Jewish people to the Irish, seeing similarities between their respective diasporas.

'The reason the Irish were so successful in America and elsewhere, Pixie, was that you are like the Jewish people,' he reflected. 'You looked after each other and looked out for one another.'

It was an interesting slant and one that I had not thought of before. Yet, László as an observant outsider could sum it up quite clearly. Even as he went about the most mundane of tasks, he was always ruminating about the world and its people. The lawn was in constant need of cutting so all summer long he would sit on his *Rasentraktor*, as he called it, and happily let the lawn tractor work its magic.

I especially loved wintertime when an endearing soft coat of snow silently crept over the land. On the terrace we would watch the village children tracking through the fields, pulling their sledges up the little hillocks and then sliding down to screams of laughter. The air was also filled with their pet dogs running and barking in excitement beside them.

Sitting out on the terrace, László would sometimes reminisce about his beloved homeland. He often spoke of his mother, and as he did so, it was obvious that he had adored her. The tight bond and genuine fondness for his brothers was still there; especially Zoltán who resembled him so much and who had wanted to live near him over the years. By all accounts, Zoltán was still alive. The time was never so right for László to visit his family in Hungary. Living in Luxembourg in the late 1990s we were both healthy, had no ties and were both free to travel. I could tell there was a niggling desire to return on his part, but one clothed in doubt.

Any time I broached the subject of visiting his family, he would inevitably reject the suggestion.

'No, I am too old now,' he said, 'and I do not have the courage. It has left me.'

He had convinced himself that he could never return and was troubled by events in his past.

'I was a stupid monkey when young; I should have listened to my father.'

Despite my attempts to open up the past, it was a closed book.

* * *

215

From my earliest days in Drinklange, while László was engrossed in work or having his ritual afternoon nap, I explored the local countryside. I would go for long leisurely walks on my own through the nearby woods. There I found many crooked narrow manmade tracks or pathways going hither and thither in all directions. Sometimes as I meandered along overhanging tree branches would brush against my face and hair in a rather enchanting way. Birdsong invariably accompanied me and my eyes and ears would prick up at a squirrel scampering up a tree or the rustle of some little creature seeking a secure hiding place.

I mostly rambled through the woods alone but occasionally László, when free, would join me on my wanders. Wildflowers were aplenty in the hedgerows and woodlands that I passed on my walks. Though often sorely tempted to pick bundles of the wild garlic, violets, parsley, purple vetch, buttercups and valerian and display them in a vase at home, I did not. László did not approve of cut flowers and would not have them in the house. It was not because of allergies or a belief in bad luck.

'But why don't you like cut flowers,' I asked him, amazed that anyone would object to them indoors.

'Why? Why destroy the nature?' he replied.

It was another foible of László's that I learned to live with. That said, I did make an exception when visitors were coming and would take wildflowers from the garden and arrange them in a posy. Flowers always reminded me of Aunt Kathleen. She had initiated me, as a young woman, into the secrets of flower arranging, giving tips on how to display and to preserve flowers, which vases to use for which flowers, when to replenish the water, and how and when to crush the ends of stems.

In hindsight, I realised that László's act of buying me a bouquet of flowers on my first visit years earlier had indeed been an exception to his rule. It was done solely to make me happy and mark my first visit in a grand gesture. Being close to nature was important to him, and observing a garden full of flowers was a better way to appreciate nature to him. Interior décor also mattered. The rooms in our house were always painted in green or blue; green especially as it was a harmonious colour that put him at ease. It was a throwback to his days as a professional musician when before a concert he and his colleagues could rid themselves of any tension or anxiety in the green room.

In the first year or so, living in the rural idyll of Drinklange, I seemed to be on a 'forever holiday'. But that feeling all too soon came to end. During my woodland and open country walks, I was often confronted by vicious dogs that distressed me and curtailed my movements. Also, many of the neighbouring properties had fearsome guard dogs. The outcome was that I was confined to the house more and more, unable to conquer my fear of being attacked by aggressive dogs. I had always loved dogs, at least as trained house pets, but these German Shepherds, pit bull terriers and Rottweilers were something else altogether. László, as ever, had a solution.

'Take a walking cane with you,' he suggested, 'and if an aggressive dog approaches, tap the ground firmly.'

His advice chimed with what my father had once said; it worked but didn't rid me entirely of my nervousness. Instead, I decided to join a small walking group from Troisvierges – safety in numbers. If I thought they would quietly stroll through the woodlands at their ease, then I was in for a rude awakening. Upon arrival at the meeting place, I found about four or five people in their thirties and forties each carrying two poles and looking very skilled and organised. As we started out, I very quickly realised that my first observations were correct. My companions were neither interested in wildlife nor enjoying the beauty of the countryside, for they all walked with heads bowed and a determined air. Nordic walking, a new fitness activity, had become all the rage, but sadly it was not for me.

Spending more time at home, I had to occupy my time in some fashion while László was absorbed in his work. My childhood love of writing re-emerged and I took to corresponding with family, relatives and friends and also writing poetry. Luckily, travelling about was not a problem, as I had the use of László's car and could cycle around freely as well. One of the most satisfying things I did was to join the local church choir, called the Saint Cecilia Choir. This was important as it was a way of getting to know the locals and, of course, socialising. Most of the hymns, however, were very different to those at home in Ireland or in Britain. For example,

'Schau Heiliger Apostel, O Willibrord' was dedicated to Willibrord, the patron saint of Luxembourg; another was a Christmas carol 'Ein Kind geboren zu Bethlehem', arranged as a Bach Cantata; and 'Léif Mamm, ech wees et net ze soen' was in honour of the Virgin Mary.

László came to my rescue, as he always did, and got hold of the church hymnal. By playing his clarinet very slowly, he made a recording of each hymn so that I would eventually have the tune in my head. Before long I was able to master the task and sing along with the choir, thanks to him. Singing also lifted my spirits in more ways than one.

Making trips to Troisvierges and weekly ones to Luxembourg City on the train brought a measure of diversion as well. The journey was always breathtaking, gazing as I did at the magnificent forests and rivers and seeing farmers working in their fields. To catch a glimpse of a sparrowhawk gliding across the vastness of blue sky or a heron standing in absolute stillness on a riverbank, or a fox shyly peeking out from its den, was awe-inspiring. All these images I would relate to László, who could chat for hours about wildlife.

Within a year of moving to Luxembourg I made the acquaintance of a young Irish artist, Anne O'Dowd-Wenner, who was to become a dear friend of mine. It came about through visiting an art exhibition at a nearby hamlet where Anne's paintings were on show. When my gaze rested upon one of her paintings, I was taken aback. It was of a tiny picturesque stone chapel seemingly suspended on a lake in low-lying mountains. I instantly recognised it as Gougane Barra in County Cork near the Kerry border. It was the scene of my childhood summer holidays. I was overjoyed to learn from the exhibition organiser that the artist lived not too far away in Clervaux. And so Anne, hailing from County Kerry, entered my life. She spoke the local Luxembourgish dialect perfectly and like myself was in love with this fairyland Grand Duchy.

Luxembourg had become a secular state, though many of its people were baptized Catholics. Believe it or not, it was illegal for the government to collect statistics on religious faiths and beliefs. Other than among Anne and me, religion was never a topic of conversation with our neighbours. As I grew older, the fervour of my own faith, such as it existed in the convent, waned but I still found Catholicism vital. Sometimes I would go to mass in the company of Anne at the Benedictine Abbey in Clervaux, a half-hour drive away, or to Notre Dame Cathedral in Luxembourg City. Afterwards, we would adjourn to a nearby café to enjoy a coffee and a long conversation. Importantly for me, we shared confidences and I could talk about my feelings of isolation, whenever they emerged.

Troisvierges too had a Catholic church, St Andrew's, though I rarely frequented it. Walloon pilgrims had named the village after three virgins, Saint Fides, Saint Spes and Saint Caritas – faith, hope and charity – who had become martyrs during the early Christian church. One of the attractions in the village was a fountain outside the civic offices with a sculpture of the three virgins sitting around it.

Other hamlets near Troisvierges – Huldange, Wilwerdange, Basbellain, Goedange and Binsfeld – had a wonderful network of social activities. There were house gatherings where the local gossip and news was exchanged and you could enjoy tea or coffee and sandwiches and cake. It was gratifying that the people were so friendly and wanted to make me feel welcome. Markets with fruit and vegetable stalls, which occasionally sold plants and flowers, were also a regular occurrence. Sometimes I would go there or to the garden centre with my neighbour, Ida Choinier, who had a great love of plants and flowers.

Middle-aged Ida was our closest neighbour. She watched over Drinklange and the other hamlets like a guardian angel, so much so that I called her the Angel of the North. Despite how thin and delicate she looked, her workload was enormous. Nothing was ever too much trouble for her and she came to people's rescue if they could not cope: she cleaned houses, she washed, she ironed, she repaired clothes, and if unwell she would nurse you. All her work was carried out with trademark benevolence and she was the living embodiment of a heroine. Sometimes, however, I wished she was appreciated more by people, for goodness can often be taken for granted. She and her husband Raymond, a tall well-built man, and their son Ronnie, a bright clever youth, became our good friends and could be relied upon in times of need. In wintertime, László would purchase firewood from them for our kitchen stove.

As the months went by, I took on some work to occupy myself and at László's encouragement. Knowing how much he needed work for his own sanity, he was eager that I should do the same.

'It does not matter what you do, Pixie,' he urged. 'Just be occupied.'

In the event, I gravitated towards children and had no trouble finding work. First, I gave English lessons in Luxembourg City to a young French child, named Anna-Marie. For a seven-year-old, she was rather quaint in her ways, both in dress and in manner. Her petticoat dresses and booties seemed old fashioned and when she spoke, no doubt from imitation, it was with the authority of a grandmother. It all made for a very amusing job. I also sometimes helped youngsters in the nearby hamlets of Troisvierges, if their English schoolwork was proving a challenge.

However, the job that gave me the most satisfaction was caring for the baby of a charming young American couple who hailed from Chicago. It lasted just under a year before they returned to the United States for good. Henry, the father, was tall and dark-haired and worked as a banker in Luxemburg City. Jane, the mother, was also very tall with fair hair and blue eyes and had a most generous manner. Their baby, Daniel, was a real darling. At three months of age, he was forever smiling and gurgling with laughter. He had inherited his father's brown eyes and dark hair, and it was pure joy to care for him. Each weekday, I would make the hour-long train journey to Luxembourg City where they resided. At their home, I would spend a couple of hours playing with Daniel or wheel him in his pram around the many beautiful parks in the city. I was eager for him to notice life teeming about him; pointing out trees and flowers, especially the abundant roses, birds in the air, and ducks on the pond.

Caring for Daniel made me realise just how much of an affinity I had for children – indeed I was very fond of my nephews and nieces. That said, I never wished to have any of my own. My mother had actively discouraged it when I was a young woman.

'Eibhlín, I advise you not to have any children.'

Perhaps the fact that I had been a delicate child and teenager still weighed on her mind. Though never a diabetic, I was prone to fainting attacks from low blood sugar that persists to this day. As a child, I was taken to the Old Richmond Hospital and underwent many tests at their neurological department but nothing untoward was found. The consultant advised my mother to have me carry dextrose tablets at all times!

* * *

If I have created the impression that László buried himself in work, day and night, then it is false. His love of music never waned and he still found time to help music students whenever he could. This was something he did all his life and continued well into his eighties. There was one student I recall in particular. André was a young Frenchman who had studied for his final clarinet exams and showed great promise. He was the son of friends of László's from his days in Echternach, but the family now resided in Luxembourg City. They asked him if he could help advance their son's career. László, who had been tutoring him privately for some time, got in touch with an old music colleague in Vienna. Following this intervention, André was ultimately taken to the USA on tour. It was an opportunity the young man never forgot. It gave great personal satisfaction to László knowing that talent had won the day.

Care and attention was still lavished on László's beloved instruments. He was meticulous to a fault in the cleaning and maintenance of his clarinet and saxophone. Sometimes he would drive down to Selmer's in Paris to purchase items he might require, such as new mouthpieces or reeds. Our house was still filled with music, especially in the evenings. There was plenty of music to choose from our combined record collection, which had grown enormous. The strains of Chopin, Berlioz, Debussy, Wagner and Verdi – his particular favourites – would waft through the air and were especially stirring on cold winter evenings. The Troisvierges Plateau had the dubious honour of being the coldest and wettest area in Luxembourg, so our kitchen stove worked overtime in winter.

Aside from German Romantic music, László had a liking too for sober and melancholy works. Verdi's Requiem, with its choral masterpiece, was a work that had a profound effect on him each time. As a tutor, László was skilful and even schooled me further in music appreciation. He once gave me a biography of Claude Debussy to read but alas I had

221

to abandon it after a few chapters. Debussy's notorious and dissolute private life got the better of me. And I blush now when I think of how prudish I was at the time. If truth be told, the private life of many a composer was scandalous. Maybe it's the price of creativity and passion combined – I'm not sure. Two of László's favourite books in English were the *Opera Guide* and *Concert Guide* written by Gerhart von Westerman. This collection was akin to a music bible, listing the concertos, symphonies and oratorios of nearly three centuries as well as the plots, music and histories of a thousand operas. Perfect reading for long winter evenings in Drinklange.

* * *

Living in rural Drinklange could be isolating so the arrival of an occasional visitor from Ireland was a welcome pleasure. Granted, I received phone calls from family and friends in Dublin filling me in on the news at home but it was not the same. The four-bedroomed house was so spacious that it was a shame for the rooms to go unoccupied. In fact, one year, I decided to operate a summer guesthouse. As a result, a lovely young Irish couple, Paul and Maureen Conroy, and their two children came to stay. They too fell in love with the locality and its relaxing ambience during a short holiday. Paul, like so many people, found László fascinating. Years later he told me that he was sorry his young children, Paul and Denise, had not been older to appreciate hearing real-life accounts of the part Hungary played in the Second World War and the communist aftermath. Listening to László describe apartheid in South Africa, he said, had been a real privilege for him.

Our friends Maurice and Yvonne visited several times as well. They would hire a car at the nearest airport and drive through the border countries, deriving as much pleasure from the rural landscape as we did. Upon learning their plane had landed and they were on their way, László would straightaway make preparations for a meal and work steadily on a Hungarian dish or his favourite Wiener schnitzel. No restaurant could cook this dish better and, besides, László rarely ate food which he himself did not prepare.

The guest bedroom was located on the first floor and László strove to make their stay as pleasant as possible. In later years he added more facilities to the upstairs bathroom for their greater comfort. Maurice and Yvonne found that László was the soul of hospitality. Yet László had certain views where generosity was concerned. If Maurice and Yvonne brought what László considered a lavish gift, then László would feel obliged to match it. So, thereafter, they would often bring a lovely bottle of wine, which he appreciated.

Seeing that László liked to do the cooking, I would lay the table with an Irish linen tablecloth and crystal, wishing to complement his dishes and create a welcoming atmosphere. There was no denying that László was particular about cooking, even Maurice and Yvonne could see food had to be prepared like it were a kosher restaurant. Many a Hungarian dish was meticulously cooked to perfection: cabbage soup, stuffed green peppers, sauerkraut, stuffed kohlrabi leaves – a kind of turnip cabbage – goulash, beef paprika stew, paprika chicken, pork cutlets, and Hungarian salad.

Before each meal I would say grace and when Yvonne and Maurice were present it was recited in Irish. Afterwards, László would gesture to eat saying *bon appétit* with a broad smile and rarely said *jó étvágyat*, its Hungarian equivalent. No matter what László served up, it was guaranteed to be tasty. And each dish was rounded off by mouth-watering puddings such as jam pancakes (*palacsinta*), strudel filled with poppy seeds or walnuts, or a favourite of ours, poppy seed roll (*beigli*).

There was no shortage of after-dinner conversation. László would fix his gaze on Maurice and hours of talk would follow. After Maurice's father died in February 1998, László had become a father figure to him. In fact, the ultra-private and reserved László never talked to anyone like he did to Maurice. It probably helped that Maurice was a history teacher and a good listener, and could recognise a good story when he heard one. After all, his father was the esteemed Irish writer, Bryan MacMahon, so storytelling was in his blood. In later years upon retiring, Maurice penned an account of his own experiences as a teacher at Dublin's St Benildus College in *Mr Mac: A Blackboard Memoir*. I could tell that he made history come alive for his students.

Maurice would say that he taught history out of a cold book, while László was a walking history book. His life story was riveting and, to Maurice, László was upfront, honest, warm, measured and precise. His precision could be exasperating at times, though, especially where correct pronunciation was concerned. Pronouncing the name of the Czech composer Dvořák, for instance, would stump many a person and László would correct Maurice's pronunciation each time.

It was true that the more László trusted you, the more open he became. But only to a point. There were chunks of his life story that still remained hidden, compartmentalised, hermetically sealed. So many different strands, so many different drawers. It was where his first two wives, Etelka and Anna, and daughter Lívia, were tucked away. Even I did not know of their existence until after his death! So too were other family secrets and his treatment at the hands of the communists. His relatives never found their way into conversations with Maurice and Yvonne either, perhaps with the exception of his father István. Maurice judged that László had a very strong ethic, integrity, honesty and modesty inherited from his father.

It was clear to them that László was parsimonious or shrewd with money. Perhaps it was due to his personality, Calvinist upbringing, but more likely, as Maurice realised, that he had learned the hard way to manage money through the wars. Those years forced him to live on his wits, to become resilient. He had the survivalist mindset of a refugee, keeping his head below the parapet but always on the lookout for opportunities to better himself. He was willing to take risks to survive, where others would fear to tread. That single-minded focus of improving his lot stayed with him all his life – whether buying small amounts of gold on the black market to trade in or buying a property like Adelaide Road to earn a living or the myriad houses he renovated.

Yvonne and Maurice's visits always seemed to fly by. Sometimes we would drive to the nearby lakes at Weiswampach and walk along the shores, while László was occupied in the house. Weiswampach was always a hive of activity, with many a campsite on its shores and water sports galore. Other times, they would make excursions farther afield in their hired car. László considered them close friends, as soul friends or *anam cara* in Irish, and responded to their sincerity. He was always a little sad when it came to their departure and would hug Yvonne.

'Will I be here next year to greet you?' he would ask wistfully.

Then he would turn to Maurice and, perhaps forecasting his own end, would utter light-heartedly.

'Nothing but the ovens … Goodbye Honolulu!'

His mention of the ovens was a reference to cremation. As for 'Goodbye Honolulu', a song from his past, which for him meant once life was over you moved on to the next. There was no guarantee of a heavenly afterlife. Yvonne and Maurice's visits were a comfort to us. To them perhaps we must have been an unusual couple, with my mothering ways and László's paternalism. I suppose in our own ways both of us were vulnerable and wanted to look after each other.

* * *

I must admit that living in Drinklange, high up in the wooded plateau of the Ardennes, with all its attendant remoteness, isolation and solitude, was exactly what my soul craved at times. As a child and teenager, I had the romantic notion of being a medieval anchoress like Julian of Norwich and living alone with God, attached to some monastery or other! Her philosophy of love and compassion inspired me. So my life with László, although austere, was an asceticism and simplicity that helped me partly fulfil those girlhood dreams. Much and all as I enjoyed human interaction, I could only handle it in small doses. In Drinklange, as mentioned before, the thrill of walking through woodland and open countryside was a salve to my soul. Later when confronted by vicious dogs more and more, life in Luxembourg completely changed and once again those old feelings of being a caged bird resurfaced.

There were episodes throughout my life when I could feel very down, the caged-bird condition, or as though I were lost and could not find myself. I had then relied on my own resources for healing and finding a way back through the darkness. László had long recognised that I was restless and encouraged me to seize whatever opportunity presented itself. Sometimes he had the measure of me far better than I had myself.

'You're whimsical, Pixie,' he said softly, 'and I understand.'

He therefore made sure that I got away regularly. And so I would return to Ireland alone each summer for a month and catch up with my family and friends. Sometimes there were funerals to attend, such as the passing of my aunts, Ida and Vera. Sad times, but offset by knowing how full and fulfilling their lives had been. Any chance to meet with friends and acquaintances elsewhere was taken up too. Part of me felt guilty that I was bailing out on László. Only for the fact that he was in reasonably good health and constantly occupied did I take off with such relish. On two occasions, he did travel to Ireland with me and we brought back furniture, much of it the dining room set bought as a wedding present. The second and last journey was also prompted by László's decision to sell the house in Foxrock. It brought to an end the property he held in the country and seeing Dublin again – you could say his adventure in Ireland was over.

Setting off to new places set my spirits soaring. I once took a train journey to Passau via Munich to visit an Irish friend Nikie de Renzy and her German husband Erwin and their two children. Nikie, of Italian extraction, and I were linked in so many ways. Her grandmother had been a friend of my Aunt Kathleen; her mother had been my next-door neighbour in Foxrock; and Nikie and I had been nursing colleagues at one time.

The week-long trip was exhilarating from the moment I stepped onto the train. I opened a map and traced the stops as the train sped along, marking out many interesting landmarks on the way. My mind was refreshed with every picturesque Bavarian town and village we passed. The journey had been amusing, to say the least. The train compartment was occupied by a caricatured German family. The parents and four teenage children sat ramrod straight, proper to the nth degree without a hair out of place, and silent for their entire journey. Their silence was rather unnerving and didn't prompt any kind of conversation between me and the other occupant of the compartment, another German woman. Two hours later the family disembarked causing the woman to launch into conversation.

'Thank God, they're gone!' she exclaimed. 'That's not the norm.'

In compensation, we had a great chat for the remainder of the journey. At Passau train station, Nikie and I embraced. Seeing the Danube in Passau made me think of László, but it looked even more majestic, being the confluence of it and the Inn and the Ilz rivers. Nikie lived not far from the town in a village called Hunding near the Austrian border. There was great excitement in the household as Erwin and his brothers were building a new house for Erwin's family. That fraternal bond was impressive and reminded me of the Irish in days gone by sharing such work. Indeed, we have an old Irish word for a work group of neighbours – *meitheal*. The family made me feel so welcome and the week passed quickly, but all too soon it was time to return to Luxembourg.

On another occasion, the American couple, Henry and Jane, asked me to join them for the summer at their home in downtown Chicago. This was in 1998, and I jumped at the chance. The invitation was also extended to László, but he gracefully declined. He disliked flying and nothing would induce him to get on an aircraft. Also, I guess that in his life he had seen enough of foreign places. However, as selfless as ever, he insisted that I should take up the offer.

'You should go, Pixie,' he said.

'But I don't want to go without you,' I replied. 'It's too far away and three months is a long time.'

'No, you should go; it will be a wonderful experience.'

He was right. Life should be one long adventure and Chicago was an opportunity not to be missed. And so I went for three months with his blessing but not without a dollop of guilt. Once there, I wrote letters two or three times a week giving accounts of my days and the rollercoaster of emotions evoked. Always with an eye on costs, he preferred my letters to phone calls. Chicago was a dream city, bursting with vibrancy. I had stepped into an extraordinarily privileged world, which was something new to me. Jane and Henry lived in a towering apartment complex of absolute luxury; as you walked into the building, doors were held open by uniformed doormen, leading to a vast lobby with reception desk and staff to cater for your every whim. Jane had rented a large apartment for me on

227

the thirty-sixth floor with every conceivable comfort. The wall-to-wall and floor-to-ceiling glass windows revealed panoramic views of much of the city. The sight was breathtaking, especially the Chicago skyline at night. My eyes devoured each new sight: the neverending trains going hither and thither, the bustle at street level below and the people going about their business. To me, they looked like the painter Lowry's matchstick men!

I particularly enjoyed regaling László with my visits to the sprawling Grant Park on the shoreline of Lake Michigan. Its annual, free open air concerts held at midday and evening time were magnetic. The tradition of this ten-week-long summer music festival had started way back in 1931, when, in a response to the Great Depression, the mayor had sought to lift the morale of city-dwellers. Another example of the healing power of music, a practice much approved of by László. Everything from Brahms's First Piano Concerto to Bizet's Carmen to Gershwin classics was on offer. At times like this I particularly missed László's company, knowing that he would have savoured the setting and the music.

Occasionally, I brought baby Daniel along, for I could tell that he loved music when he responded to it at home and had a good ear. Other midday concerts were held at the adjacent Art Institute of Chicago, famous for its collections of American art and Impressionism. Luckily for me, it was very child-orientated and Daniel was welcome. The works of Bartók were played on one occasion and I was eager to attend. Admittedly, the music was quite difficult and not easy on the ear, yet also very beautiful. Realising that it might not be to Daniel's taste, I was prepared to take him away at the first sign of a disturbance. But I need not have worried. Lying in his pram, Daniel was captivated by the music: legs kicking, hands clapping, cooing up at me. After the performance, the pianist, a tall young man, approached us. He was smiling from ear to ear.

'I'm so pleased to see a baby enjoy the music,' he said to my surprise. 'He could be a great musician one day!'

From music to art to sports, the city was ablaze with culture and recreation. Considering the apartment was so spacious and the city so vibrant, I invited my sister Áine and brother-in-law Gregory, living in Boston at the time, to come for a visit. However, their busy schedules and the short notice meant they were sorry at not being able to join me. As part of the holiday, Jane and Henry arranged for me to have a week off. I chose to go to Syracuse in New York State to visit maternal cousins. More Maddisons – but this time showing me American hospitality. The high point was visiting the grave of Uncle Thomas, my mother's brother, who had died the previous year. While in Syracuse, I also found a Hungarian cookbook to my great delight. Needless to say, I purchased it straightaway and couldn't wait to show it to László and imagined the endless hours of cooking that lay ahead.

After my return to Chicago, the family and I journeyed to the lake district of Wisconsin where we joined Jane's parents, who also had a holiday home in the region. Both homes were substantial buildings that overlooked large lakes. They reminded me of those white clapboard houses found in New England that conjured up an image of homemade blueberry pie, Thanksgiving and solid American values. The two houses were well fitted out with all possible modern conveniences and were very relaxing. Unfailingly hospitable, Jane lodged me in a bedroom that fronted the lake, glistening in the hot summer sunlight. Any free time was spent walking the forested shoreline, breathing in the fresh clear air and thanking my lucky stars. Time seemed to race by because all too soon we were back in Chicago and preparing to return to Luxembourg. Even little Daniel was now crawling about and on the go. The entire trip had been exhilarating. I came back to Drinklange refreshed and revitalised.

On my return home to László, poesies of sweet pea adorned the bedroom and a lovely meal awaited me. Such was my exuberance after my holiday that had I been younger – and László of course – I would have asked him to relocate to the Windy City permanently. It made me realise that I would need regular breaks away if I was to be content in Drinklange in the long term. However, that realisation was tempered by the fact that László was in his sunset years. That knowledge hung over me like a death sentence. Sadly, Jane and Henry and little Daniel returned permanently to Chicago at the end of the year, but I will never forget their kindness and generosity.

13.

A Great Light Goes Out

Clouds beyond clouds above me,
Wastes beyond wastes below;
But nothing drear can move me;
I will not, cannot go.

From 'Spellbound' by Emily Brontë

ONE of the lessons of life I came to learn was that pleasure is inevitably followed by pain. One June afternoon in 1999, László and I were grocery shopping in the village of Wemperhardt on the Belgian border, availing of one of several large, well-stocked supermarkets there. Returning home, we were involved in a dreadful road traffic accident.

Our car collided with a red Ford Orion not far from the village; the driver had pulled out suddenly from a petrol station and László had crashed into the back of his car. My head hit the windscreen and left me unconscious at the scene, while László was badly injured. The driver was unscathed but had he not dropped his wife and child off minutes earlier, I dread to think of the carnage. With typical Luxembourger efficiency, the emergency services responded quickly and we were taken by ambulance to Wiltz, where the northern regional hospital was located. There László was treated for a fractured sternum. Thankfully, I regained consciousness before the ambulance arrived but was rather muzzy and disorientated and had a torn right shoulder ligament as well as a fractured sternum.

Nothing but painkillers, quiet rest and physiotherapy would get those bones to heal.

With rest we both recovered somewhat and after some weeks were discharged. I must say our treatment and medical care at Wiltz Hospital was second to none. Efficiency, courtesy and expertise were on display throughout our stay. At home once more in Drinklange, I soon found that I was unable to cope, having lost power in my right shoulder and arm. Meanwhile, a weak and feverish László was finding recovery difficult too. My neighbour Ida was a blessing, but she could hardly don a nurse's uniform and tend to us day and night. Thus, after a couple of days at home, both of us were readmitted to hospital for a further few weeks – luckily we had a private room together. This time László had to undergo surgery to remove his gallbladder. But after surgery, he developed a high fever. He was on fire and delirious. Thinking he was about to die, László prayed hard to his mother to come to his aid that night.

'Pixie, my mother came to me,' he told me the next morning, feeling much improved. 'She cured me.'

The injection of steroids into my shoulder and physiotherapy helped put me on the road to recovery. However, the accident took its toll and undermined our confidence; it was some time before we recovered our independence and ventured out once more.

Some people are magnets for things happening to them – good and bad. I wondered whether or not László and I were such people. My accident set me thinking about a previous accident I had while a student nurse in Dublin. Memories of me coming off duty one evening sprang to mind. Happily riding along on my Honda 50cc motorcycle, I had approached the junction of North King Street and Church Street when suddenly a car sped across the junction and ran straight into me, leaving me with a broken nose, damaged left hand and wrist, and a strained back!

Concerned that I had not arrived home, my parents phoned the hospital asking had I finished duty, only to be told that I had left at half past eight. Alarm bells rang and the hospital authorities along with my parents got in touch with the Gardaí. On hearing of an accident at Church Street, various hospitals around Dublin were contacted to find my whereabouts. At last

I was found and transferred to St Laurence's Hospital, where I underwent surgery. After some weeks I returned to nursing duty and was reunited with my treasured Honda 50 once again! I had made a good recovery then, but now in my fifties I was much older with my healing powers not at their peak.

* * *

László's brush with death set him thinking about his family and homeland again. Our house sometimes felt a little like a Hungarian enclave – I had embraced Hungarian cuisine wholeheartedly, especially baking, after purchasing the cookbook in Syracuse. László taught me all I know for sure. I loved to make Hungarian biscuits, where ingredients could be sprinkled on top of the biscuit or mixed into the dough. These included fresh and dry cheeses, cabbage, black pepper, hot or sweet paprika, garlic, red onion, sesame seeds, sunflower seeds or poppy seeds. More and more memories of Hungary surrounded him as I tried out various recipes.

However, the car accident had seemed to bring unfinished business to the fore. Later that summer Yvonne and Maurice paid us a visit, which coincided with the total solar eclipse in Europe in 1999. Southern Luxembourg was on the path of totality, so we all set off early in the day to witness it or at least to get as close as possible. Somewhere near Diekirch we joined a small group of people milling around the car park of a shopping centre with eyes or rather eclipse glasses trained on the rather cloudy morning sky. We were too far north to experience day briefly becoming night, but the sky did darken and the air grew cold. There was a palpable stillness and the birds fell silent. Nature is sometimes the finest kind of entertainment. And it can also bring moments of great clarity.

László's desire to visit his homeland and his relatives was now conveyed to Yvonne and Maurice. In hindsight, I believe at that time he wanted to be reunited with Lívia, his daughter. Several attempts had been made to return to Hungary since the fall of communism but I reckoned he was still too afraid, fear of arrest being uppermost in his mind. Whenever he talked about the Russians in my company, he would break into a cold sweat and a deathly pallor would appear on his face. It left me in no doubt that he was not ready to face his demons. Finally, however, plans were hatched to travel overland to Budapest in his Volkswagen, all four of us, in 2000. The route was mapped out, via Germany and Austria, and everything was arranged. It seemed to boost László's spirits to my great satisfaction, and I hoped for once that he had overcome his fears. However, a few weeks before our departure, László called a halt. I was as shocked as everyone else.

'I cannot drive all the way to Budapest,' he announced. 'I'm not able to do it.'

'We could stop off somewhere in Austria and stay overnight,' Yvonne suggested.

At first that seemed to satisfy László but later he pulled out again. It is true that he liked to control things when planning a journey and was loath to rest overnight during a long distance drive, given cost was a consideration. This time, however, he would not be in a position to control where three other people wanted to stay. There was also the matter of not being able to control our reactions to the discovery of his past, in particular his daughter. In my opinion, the fear that his life would unravel before our very eyes was too much for him. He was conscious that during that period I was a religious fanatic and ultra-nationalist. Thankfully, that's all changed now, but at the time I would have disapproved of ex-wives or an abandoned daughter. There were also the possible reactions from his daughter and her family to contend with – would they reject or rebuke him? In the end, his courage failed him. So with the journey cancelled, László's fears were left to marinate once more.

The arrival of the new millennium earlier that year had also signalled a change in László. He spoke of his wish to adopt a child, a Hungarian in their early teens. First he broached the subject of the adoption with me and I agreed. A teenager would bring life and energy to the house after all. Then he talked to Nicolas and Maria about the matter, but their advice was to abandon the idea altogether.

'László, you're too old and so is Eibhlín,' said Maria.

'It wouldn't be fair to the child,' added Nicolas.

In hindsight, I realise that it was probably a grandchild that László had in mind. His daughter Lívia by then would have been sixty and László was somehow aware that she had married and had a family. The knowledge that cold water had been poured on such yearning touched me deeply. If only he could have seen a way to be open with us without fear of sanction or condemnation. It was such a pity. I would have welcomed a grandchild or a grandniece or grandnephew into our home with open arms. Had László received approval of the adoption, perhaps he would have been more inclined to reach Budapest. I'll never know.

* * *

To me, making a house a home always meant having links to the past. Just as László's family photos were important to him, so too were my family photos and portraits. In fact, László loved to scrutinise my family tree – drawn up in my twenties at my mother's urging – mounted on the dining room wall. It intrigued László that my heritage seemed somewhat poles apart. On the one hand, as I mentioned, I was an ardent Irish nationalist but, on the other hand, quite a lot of English blood coursed through my veins.

I had also inherited my father's conservatism and my mother's liberalism. My own nationalist leanings abated during my years in Luxembourg, aided by László and circumstances. Perhaps being away from Ireland and my getting older – when passions grow tamer – meant the Troubles in Northern Ireland lost their intensity. The signing of the Good Friday Agreement on 10 April 1998 in Belfast meant the peace process had brought an end to the violence. Live and let live, *leben und leben lassen*, became my guiding principle in Luxembourg.

Like László, the past was constantly alive in my head. Conflict on both sides of the sectarian divide had been the experience of my mother's family, the Maddisons, in Ireland. Having been cut off by his English clergyman father, my great-great-grandfather Alexander McCrae Maddison seemed to have flourished in Northern Ireland during the nineteenth century. His son Roland John George studied medicine and law and became Taxing Master of the Four Courts in Dublin. Roland's two sisters, the musically gifted Hilda and Maud, set up and ran their own music school in Coleraine, about sixty kilometres from Belfast. However, all that success changed in the early nineteenth century as Ireland trod the road to political independence.

Clearly a man of strong convictions and passions, Roland's son, my grandfather, Roland Guy Maddison, converted to Catholicism, despite his Anglican upbringing, in order to marry his Dublin-born wife Annie. They lived at first on Agincourt Avenue, a street of elegant Victorian redbrick houses off the Ormeau Road in Belfast, and were blessed with three daughters at the time. His conversion also resulted in somewhat poorer prospects, working as an electrician at the shipyards of Harland & Wolff.

It bode ill for converts, however, given the period. As the War of Independence raged in the South, there were reprisals by loyalists, the Orange Order, for any British officers killed in the course of the conflict. For example, a three-day pogrom took place in Belfast in 1920 after the death of Lieutenant-Colonel Gerald Smith in Cork at the hands of the IRA. Mob rule reigned after the funeral of Smith, a native of Banbridge, County Down. Loyalists chased Catholics from their jobs, especially from the shipyards, and burned their homes and businesses.

Members of the Orange Order had heard of my grandfather's conversion. One day, while he was at work, a large group of loyalists surrounded him, tortured him and dragged him towards a furnace where he was to be killed. A crane driver observed the mayhem below and with quick thinking lowered the grab for my grandfather to clasp onto. This he did and was pulled to safety. The crowd refused to leave, however, and were still baying for blood. A local rector was sent for and somehow calmed down the angry mob before taking my grandfather to the rectory for safety.

Subsequently, the family home was daubed with red paint, a sign for them to leave the area. My grandmother Annie and the three children were taken to the home of her parents-in-law, the Maddisons, near the Botanic Gardens, for safekeeping. Witnessing terror on the streets of Belfast became the norm for my young aunts.

'I remember, though I was only three,' said my Aunt Irene, 'seeing a man being dragged and bound to the wheel of a cart; the horse was then whipped and galloped off. All my life long I could hear the terror as the man cried out in pain. This horrific sight never left me.'

Meanwhile, my grandfather was spirited out of the North. He made his way to Dublin, where his sister, my grandaunt Ida, lived with her husband and children, two of whom where Kathleen and Nora. Coincidently, Ida had also married a Catholic, Michael Moore, who in time would become a member of the Fianna Gael party. With my grandfather safely settled in Shankill, County Dublin, he sent for Annie and the three children to join him. They kept their heads down, especially whenever my mother and her cousins Nora or Kathleen travelled north to visit their Maddison grandparents in Belfast. The story goes that if my mother and her family wished to attend mass on Sundays, they needed the protection of the police or military. The violence had a catastrophic effect on the Protestant Maddison family. Once my great-grandfather died, all my Maddison relations left Northern Ireland and resettled in Canada, the USA or England. Today, there are very few Maddisons left in Ireland. Most of them are sprinkled all over the world.

The beatings and torture that my grandfather had earlier received at the hands of the loyalists left him deaf and with a blood disorder that required treatment for the rest of his life. For this condition he attended the Meath Hospital at Heytesbury Street in Dublin. So when it came to torture in Ireland both sides knew how to mete it out.

My grandfather's disability also put him at a serious disadvantage during the rest of the War of Independence, where the Black and Tans were concerned. A Black and Tan unit was on patrol one day when my grandfather was walking to visit his sister Ida, who lived in nearby Shanganagh. Ida was aware that her brother was due to visit but also mindful of the presence of the Black and Tans in the vicinity.

'Kathleen, quick as you can, go out and meet Uncle Roland,' her mother urged. 'He might be in danger being deaf.'

Kathleen did as she was told and on the street could see her uncle up ahead. She also observed a Black and Tan unit behind him.

'Stop, stop!' they bellowed at him.

Obviously, my grandfather never heard them and the unit raised their guns menacingly.

'He's deaf, he's deaf, he can't hear you,' Aunt Kathleen roared, running towards them.

Luckily, both Kathleen and my grandfather were unharmed and lived to tell the tale.

As I mentioned earlier, my nationalist feelings and, indeed, fervent religiosity had started to abate when cloistered in the Carmelite monastery in the mid-1980s, but the period living in Luxembourg truly sealed it. In Luxembourg, I came to a better understanding of myself, tortured as I was between nationalism and affection for my English relatives. I now prized love and compassion above all else. When researching the family tree in my twenties, I had visited Maddison tombs in Lincoln Cathedral and Newcastle Cathedral as well as Maddison country estates and houses in Lincolnshire, such as Partney Hall. On each occasion, I was received graciously and presented with gifts, particularly photographs of family portraits. One that captured my imagination was of a grandaunt Theodosia Maddison, a beautiful and haughty young woman born in 1783 and attired in a magnificent gown. Another was of middle-aged Colonel George Maddison, born earlier that century, dressed in military uniform. These photos were enlarged and framed by me for posterity. I still feel a connection to these people, in particular, my mother's eighteenth-century portrait of Cousin Sarah – her image faithfully rendered in oil – though centuries and situations divide us.

I knew there were contradictions within me; with my heritage and with my personality. Always wanting to take flight like a bird, soar away, whether it was to convents or hospitals or foreign countries, but beset with homesickness too that would bring me back home. Would it be the same when László died, I wondered? The philosopher Hegel said that contradiction is a higher form of truth, and I believe it is. It is not a defect or fault to change your mind; to try different things, to succeed or fail. Just as the weather can be unsettled – and we in Ireland know all about that – life is constantly about flux and change. Recognising and accepting that fact is what makes life so challenging and rewarding.

I could see that László too lived with contradictions – having so many family secrets – but he found a way to control them, despite the sadness. I was reconciled to the two strands of my ancestry and proud of both. In fact, I came to treasure my family history. And so László could understand why I needed to take myself off to Ireland each year. Seeing how revitalised I was after each visit was proof enough. There was one trip during the early 2000s, in particular, when I had attended a literary festival in the town of Westport, County Mayo with some family and friends. The spring weather had been exceptionally warm and sunny and we had availed of it and travelled out to Achill Island, one of the remotest spots on the Western seaboard. To me, this was the hidden jewel of Ireland along its Wild Atlantic Way and seemed to imbue me with strength and vigour. It was an anchoress moment, linked instantly to both God and nature.

On my return home, László had filled my bedroom with wild lilac blossoms – another exception made on my behalf. The gesture filled me with such happiness and gratitude that I penned a few thoughts.

> Into my room
> Of sweet perfume,
> An ocean of lilac
> To greet me.

Looking at the above words, I lament being so selfish, taking those breaks away from László.

* * *

Though he had survived the car accident and made a good recovery, my husband's years were numbered. His decline in health, in retrospect, began around the year 2000 at the age of eighty-five. The phenomenal energy that had marked his life seemed to be slowly fading away and he preferred to stay at home more and more. He would listen to music and watch the television news – the big talking point that October was that Jean, the Grand Duke of Luxembourg, had abdicated to allow his son Henri to succeed to the throne.

Heart trouble was soon diagnosed and László underwent surgery to insert a pacemaker, which helped a good deal. Of course, deep down, I knew that he was getting older and tried not to dwell on the fact. The thought of his death left me with feelings of intense sorrow. It was a kind of anticipatory grief I suppose, being certain of the inevitable end of his days.

In the last few years of his life his decline unavoidably left me confined to the house more and more. I began to write my life story through the medium of poetry and absolutely loved it. Since early childhood my mother had encouraged me to write; I felt grateful to her because writing became a coping strategy for me in the new situation in which I found myself. I can never claim to be a great poet, but it gave me enormous satisfaction to see my thoughts take shape on the page and craft images, as I did with watercolours. While my thoughts seemed to flourish on paper, like a budding flower unfolding, the reverse was happening to László. His life was slowly contracting, drawing in all his energies and thoughts, the petals receding and shrivelling.

Sitting out on the terrace, in silence mostly, we watched the lights of little villages in the far distance often twinkling and dancing as the night drew in. It occasionally triggered certain memories in László, who would turn to me.

'Pixie, look across at those lights,' he said, pointing to farmsteads in the distance, 'it reminds me of my escape from Hungary.'

'Does it feel very real, László?' I asked.

'Yes, I can picture myself walking across the fields towards Austria.'

Though unaware of my husband's family secrets, I could tell that his family were still very much in his heart. Our east-facing terrace had always been a mecca for me. For years during the warm summer months, I would rise before dawn, perhaps at four or five, and sit outside on the terrace. In solitude and silence, I would listen to the world around me with its deafening quietude and stillness, observing the sun climb slowly into the sky and cast its glowing pink shadows over all. Meanwhile, I would gradually become aware of the dawn chorus, an orchestra of birdsong, in my midst. In these moments, I would rejoice at having married László, having taken his name. Gede. Doing so meant something noble to him.

'Pixie, I gave you my name.'

Continuing to look eastwards, I would bring to mind all my unknown Gede family and blow kisses to them and send my love far into the distance.

László finally could fight his demons no longer. In April 2005, perhaps foreseeing his death, he spoke about returning to Hungary for the last time. We took the train from Troisvierges to Luxembourg City and went to the Irish Embassy to ensure both of our passports were in order; László was still an Irish citizen and nothing would induce him to relinquish that state of affairs. Everything was satisfactory. At the information desk in the Gare de Luxembourg, we checked the times and routes of trains to Budapest. As we were leaving the desk, I turned to László and was taken aback. The blood had seemed to drain from his face, now thin and gaunt, and his whole appearance was corpse-like.

'Oh, László, you're dying,' I said silently to myself.

My only concern was to get him home as quickly as I could and put him to bed; there was no energy for Hungary now. Rest did restore László somewhat, but his heart and kidneys were failing. With him growing ever more feeble, the driving fell to me now and management of the household. I consoled myself in a book called *Simple Abundance: A Daybook of Comfort and Joy* by Sarah Bán Breathnach. In it she describes her life's journey on the road to positive thinking and positive living. Thus emboldened, I started a 'Gratitude Journal', where I would record five good things to say each day. There was no shortage of blessings to give an account of: László, my parents, my brother and sister, loyal friends, flora and fauna, especially watching birds splashing on a birdbath or an electrifying summer storm. Each month I drew an accompanying watercolour of local scenes, such as a bird on a tree with lilies and daffodils. I set down my private thoughts along with concerns for my husband's health. All the writing had to be carried out though positive eyes, a positive mind. No negativity whatsoever was entertained. Everything had to lead to a positive self; this gave me solace and was most rewarding as I faced each day of László's decline.

The local doctor, Edy Mertens, was a remarkably gifted and caring person; his visits would not alone perk László up but me too. László's ninetieth birthday was in June that year and Yvonne and Maurice came to celebrate it. They arrived the week before and brought a large bottle of Paddy's Irish whiskey to mark the occasion. László was particularly fond of Yvonne and would regale her with stories of his music days: evenings when he played with Goldwin Gede in cafés and bars, and later in Lake Balaton during the summer months with his colleagues from the Opera House. It was a very happy period for him, as Yvonne would later recall. Yes, they really were the golden years of his life. Aside from his talent, they had come about through sheer drive and determination not to mention hard graft.

'He believed that you made your own luck,' Yvonne recalled. 'There was no such thing as being lucky. You got what you worked for. That was his philosophy.'

When it came to the couple's departure, László bid them his usual farewell.

'Will I be here next year to greet you?'

We all smiled, not having the heart to say anything.

'When I close my eyes, put me straight into the oven. I want no church service, no Catholic priest, no clergy of any kind!'

By a strange coincidence his brother Zoltán died the following month in July. The news did not reach László but I wonder did he feel his passing in any way. A special fuss of László's ninetieth birthday was also made by the Troisvierges town council. A few days after his birthday, one of the officials phoned me and asked if they could visit László to wish him a happy birthday. Two representatives arrived with a bottle of champagne and a small gift, and spent a couple of hours sitting on the terrace chatting to László. It was such a kind gesture by the authorities and so lovely for László, who thoroughly enjoyed it.

In August, László's health began to fail further and he was confined to bed for longer periods. His nights were restless and I was afraid to leave his bedside. A biography of Franz Liszt in Hungarian – a treasured item – was kept on his bedside locker and occasionally he would take it up and read a few passages about the piano virtuoso. Sometimes he would translate passages – of his compositions and travels throughout Europe – and read them to me. The record player too was pressed into service time and again, playing favourites from Liszt, Beethoven, Brahms, Mozart, Verdi, Wagner, Mahler and Bartók. I felt as if music would usher him into the next world.

Then one morning out of the blue, he turned to me and said something wholly unexpected.

'Bring me to your God, Pixie. I want to thank him for sending you to me.'

Despite his weakened state, I drove him to the Benedictine Abbey in Clervaux, and we sat before the altar in silent prayer for about thirty minutes. The chapel where Anne and I had often come to mass was not the scene of a deathbed conversion, however. Organised or formalised religion never appealed to László, though raised in the Calvinist faith. Yet his appreciation of the natural world, not to mention his cherished music, proved that he was rich indeed on a spiritual level. Following this visit, he seemed more relaxed and satisfied. The visit seemed to clarify his thoughts.

'I want us to return to Ireland, Pixie. Can you make the arrangements?'

'László, I don't think you're well enough to travel.'

'I am. Can you organise a quick sale of our property?'

'Are you sure this is what you want?'

'Yes, I'm absolutely sure, Pixie. Buy two airline tickets as soon as possible.'

We had long since sold the house in Foxrock, so László insisted that we return to my apartment in Dundrum. And so I booked two tickets for October and made contact with a removal firm to take back some of our belongings to Dublin. In retrospect, László was making arrangements for my return to Ireland after his own death, though I did not fully comprehend this fact at the time. That kind act, in the face of his impending death, was caring, considerate and thoughtful beyond belief. It epitomised his whole life in putting others first.

Sometimes he would feel well enough to sit on the terrace for half an hour or so. Wrapping him in blankets, I would assist him to the sun lounger and place no less than three large umbrellas, as sunshades, over him. Being out on his beloved terrace boosted his spirits no end before his energy would flag and a return to bed was in order. In mid-September his condition deteriorated further. His appetite was now gone, his heartbeat irregular, his kidneys had failed and a urinary catheter was inserted. I nursed him at home with the help of Dr Mertens and some visiting nurses, who came to also monitor his condition. I especially recall a young German nurse whose humanity seemed to shine like a beacon of hope and love, as she knelt at his bedside and spoke softly to him.

Despite his condition, László was still thinking of others.

'Pixie, young people should have a home,' he said, his voice feeble. 'Being homeless is a terrible thing.'

'Of course, it is László,' I agreed, unaware of what precisely prompted his words.

In the week prior to his death, my heart was sinking fast and that homebird feeling began to take hold of me once more, just as it had during the final days in the monastery in Kilmacud. I phoned Eoin and asked if his daughter, my niece Denise, could come and stay for a while, as I was finding life a little stressful.

'Eibh, I'm so sorry, she's about to take off on a trip with some friends for a year,' he said. 'It's a working holiday, touring the world after all her studies.'

'That's all right, Eoin. I'll be fine.'

Though disappointed, chatting with Eoin lifted my spirits somewhat. I thought that László might hang on, as we were due to travel back to Ireland anyway in a few days' time. It was not to be, however, as László took a turn for the worst.

A day or two later Eoin phoned with an offer of assistance from his wife Josephine.

'If Josephine travelled over, would that help?'

By then I knew that László's days were limited.

'Not to worry, I'll be able to manage.'

Talking about László with Eoin, whom I was always close to as a child, brought great comfort to me.

In the early morning of 13 October 2005, László's soul returned home with his parting words.

'Find … find … find…'

It would take me a few years to learn that in all likelihood it was his long-lost daughter Lívia that he wished me to find, which I did. As I looked upon his sensitive face, from which life had just ebbed, I had an overwhelming feeling of love and gratitude. Gratitude not only for me but for all those people he had quietly helped throughout his long life. All those bygone years are now cherished memories of when my László came to me and gently took my hand and helped restore my lost confidence and led me into the exquisite light of a new life.

He inspired me and I take comfort from a few lines from Robert W. Service's poem 'The World's Alright' that my dear father used to recite to me:

> Be honest, kindly, simple, true;
> Seek good in all, scorn but pretence;
> Whatever sorrow comes to you,
> Believe in Life's Beneficence.

EPILOGUE

MY quest to trace László's origins and the object of his deathbed request began in earnest in 2006, the year after his death. By then my intense grief had abated somewhat and I had mustered enough strength and energy to travel to Hungary. As I mentioned earlier in the book, I had arrived in Budapest in May 2006 with Maurice McMahon. The trip had been bitterly disappointing for me because the Liszt Academy of Music had not accepted my gift of three small apartments in Budapest for student accommodation. However, they did accept my donation of László's two clarinets and his extensive music collection, scores of old and rare pieces of music, in addition to a few small items. My hope was that many young students would have the pleasure of their use one day, and perhaps some of László's own descendants could be counted among that number!

The real progress was made when we visited Debrecen, the place of his birth. On that trip in August 2006, Yvonne McMahon and I had unearthed quite a lot of information about his parents and grandparents. After that, my eyes were firmly trained on Budapest. I installed myself in one of the apartments I had purchased, on the Pest side of River Danube, where I could immerse myself in the sights and sounds of this true Paris of the East. It was a way for me to reconnect with László and experience, albeit at some remove, his city and all that he loved about it. Doing so brought his spirit all the more closer to me.

By September that year I was itching to find László's house on Napsugár Street – the seat of much joy and strife over the decades. Yvonne and I set off and at Blaha Lujza tér metro station asked an office clerk for directions to Napsugár. To my amazement and gratitude, she ushered us into an office and consulted several clerks busily working away.

'What's the best way to get to Napsugár Street?' she asked.

Among themselves, they discussed the easiest route for us to take. While one clerk looked up a map, another drew diagrams and wrote street names on a sheet of paper and handed it to us. They were excellent directions, I must admit, and without them our task would have been far more difficult. Blaha Lujza tér was one of the busiest metro stations in Budapest, a transport hub thronged with people scurrying hither and thither at all hours of the day and night. Yet once again, we experienced kindness and helpfulness that were to become hallmarks of our trips to Hungary.

Before long Yvonne and I were aboard a metro heading across the river to Batthyány tér station, and from there two bus journeys eventually brought us to the Napsugár district. There, we headed up into the Buda Hills and hoped for the best. I clutched a photo of László's house, thinking it would help us in our search. In fact, I was so keen to find the house that I even whispered a short prayer for success. The search became fruitless after a while, however, and we had to admit we were lost. The area was full of narrow tree-lined streets with many a villa tucked away behind neat railings or stone walls. The intrepid Yvonne, however, was undaunted. Observing her surroundings, she knocked at a nearby house and the owner soon appeared. In my broken German with a smidgeon of Hungarian thrown in, I asked for directions, while I held up the photo. Taking it in his hands, he looked at the photo and smiled.

'Yes, you need to retrace your steps,' he replied in German, 'just walk further up into the hills.'

And so off we went, climbing higher and higher along meandering streets and lanes. By now, mid-afternoon, the sun was still beating down upon us and I began to feel very warm and faint. I looked down the long length of one road and, in the distance, saw a car parked at the roadside. Beside the car stood a young man and woman with what I presumed were their children. A feeling suddenly came over me, something telling me to hurry up, that this was the house.

'Yvonne, this is it! Quick, quick, let's catch that man.'

Well for two women not exactly in the first flush of youth, Yvonne and I moved very quickly.

By the time we reached the car, the woman and children were settled inside, while the man was just about to climb in. Exhausted and panting, with the photo firmly in hand, I ran towards the man. Yvonne was not far behind me.

'The Gede house, I'm looking for it,' I spluttered, having mustered up some German words.

I need not have worried for the young man spoke perfect English.

'It is here,' he said, pointing to the house in front of us. I had learned from László, years earlier, that Irén's niece Monika was the last known occupant of the house.

'Is Monika alive?' I asked, hoping against hope.

At that, he threw back his head and laughed.

'I'm Gyula and Monika is my mother,' he replied, 'We've just been visiting her.'

At the mention of the word 'we', he had waved his hand over the occupants of the car, his family. After introductions, Gyula's wife drove off with the children, while Yvonne and I were escorted up through a rose-lined driveway towards the house. A woodland garden was to my right and my eyes quickly sought out the many peach trees that László had planted.

'Are you okay, Eibhlín, can you manage all this?' Yvonne enquired quietly.

'Yes,' I nodded, as we approached the door.

The door opened wide and there stood Monika and her husband Friedrich, both in their sixties. Neither had a word of German let alone English, but thankfully Gyula acted as translator. Invited inside, we walked down a long hallway with rooms to our right and on into a rather dark dining room at the gable end of the house. Old photos graced the room and the window overlooked the front garden. I immediately felt caught in a time warp. We had stepped into László's life of bygone years. In one corner of the room stood a piano and my heart skipped a beat. I thought of the music students who had come for lessons in those days long gone, trekking up the hills as we had, and savouring all that László had to impart.

'This belonged to László,' said Gyula, translating for his mother, who had pointed at the piano. I smiled.

Over refreshments, we chatted about László. Monika had been unaware that he had remarried after her aunt's death. She reminisced too of the trips to Ireland in the 1970s along with her husband and children to visit László and Irén. Inevitably, the subject of Irén's daughter Marie, and Monika's first cousin, surfaced. Monika wondered had I had any communication from her in Canada. I shook my head and said no. After László's death, I had approached the International Red Cross to find her whereabouts but sadly they were unsuccessful. On a piece of paper, I wrote out my telephone number and email address and gave it to Monika. In due course, Marie did get in touch with me and I passed on her mother's personal effects that had remained in László's possession. As dusk fell, Yvonne and I said our goodbyes. I gave Monika a big warm hug and left, feeling glad that László's old home was well cared for and loved. The visit had been wonderfully relaxing and pleasant.

'Eibhlín, I tell you, that house is as László left it,' Yvonne whispered in my ear. 'He could've just walked out of it yesterday!'

Finding László's house had indeed been a boost to my spirits but I had no luck finding any of his Gede relatives at that stage. Then to my surprise in 2008, I received an email asking was I, by any chance, the wife of László Gede, a professor of music who was born in Debrecen in 1915. The sender was Éva Gede Tóthné, daughter of István, László's brother. I was dumbstruck and over the moon by this bolt from the blue! Interested in family history, she had come across my name in Hungarian social media – most likely from a relative of Marie's. We became close friends, following this initial enquiry, and I look upon her as a dear sister. To this day, we speak a rather broken German when we meet. All our email correspondence is translated by Éva's good friend Kati, a fellow Hungarian, living in the USA. So without the hard work of Kati, my friendship with Éva would never have flourished.

The day I got to meet Éva was one of the most memorable of my life. It happened in May 2009 at the Szőnyi Panzió Hotel restaurant in Budapest. Kathy Watts, my good friend and confidante, accompanied me and there we met Éva and also László's nephew. What a most interesting afternoon we spent exchanging stories as we attempted to complete the family jigsaw puzzle piece by piece. Éva, with her genuine warmth and charming manners, reminded me so much of her dear uncle and I felt an immediate bond of kinship. Her husband Rudi Tóth also joined us that day. László's nephew, son of Zoltán, was named after László and lived in Székesfehérvár, a city in central Hungary. A gallant Hungarian accompanied by his wife Éva, László arrived with two bouquets of flowers, one for his cousin Éva and the other for me.

László held a striking resemblance to my László not only in looks but talents too; he had inherited the Gede gift of music. A former lieutenant-colonel in the army, László had graduated as a conductor from the famous Moscow Tchaikovsky Conservatory in 1983. Thereafter, he was the conductor of the Military Brass Orchestra of Székesfehérvár between 1983 and 2001. It was a deep pleasure to later learn in 2013 that László was appointed conductor to the Youth Brass Band of Székesfehérvár. So many parallels with my László!

I told Éva and László of the affection my husband held for his paternal grandmother, Julianna Kálmán Gede, and how over the years he had spoken kindly of her. It was obvious to me that he greatly loved and respected her. Coincidentally, Éva had an old sepia-toned photo of this grandmother in her purse and showed it to me. My eyes fell upon a woman with a rather severe expression, reminding me of how rigidly people posed for the camera in those days.

'László said she was quite soft-hearted in fact,' I told them, as I examined the photo, searching for family resemblances. László had said she had lived to a great age and that his mother had cared for her and later his stepmother. Looking back on that meeting now and witnessing and observing the sincerity and kindness of these people are indeed treasured moments.

I grew to love Budapest and would travel back and forth over the years to Hungary, always searching for more family relatives and ways to ensure László was not forgotten in the city in which he had flourished. In 2013, while on a visit to Debrecen with Éva and her husband Rudi, we visited the Gede family grave. By now Éva and I had erected a new marble tombstone for the grave of Papa István and Mama Zsuzsanna. In the cemetery I was shown the monument dedicated to the Balog and Kálmán families who had contributed to the restoration of the Great Reformed Church destroyed during a devastating fire in 1802. They also brought me to Hajnal Street where László was born and grew up. Heavy wooden gates now formed the entrance to this property. As I managed to look through a small grating, I observed a large courtyard surrounded by buildings, some of houses and others apartments. I realised that this extensive property had at one time belonged to Papa Gede, who had wished to provide for his sons and their families. But now sadly it seemed vacant and rather neglected, having passed out of the hands of the Gede family.

Discovering the existence of László's daughter Lívia, courtesy of his Hungarian State papers, was an extraordinary moment for me. I knew I could not rest until I had tracked her down. A solicitor, Wera Hegedűs, kindly offered to do this for me. Wera's efforts in tracing Lívia were immense. The correspondence between Lívia and me was conducted through Wera, and I certainly respected Lívia's privacy in not wishing to meet me. Learning of Lívia, her five children and her fifteen grandchildren, of whom I knew nothing, was an answer to a deep-seated hope. It was also a comfort to me that László's extraordinary gifts and talents would live on. Lívia too had inherited the Gede gift of music and was an accomplished pianist. Not to my surprise, I found that László had supported the upkeep of his child until his arrest and imprisonment in 1956 and later in 1965 had made provisions for her future. I was sincerely glad to have found Lívia and happy to pass on mementoes of her father. I felt I had carried out his final wishes and that in his own strange way he had wished me to know of his past, though unable to reveal it during our years together. It had been a tragic loss to him. Being in occasional email contact with Lívia's daughter Krisztina since November 2011, however, is a good link with the past, especially knowing that László's grandchildren and great-grandchildren are so musically talented.

The passing of László had a deep impact on me. During those first seven years or so after his death I was all mixed up, or *trí na chéile* as we say in Irish. Once more I could not seem to find myself; I felt cast adrift and did not know what I was doing. But for my siblings and close friends, I would truly have been lost. Thanks to their guidance, they kept my mind focused and my feet grounded.

The journey and research I had to undertake in order to fulfil dear László's request was very personal to me. The facts, surprising at times, speak for themselves. I make no judgements; I have only admiration. Not everyone is as fortunate as I in loving a remarkable man, good and kind, and for this I am eternally grateful. My memories and story are but a small tribute to a husband who gave real meaning to my life.

Ní imithe ach romham atá sé.
Not gone, only before us.

Solas na bhFlaitheas ar dá anam uasal
agus leaba i measc na naomh go raibh aige.
May the light of Heaven shine upon his noble soul
and may his gentle self find rest among the saints.

Pihenjen drága lelke.
Rest precious soul.

ACKNOWLEDGEMENTS

Many dedicated people have helped me to create this memoir. My grateful thanks go to Antoinette Walker, writer and editor, for taking on the difficult task of guiding me to its conclusion. Her enormous hard work and input encouraged me to search and find answers to myriad questions about László's life. I also thank Conor Graham of Merrion Press for agreeing to publish the memoir and Peter O'Connell of Peter O'Connell Media for bringing it to a wider audience. Deep appreciation also goes to Kieran Nolan of Oldtown Design and to Síne Quinn for her excellent copyediting skills.

For permission to reproduce the poem 'An Artist', I would like to thank Seamus Heaney and his publishers, Faber & Faber. In reply to my letter in 2013, Seamus wrote of how pleased he was that his poem had come home to me and for László so appositely. It was one of Seamus's favourite poems, so he revealed, and I'm glad to have something in common with the great Nobel Laureate.

Since first setting out on this journey to pay tribute to my husband, many have helped along the way. To the following, I owe a deep debt of gratitude: Maurice McMahon for his patience and giving of his time to advise and offer me feedback on early drafts; Yvonne McMahon for all her help and in accompanying me on several trips to Hungary; Kathy Watts for her support and for likewise accompanying me when meeting László's niece and nephew for the first time; Paul Conway, Helen Murphy and Gerald Tomkin for sharing their thoughts and memories of László; and Jószef Csibi for his reflections of being a Hungarian musician and émigré in Ireland.

In Hungary, there are many whose support and assistance I greatly appreciate: Éva Gede Tóthné, László's niece, for her tireless hours of research and her friend Katalin (Kati) Fodor for acting as translator, thus enabling Éva and me to correspond and understand each other over the years; Susan Keglevich, whose assistance was invaluable in translating the various Hungarian Court documents; solicitor Wera Hegedűs, based in Budapest, for her tireless energy and generosity with various transactions and for finding László's daughter Lívia; the director and staff of the Hungarian State Opera House; the director and professors of the Liszt Academy of Music, especially Matthew Mesterházi and Emőke Solymosi Tari; the Bartók Béla Zeneművészeti Szakközépiskola és Gimnázium (formerly National Music School), Budapest for providing me with invaluable information, with special thanks to György Bokor. I also thank the Hungarian Embassy in Dublin for translating Hungarian military documents vital to László's story.

When writing a memoir, there is much relying on memory and hindsight, which is not without peril. So for any omissions, errors or inaccuracies, I can only apologise in advance. Some names have been changed to protect the privacy of individuals.

Finally, I pay special tribute to my kind and caring brother and sister, Áine and Eoin, and faithful friends always there and ready to listen: Helen Murphy, Maureen Conway, and Eamon and Mary Monahan; my nursing colleagues the late Kay Cooney, Máirín Leyne, Dolores McGauran and Sheila O'Brien, and all in St Vincent's Private Hospital. To those who assisted me on this journey, blessings upon all.